RESEARCHING URBAN SPACE AND THE BUILT ENVIRONMENT

Manchester University Press

IHR RESEARCH GUIDES

Series editor: Simon Trafford

This series is for new researchers in history. By offering a practical introduction to a sub-discipline of history, each book equips its readers to navigate a new field of interest. Every volume provides a survey of the historiography and current research in the subject; describes relevant methodological issues; looks at available primary sources in different media and formats and the problems of their access and interpretation. Each volume includes practical case studies and examples to guide your research, and handy tips on how to avoid some of the pitfalls which may lie in wait for the inexperienced researcher.

The guides are suitable for advanced final-year undergraduates, master's and first-year PhD students, as well as for independent researchers who wish to take their work to a more advanced stage.

Already published
Using film as a source   Sian Barber
Doing digital history   Jonathan Blaney, Sarah Milligan, Marty Steer and Jane Winters
History through material culture   Leonie Hannan and Sarah Longair

RESEARCHING URBAN SPACE AND THE BUILT ENVIRONMENT

Jasmine Kilburn-Toppin, Elaine Tierney, Charlotte Wildman

Manchester University Press

Published by Manchester University Press
Oxford Road, Manchester M13 9PL

www.manchesteruniversitypress.co.uk

British Library Cataloguing-in-Publication Data
A catalogue record for this book is available from the British Library

ISBN   978 1 5261 3360 1   paperback

First published 2022

The publisher has no responsibility for the persistence or accuracy of URLs for any external or third-party internet websites referred to in this book, and does not guarantee that any content on such websites is, or will remain, accurate or appropriate.

Typeset
by Cheshire Typesetting Ltd, Cuddington, Cheshire
Printed in Great Britain
by CPI Group (UK) Ltd, Croydon CR0 4YY

CONTENTS

FIGURES

ACKNOWLEDGEMENTS

This guide has been inspired by our research into urban spaces and built environments from the fifteenth to twentieth centuries. We hope that something of our collective experiences of spatial methodologies, theories and archives is reflected here, and that this book might go some way toward enthusing the next generation of spatial historians. We have also been motivated to write this guide as a consequence of teaching varied spatial histories with students at Cardiff University, at the University of Manchester and on the Victoria and Albert Museum (V&A)/Royal College of Art History of Design postgraduate programme. We are indebted to our fantastic students who have engaged with space, place and the built environment with such eagerness, and who have prompted some of the research questions and methodologies in the pages which follow.

This book has been some time in the planning and writing, and we are very grateful to Emma Brennan and Paul Clarke at Manchester University Press for their support and guidance and to the anonymous reviewers who generously sharpened some the arguments and emphases. Numerous colleagues at Cardiff, Manchester and the V&A also provided invaluable suggestions for further reading and research. Finally, we are grateful to our families who have patiently lived with this guide for several years, and provided much encouragement along the way.

LIST OF ABBREVIATIONS

ANT	actor–network theory
GIS	geographical information system
HGIS	historical geographical information system
LMA	London Metropolitan Archives
RIBA	Royal Institute of British Architects
STS	science and technology studies
TNA	The National Archives (Kew, London)
V&A	Victoria and Albert Museum, London

INTRODUCTION: RESEARCHING URBAN SPACE AND THE BUILT ENVIRONMENT

INTRODUCTION

The space and built environment of the town and city have profoundly shaped social, cultural, political and economic lives for as long as humans have fashioned urban settlements. As inhabitants of and visitors to cities today, we are only too aware of how street plans, transport systems and building projects impact upon our everyday experiences of the urban environment. We are conscious too of the appeal, and conversely undesirability, of certain city spaces for socialising, consumption and entertainment. The same was true historically. Urban residents developed ways of navigating the material fabric of the city, depending upon preferences for wide or narrow streets, light or dark passageways, visibility or concealment. City inhabitants built up their own personal understandings of urban space, based on the various activities or practices, sensory stimuli and symbolic or historic associations of certain sites. As we will see in later chapters, city dwellers, such as seventeenth-century Londoner Samuel Pepys, developed subjective mental maps of urban spaces.

For historians, the examination of urban space and the built environment offers unique opportunities for exploring urban customs, mythologies, economic systems and many other features of society, politics and culture besides. Historians 'can answer old questions and pose new ones by making space a central theoretical concern'.[1] This research guide aims to equip readers with the tools to successfully carry out spatial research. Before turning to explore the rationale, methodologies and terminologies of spatially oriented historical research we begin this introduction with a couple of historical case studies. A brief consideration, first, of late medieval and early modern city walls and gates, and second, of mid-nineteenth- and early twentieth-century transport systems are useful entry -points for thinking through the meanings, experiences and what historians have termed the 'productivity' of urban spaces.

From the late medieval period, across Europe, cities were typically surrounded by walls, made from stone, brick and wood, and these fortifications were often embellished and expanded in the sixteenth and seventeenth centuries. Urban fortifications had a highly significant military and defensive role, but they also 'functioned as a kind of social filter'.[2] All visitors would encounter the walls, and entry into the city was closely regulated through guarded gates. City walls and gates ideally controlled the movement of material and perishable goods, animals, humans and infectious diseases. Individuals under exile and ban, vagabonds, beggars and religious minorities, particularly Jews, were denied access through the gates. From the late medieval period, in many Italian city states, those who desired entry would have to first provide a health certificate from their former place of residence. Non-citizens were subject to intense questioning at the city gates as to their origins, occupation and future place of residence; this does not seem all that dissimilar to the close scrutinisation of visas at international airports today.[3]

For contemporaries, city walls also had a deeper symbolic meaning. As Martha C. Howell has written, 'the walls were built almost at the same moment the urban corporation drew breath, and they survived at least as long as did a viable pretence of urban autonomy (and sometimes longer).'[4] Fortifications represented the civic independence and privileges of particular urban communities. It is thus no surprise to find that walls and city gates featured prominently in visual representations of early modern cities; for instance, collections of urban prints which circulated among wealthy travellers who wanted a memento of their excursions. Such was the symbolic weight of walls in relation to civic identity that these structures were on occasion razed by opposition or centralising political forces as a form of collective punishment and humiliation. The walls of the English town of Gloucester and the Alsatian town of Colmar met this fate in the 1660s and 1670s respectively.[5] As prominent features of the built environment, city walls had social, military, legal, political, and economic importance in the early modern period. Walls physically demarcated urban spaces, and acted as material barriers and filters, but they also had profound symbolic meanings for urban dwellers, and those excluded from such privileges.

Choosing another point of entry shifts how we think about – and with – urban space. Nineteenth- and twentieth-century infrastructure, including sewers, the telegraph and telephone, and mass transit, and the mobility and circulation they supported, emphasise the physical and immaterial links that joined together people, places and goods within and between cities. Connectivity and networks reconstitute how we think about urban space in a number of important ways. In the case of innovations in transport and communication, this is often used to explain what was distinctive about the modern, as opposed to early modern or medieval, city. Intra-urban railways, including the London Underground, the 'El' (or Elevated Railway in New York) and Paris Metro, appeared across Europe and America from the mid-nineteenth-century onwards.[6] In addition to reshaping physical environments, through the addition of elevated rails, underground tunnels, bridges and elaborate station buildings, these projects also reconfigured in a fundamental way what (or more properly where) was considered to be part of a city. Fast, reliable transportation joined together previously disparate places and reorganised urban space by absorbing into greater metropolitan areas the suburbs, towns and villages that had been on the peripheries of large nineteenth- and twentieth-century cities. This was the difference between the City of London, encircled by its city walls, and 'the Greater London Area' shown in a London Underground Map issued in 1921. The latter showed a city stretched outwards to encompass Harrow to the north, previously part of the ancient borough of Middlesex, and Wimbledon, in the south, historically part of Surrey.[7]

The ability to move people and goods around, in quantity and at greater speed, also meant that land use became increasingly specialised. Businesses could locate unsightly, noisy factories in one part of town and sell finished goods in spectacular retail destinations located elsewhere.[8] People might live, work and play in completely different parts of the city – and potentially ignore the existence of other, less salubrious locales. Underground railways, like those that first appeared in London in 1863, made the potential for disconnect even more acute. A clerk living in West London could travel to his job in the City, in the process 'leapfrogging' over some of London's most brutal slums.[9] Evidence, from the built environment to the visual arts, from newspaper reportage to first-hand accounts in diaries and letters, also reveals how new forms of transport transformed experience of the urban.[10] Passengers looked down on urban landscapes from new vantage points, like the raised railway viaduct shown in Gustave Doré's engraving of working-class backyards, and were brought into closer contact with people of different social classes in the new public spaces formed by train, tram and omnibus carriages.[11] Above all, people contended with the sense that new forms of transportation collapsed time and distance, altering the duration and feasibility of journeys, but also transforming how urban space was imagined and perceived.[12]

These short case studies establish ideas that will be explored in the book that follows. First and foremost, we hope you will agree that urban space and the built environment were creatures of historical context. City-walls and intra-urban railways were invested with meaning by the people who built, regulated and used them. Second, our case studies suggest how the values given to the spatial and environmental in the past can be accessed through a range of sources, including the built environment, the rules and regulations that attempted to modulate behaviour within cities, and representations, from paintings to maps to life-writing, which sought to capture aspects of urban life. Third, and finally, this evidence always gives us a sense of the past that is partial and value-laden. While the experiences of some types of people are captured in a wide variety of printed and archival texts, images, objects and built environments, others can be much more difficult to locate. Think, for example, of the different levels of information we might have about an early modern nobleman, who commissioned his own urban palace, kept detailed household accounts, left treasured objects to his descendants, and was represented in all his pomp and glory in an oil painting. Now think of a poor woman in the same city, at the same time. We might glimpse her in institutional records – if for example she received charitable support or was charged with breaking the peace – but getting a sense of her identity and everyday experiences requires us to be more creative in how we think with our evidence.

Before going any further, it is worth saying something about our own practice as historians. As social and cultural historians, we work on urban politics, professional and gendered identities, and the materiality of built environments in early modern Europe and modern Britain. Drawing on a range of approaches from outside history, including anthropology, archaeology, historical geography and science and technology studies, our own work uses material culture – from buildings to hand-held personal items – as a way of rethinking urban cultures. Indeed, you will notice a recurring theme in this book: how far the materiality of urban environments informed and shaped social, cultural, political and economic identities, relationships and contexts. Although our majority focus is on early modern and modern Europe, in preparing this guide, we have also reached out to colleagues in history and other disciplines. This allows us to stretch beyond our own specialisms to engage with questions and issues that motivate historians who work on other historical periods and geographies.

THE ACADEMIC LANDSCAPE

This is an exciting time to be carrying out spatial research. Since the 1970s the discipline of history has undergone a profound 'spatial turn'. In the last two decades in particular, there has been an explosion of academic interest in space and place. This is evidenced by the significant number of conferences and workshops, special issues of journals, and space-related monographs across all historical periods since the early 2000s. In recent years too, museum and gallery exhibitions have attended to the themes of space and the built environment in imaginative and innovative ways. For example, the Wellcome Collection's 'Living with Buildings' exhibition (2018/19) which explored the diverse and complicated relationships between buildings and human health from the nineteenth century to the present day.[13]

Historians Beat Kümin and Cornelie Usborne have written of 'the essence of the "spatial turn"' as 'the move from a "container" image of space [the idea that historic encounters simply happened in space] toward an acknowledgement of its mutability and social production'.[14] The exploration of the built environment, space, and place as legitimate and productive fields of research enquiry is certainly not the exclusive terrain of historians. The move towards the spatial has always been a fundamentally interdisciplinary project, with archaeologists, sociologists, geographers, and historians, among others, working in dialogue. The interdisciplinary approaches and methodologies of spatial histories are central to their appeal and interest, and also why they have frequently attracted research funding; but interdisciplinarity is also at the root of why they can be so challenging to write.

There can be no singular or straightforward explanation for the rising prominence of space as a subject of enquiry, and growing engagement with spatial theories and methodologies. Part of our explanation might lie with the growth of global history. The exploration of networks, exchanges, and connections within global histories have fostered 'experiment with alternative notions of space', far beyond customary, bounded notions of nation-states or empires.[15] The development of environmental history as a thriving field of research has also expanded our awareness of the significance of spatial matters. As historian Caroline Ford has written, a central question for environmental historians is how to perceive and interpret landscapes; whether as 'uninhabited wilderness' spaces or as composite natural and artificial sites. The work of numerous European scholars has 'focused on how the material environment was viewed, the myths and memories with which it has been invested, and its symbolic power. They explore landscape as a way of seeing'.[16]

The rising interest among historians and other scholars in the humanities in space-related research has certainly also been facilitated by the development of new technologies, notably geographical information systems (GIS). GIS uniquely enables the researcher to create a type of database, with a location stored for each item of data. Thus 'historians have been able to create dynamic, interactive digital visualizations of change over space and time'.[17] These datasets and their associated maps have so far advanced our understanding of urban growth and decay, ethnic segregation, poverty, immigration and the shifting distributions of retail establishments.[18] The sheer quantity of data available for the investigation of modern cities has meant that nineteenth- and twentieth-century GIS histories have so far predominated and have helped to uncover vivid insights into the sensory experience of cities and present new interpretations of the impact of urban redevelopment. Other ways that GIS has been used include enabling new insights into the relationship between urban redevelopment and the production of inequalities. Colin Gordon's *Mapping Decline* uses GIS mapping to illustrate and explain the decline of St Louis, Missouri as a product of federal policies that facilitated 'white flight', and charts the impact of systemic racism as a cause of residential segregation. The project used GIS mapping to highlight the use of zoning and state-initiated programmes of redevelopment, allowing Gordon to explain St Louis' ongoing problems of poverty, racial inequalities and urban problems as a failure of urban policy.[19] Its insights exemplify how spatially attuned histories can provide methods for addressing current problems of racial and social inequities that are persistent in so many major cities. Innovative research is also being carried out for earlier periods. For instance, a recent historical GIS project uniquely brought together and examined cartographic evidence and descriptive historical sources from eighteenth-century Rome. This project 'takes advantage of the geometric precision and the descriptive detail characterizing the "Nuova pianta di Roma", published in 1748 by Giovanni Battista Nolli, in order to study the city of Rome in the 18th century and its transformations'. This map took into account diverse features of the urban environment, including buildings, fountains, ruins, walls, streets and gardens. One of the most fascinating outcomes of this research project is the ability to trace the changing built landscape of antiquity, 'the archaeological heritage as it was in the 18th century, before the transformations that occurred after the unification of Italy'.[20]

DEFINING TERMS

Defining terms is one of the first jobs undertaken in any research project. This can be especially tricky in histories that grapple with space and place. By its nature, this is interdisciplinary work and, somewhat problematically for our purposes, different disciplines do not agree on what key terms like 'location', 'site', 'place', 'space' and 'spatial' actually mean. In some cases, the definitions available are even contradictory. Indeed, the fluidity of terminology is about the only thing that most commentators agree on. Leif Jerram's useful intervention is worth quoting at length:

> A significant problem is that in academic usage, place and space can both refer to many things that often overlap, with the net result that one cannot really be sure what a scholar is talking about ... At the heart of the confusion are the words 'place' and 'space,' which so often jumble up materiality, distributions, relationships, and meaning in very unhelpful ways.[21]

Let us think through some of the key differences in studies of space and place. Some disciplines, like physics and maths, engage in precise measurements of space as volume. Similarly, 'science facing' geographers and archaeologists are concerned with taking empirical (or evidence-led) approaches to place, by calculating landmasses, measuring distances, heights and depths and mapping distribution patterns. By contrast, other disciplines, including cultural geography, sociology and cultural history, regard space and place as essentially subjective.

This way of thinking proposes that 'somewhere' is not only a physical, external reality but is produced by means of the relationship between an individual's body, experiences and memories and the 'outside' world. Think, for example, of the difference between knowing the address of somewhere, as a piece of information, and knowing somewhere deeply and personally, like your childhood home. In the latter case, a sense of place is shaped by a jumble of memories and emotions, in the past and in the present.[22]

But even within this variety, there is broad agreement that 'space' and 'place' are somehow different. Properly grappling with the spatial means framing what makes each distinct. The definitions offered here are informed by engagement with the key thinkers and approaches discussed in greater detail in Chapter 1. Most noticeably, we take a three-fold approach by distinguishing between 'site', 'place' and 'space'. Doing this encourages understanding of the multiple ways in which 'somewhere' can be meaningful, as well as the ways in which these different facets of the spatial interact.

- **Site** means a specific, or absolute, location, as defined by, say, the grid references attached to a particular portion of the earth or an exact postal address. This recognises that places have to be located *somewhere*.
- **Place** will be used to explain how that 'somewhere' is a 'particular or lived space'. This means dealing with the specificities of what that place is like – its physical characteristics – but also the meanings associated with it. These meanings are produced through social practices, memories (individual and shared), cultural production (e.g. architecture, paintings, descriptions in novels), emotional and sensorial associations, all of which combine to make what has been described as a 'sense of place'.
- **Space** captures what is *between*: it is relative and relational. This is a much less straightforward business than this wording might suggest. Space, like all ideas, has its own history, one which helps to explain the main strands of thinking about the concept. Early modern polymaths Isaac Newton and Gottfried Wilhelm Leibniz were two major contributors to debates in seventeenth-century Europe, proposing completely divergent ideas about space. For Newton, space was absolute, unitary, stand-alone and inert: a 'thing' that other objects and events fitted into, but which remained unaffected by these. For Leibniz, space was relational: it existed only because of

the relationships between different entities.[23] This second strand of thinking – that space is created by means of relationships – has been hugely influential. The most important idea, which we will build upon in Chapter 1, is that space is not inert – an empty nothing or nowhere – but is, instead, produced, productive (insofar as it sets the terms of future interactions) and dynamic. The historical geographer Richard Dennis puts it succinctly: 'Space is not simply a container in which modern life is played out. Rather, the ways in which we conceptualise and operationalise space are products of political, economic, social and cultural processes. In turn, the organisation of space offers opportunities and constraints for the further development of those processes.'[24] What this means in plain English is that space is created through the links between places and by how these links are structured and understood. A wide range of social, cultural, economic and political factors affect and, in turn, are affected by how and why specific places are linked, how these links function and for whose benefit, and how they are represented. We might think here of the technologies (from compass and ship design, to ever more exact cartography), economic and political arrangements (mercantilism, colonialism) and impacts (trade, enslavement) that brought into alignment a series of distinct places, from counting houses in London to slave ships on the Ghanaian coast, from West Indian sugar plantations to 'polite' drawing rooms, to forge an increasingly global world during the first era of globalisation.[25]

READING THIS GUIDE

The structure of this research guide is intended to take you through the main stages of any research project. Although the broad tasks we describe are applicable to other sorts of history, our focus throughout, including the examples and case studies we use, is research projects that foreground the study of urban space and the urban built environment. The guide will help students who are undertaking original historical research. For many of you, this will be the first major piece of work of this kind that you will complete. For this reason, the guide is intended to provide you and your project with intellectual scaffolding – an overview of the historiographical landscape, questions you might ask, methods and approaches you might use; but it also advises you on how to manage the practicalities of getting your research project done on time. These two strands are at the heart of any research project – from article to multi-million-pound research project – so it is good to begin early!

The guide is also written for a wide range of students. We imagine that some of you will have a clear sense of what they want to do and why. For these students, what follows will help them get the most out of their research. But others will be completely new to this way of thinking and working. Our job is to give you a sense of what is distinctive about doing history with spatial dimensions and give you tools for beginning and developing your own project. Whatever stage you are at, think of the book as a research companion. You can read the chapters about approaches and beginning your research, then dip back in as your project develops. As this is highly interdisciplinary work, we begin with a broad overview of the main disciplines and approaches that scholars have used in writing spatial histories. From here, we move on to the practical business of the research process: how you go about shaping your research questions, choosing your methodology and locating and analysing your sources. The final part of the book will help you to manage the process of writing up your project.

Your aim in developing your research project is to contribute to our knowledge of the past – to produce a piece of work that is rigorous, original and critically engaged. To ensure that you stay on track, we advise that you draft a research proposal before you begin the bulk of your research and writing.

Research project: a common structure

1. Project summary: What is this about? What is your gap in knowledge? What are the research questions? Why is this project interesting and important?
2. Background: What has been written on this topic and by whom? Where does this work fall short? How can you build on it?
3. Methodology: What approach will you take? What methods will you use? What theoretical framework (if any) does your project need?
4. Sources: What is your evidence base? Why is this appropriate for your project? Where are your sources located?
5. Outcomes: What will be proposed at the end of your research? Why is this the 'right' format for your project?

This document will not be set in stone: you can go back and amend it as your project develops. But it is worth having a draft research proposal as a point of reference, so that you are clear about where your project sits in relation to work that has already been done, the gap in knowledge you want to address and the questions and methods you will use to achieve this.

Chapter 1 outlines some of the key theories and disciplinary approaches in spatial scholarship. In the first part of the chapter we sketch out some of the most important disciplinary and theoretical influences in the development of spatially minded research: archaeology, art history, geography and cultural history. The second half of the chapter turns to exciting new directions in spatial histories. Here you will learn more about attempts to rematerialise urban space and the use of GIS – or Geographic Information Systems. As at all other points in the guide, case studies, endnotes and recommended reading will help you to undertake further reading of your own.

Chapter 2 shows how to begin the research process. We suggest several possible starting points for thinking through and designing your project, divided here into the broad parameters of location or building type, theme or concept and body of evidence. These different approaches are explored through a number of concrete case studies of spatial histories, demonstrating how these research routes work in practice. The final sub-section provides some wide-ranging advice for formulating useful research questions.

Chapter 3 will help you to identify appropriate methods, approaches and theoretical frameworks for your project. There are many different ways of doing a research project. With these multiple possibilities in mind, the key job of the methodology section is to convince your reader that you have selected the right 'tools' for the job. To help you frame your project, we have identified four routes into spatial histories: personal testimony (including diaries, letters and oral interviews); focus on a building or built environment; histories that foreground networks; and finally, work that engages with representation of urban space and built environments. In each case, we include a broad overview of how historians have used this approach, including the questions they have asked, the methods and theories they have engaged with and sources they have used, citing case studies that demonstrate the 'nuts and bolts' of its application.

Chapter 4 introduces the wide variety of primary sources that can help your investigation of urban space or the built environment. In addition to giving advice about how and where to begin looking for evidence for your project, this discussion also provides an overview of different categories of source material. These are loosely grouped as: buildings and built environments; archival materials (like inventories, government regulations, contemporary descriptions); visual (such as plans, maps and photos); material cultures; and oral history interviews.

Chapter 5 explores how you can analyse your sources to best effect. It discusses the strengths and limitations of primary source types in relation to spatial histories, including buildings, archival materials, personal testimony, visual sources and material culture.

Chapter 6 concludes our all-round consideration of the research process by looking at the different ways in which you might present your dissertation or research project. We offer guidance on the organisation of ideas and text that will help you to show to best effect your original archival discoveries and novel connections between buildings, landscapes, ideas, objects and cultures. The chapter provides models for structuring your dissertation, as well as guidance on the most effective ways to reference the material and visual sources essential to spatial histories, such as buildings, material cultures and maps.

NOTES

1   P. Arnade, M. Howell and W. Simons, 'Fertile spaces: the productivity of urban space in northern Europe', *The Journal of Interdisciplinary History*, 32:4 (2002), 515–48.

2   D. Jütte, *The Strait Gate: Thresholds and Power in Western History* (New Haven, CT: Yale University Press, 2015), p. 225.

3   *Ibid.*, pp. 225–6.

4   M. C. Howell, 'The spaces of late medieval urbanity', in M. Boone and P. Stabel (eds), *Shaping Urban Identity in Late Medieval Europe* (Leuven: Garant, 2000), pp. 3–23 (p. 5).

5   C. R. Friedrichs, *The Early Modern City, 1450–1750* (London; New York: Longman, 1995), p. 24.

6   See for example: R. Dennis, *Cities in Modernity: Representations and Productions of Metropolitan Space, 1840–1930* (Cambridge: Cambridge University Press, 2008); C. López Galviz, *Cities, Railways, Modernities: London, Paris, and the Nineteenth Century* (London: Routledge, 2019).

7   A. Forty, *Objects of Desire: Design and Society since 1750* (London: Thames and Hudson, 1995 [1986]), p. 236.

8 K. D. Revell, 'Regulating the landscape: real estate values, city planning, and the 1916 zoning ordinance', in D. Ward and O. Zunz (eds), *The Landscape of Modernity: Essays on New York City, 1900–1940* (New York: Russell Sage Foundation, 1992), pp. 19–44; D. Harvey, *Consciousness and the Urban Experience* (Oxford: Blackwell, 1985), pp. 92–6.

9 Dennis, *Cities in Modernity*, pp. 322–3.

10 L. Nead, *Victorian Babylon: People, Streets and Images in Nineteenth-Century London* (New Haven, CT: Yale University Press, 2000), pp. 34–46; Dennis, *Cities in Modernity*, pp. 1–2.

11 M. Daunton, 'Introduction', in Daunton ed., *The Cambridge Urban History of Britain. Vol. III: 1840–1950* (Cambridge: Cambridge University Press, 2000), pp. 9–10, 37.

12 For a useful overview and critique of 'time space compression' and the experience of modernity, see: J. May and N. Thrift, *Timespace: Geographies of Temporality* (London: Routledge, 2001).

13 'Past Exhibitions: Living with Buildings', *Wellcome Collection*, https://wellcomecollection.org/exhibitions/Wk4sPSQAACcANwrX [accessed 23 January 2020].

14 B. Kümin and C. Usborne, 'At home and in the workplace: a historical introduction to the "spatial turn"', *History and Theory*, 52:3 (2013), 305–18 (p. 307).

15 S. Conrad, *What Is Global History?* (Princeton, NJ: Princeton University Press, 2016), pp. 64–5.

16 C. Ford, 'Nature's fortunes: new directions in the writing of European environmental history', *Journal of Modern History*, 79:1 (2007), 112–33 (pp. 115, 120).

17 R. Kingston, 'Mind over matter? History and the spatial turn', *Cultural and Social History*, 7:1 (2010), 111–21 (p. 111).

18 D. A. DeBats and I. N. Gregory, 'Introduction to historical GIS and the study of urban history', *Social Science History*, 35:4 (2011), 455–63.

19 Colin Gordon, *Mapping Decline: St Louis and the American City* (Philadelphia, PA: University of Pennsylvania Press, 2008); http://mappingdecline.lib.uiowa.edu/ [accessed 15 June 2021].

20 K. Lelo, 'A GIS approach to urban history: Rome in the 18th century', *ISPRS International Journal of Geo-Information*, 3:4 (2014), 1293–316 (pp. 1295–6, 1309–10).

21 L. Jerram, 'Space: a useless category for historical analysis?', *History and Theory*, 52:3 (2013), 400–19 (p. 403).

22 See discussion in Y.-F. Tuan, 'Space and place: humanistic perspective', in S. Gale and G. Olsson (eds), *Philosophy in Geography* (London: Reidel, 1979), pp. 398–400, 410–11, 416–19.

23 J. Agnew, 'Space and place', in J. Agnew and D. N. Livingstone (eds), *The Sage Handbook of Geographical Knowledge* (London: Sage, 2011), pp. 316–30 (pp. 316–21).
24 Dennis, *Cities in Modernity*, p. 1.
25 See for example: S. Gikandi, *Slavery and the Culture of Taste* (Princeton, NJ: Princeton University Press, 2011); M. Finn and K. Smith, 'Introduction', in Finn and Smith (eds), *The East India Company at Home, 1757–1857* (London: UCL Press, 2018), pp. 1–20.

RECOMMENDED READING

J. Agnew, 'Space and place', in J. Agnew and D. N. Livingstone (eds), *The Sage Handbook of Geographical Knowledge* (London: Sage, 2011), pp. 316–30.

W. C. Booth, G. G. Colomb and J. M. William, *The Craft of Research*, 2nd edn (Chicago: University of Chicago Press, 2003).

L. Jerram, 'Space: a useless category for historical analysis?', *History and Theory*, 52:3 (2013), 400–19.

R. Kingston, 'Mind over matter? History and the spatial turn', *Cultural and Social History*, 7:1 (2010), 111–21.

B. Kümin and C. Usborne, 'At home and in the workplace: a historical introduction to the "spatial turn"', *History and Theory*, 52:3 (2013), 305–18.

THEORIES AND APPROACHES TO SPACE AND PLACE

INTRODUCTION

In the Introduction we saw how scholars of diverse disciplines have undertaken spatial research, broadly defined. Spatial scholarship often involves the adoption of varied theories, approaches and methodologies. Historians engaged in spatially oriented research and writing today have thus inherited a rich multidisciplinary academic heritage. As you plan and develop your own research project it might be useful to reflect on how you are building upon these approaches. You might also be extending or challenging existing approaches. Your contribution or intervention may be through the use of particular primary sources (such as architectural plans, or census records), or by the theoretical lenses and methodologies through which you interpret and present your evidence.

In this chapter we outline some of the key theories and disciplinary approaches in spatial scholarship. Such is the richness and breadth of spatial research in the humanities and social sciences from the 1970s onwards that we cannot possibly offer a comprehensive guide. Rather, our intention here is to sketch out some of the most important disciplinary and theoretical influences in the development of spatial research and to encourage you to undertake further reading of your own. We present disciplinary approaches in separate sub-sections in this chapter, so as to organise the material in a coherent way, but readers should be aware that these scholarly approaches have acted, and continue to act, in mutually enriching ways. Moreover, we should be mindful that writing about and representing space, particularly interpretations of urban space, was hardly a new phenomenon in the twentieth century. We have already encountered the medieval and early modern practice of depicting city walls in drawings, prints and paintings. In Chapter 3 we will meet a seventeenth-century diarist who described in great detail the human activities and built environment of his city. The history of writing about and representing towns and cities is an enormous theme, which deserves greater attention than we can provide here in a research guide.[1] The point is that for as long as humans have built, inhabited and encountered urban space, they have also attempted to make sense of it through words and images.

Our discussion of theories and approaches begins with how archaeologists, architectural historians, geographers, sociologists and cultural historians have engaged with space as a central research concern. The second section of the chapter explores significant trends in spatial research today, what we might describe as the 'state of the field'. Our focus here is on materiality and space, and GIS and spatial histories.

ARCHAEOLOGY

Place and space have always been central research concerns for archaeologists. As social archaeologists Robert Preucel and Lynn Meskell write, 'the mapping of peoples and cultures across space and time as evidenced by the distribution of artefacts, households, settlements, and monuments is one of the most basic forms of archaeological analysis'.[2] In their investigations of the buildings, tools, burial sites and other material remains of past societies and cultures, spatial analysis has been an especially helpful tool in uncovering patterns of behaviour and social organisation.[3] For example, a highly influential study undertaken in the 1970s, published as *The Early Mesoamerican Village*, used spatial analysis to examine household and community formation, essentially cultural change, in agrarian settlements of the Oaxaca Valley, Mexico, c. 1500–500 BCE.[4] Along with social geographers, archaeologists have also pioneered the exploration of wide-ranging scales of spatial analysis: from vast landscapes right down to individual households. Research into archaeological landscapes has stressed the reciprocal relationship between natural environment and sociocultural features. The landscape is not a passive backdrop but actively shapes human activity, experience and memory.[5] In an influential work on the human experience of landscape (or the 'phenomenology of landscape'), Christopher Tilley charted the reciprocal and shifting relationship between landscape (including natural and artificial aspects) and human habitation over vast swathes of time. For example, Tilley contends that with the development of herding societies in the Neolithic era, 'the movements of animals would physically inscribe these paths across the landscape much more prominently than the feet of hunter-gatherers following the movements of game, and it would become increasingly difficult (both in practical and symbolic terms) to take different ways'.[6] Landscape and human activity shape each other.

At the micro-level of the individual household, too, the emphasis in archaeological research has been on the ways in which the built environment and human activities and behaviours are mutually reinforcing. Writing about early modern domestic environments and their inhabitants, archaeologist Matthew Johnson has stressed the ways in which 'the house and social life acted recursively, back-and-forth on one another'.[7] Humans designed, built and materially adapted their homes, but the experience of living within particular structures reciprocally shaped human behaviour and attitudes about gender, class and intergenerational relations. We will see later in this chapter that this powerful idea of reciprocity has also been taken up and developed within the field of cultural history.

ARCHITECTURAL HISTORY

The discipline of architectural history is located at the intersection of studies of the built environment and history. Architectural historians typically have training and expertise in the interpretation of building designs and built space. Historians who are interested in engaging with the built environment thus have much to gain by paying attention to the work, primary sources and methodologies of architectural scholars. Traditionally, architectural history was focused on the attribution of buildings to particular architects and patrons, and an examination of the individual architect's influences and motivations. Since the 1960–70s, impacted upon by the wider 'cultural turn' in the humanities and social sciences, architectural scholarship has been much more attuned to the wider social, political and cultural contexts shaping and shaped by built space.[8] As architect and architectural historian Swati Chattopadhyay explained in an article on the state of the field:

> Initially lodged within art history (and its traditional concerns with style and iconography), architectural historians have variously redefined themselves as historians of the built environment (in the 1960s, closely

tied to the development of environmental design and planning), as historians of the cultural landscape (beginning in the 1970s, related to the study of folklore and vernacular architecture, and grounded in structuralism and the new class analysis of the 1960s), as cultural historians (influenced by poststructuralism and the cultural/textual turn of the 1980s), and as historians of spatial practice (inspired by the spatial turn in the 1980s and the critique of capitalist production of space).[9]

The range of built spaces considered worthy of examination has also vastly expanded since 1970. Architectural histories thus include not only the grand houses of the gentry and aristocracy by renowned designers and patrons, but also ordinary homes, streets, shops and public spaces. Some pioneering works in architectural history have explored buildings and themes as varied as embodied space in seventeenth-century Neapolitan convents and consumerism and globalisation in twenty-first-century shopping malls.[10] In Chapter 5 we will consider how the visual and material sources and methodologies used by architectural historians might be useful in your own research project.

GEOGRAPHY

Where history's main organising principles are time and temporality, geography is the discipline that deals most explicitly with space and place. Like many of the approaches considered here, geography is 'quintessentially an interdisciplinary tradition when its various "parts" (physical and human, cultural and economic, etc.) are considered together'.[11] What follows is not intended as an exhaustive survey. Instead, it sets out key 'turns' in geographical practice since the 1980s that will be of special interest to historians: 'new' cultural geography, critical human geography and historical geography. In each case, we will see how these approaches have expanded the horizons of geography as a discipline to show how space and place underpin all manner of social, cultural, political and economic experience in the past and present.

'New' cultural geography

Like spatially attuned historians, advocates of the 'new' cultural geography took on ideas from outside their discipline, including the 'new' cultural history discussed below.[12] Understanding its aims requires us to reflect on how proponents redefined the relationship between culture and landscape. First and foremost, this required cultural geographers to move beyond a paradigm (or model) that viewed the relationship between human culture and landscape in terms of the former's impact on the physical world.[13] Second, it meant asking anew how 'culture' should be defined: moving from the notion of a singular, elite intellectual and artistic canon (in the sense that 'culture' might be enjoyed at the Royal Opera House) to engaging with a plurality of *cultures* on their own terms.[14] In doing so, 'new' cultural geographers built on the pioneering work of Stuart Hall and the Centre for Contemporary Cultural Studies at the University of Birmingham on popular and youth cultures, and subculture. The broad focus of this work is how cultures – always plural – are meaningful. In Clarke et al.'s famous formulation, culture refers to the way, the forms, in which groups '"handle" the raw material of their social and material existence'.[15] Open-ended and inclusive approaches to the subject encouraged scholars from across the humanities to look at the multiplicity of ways in which cultures, as the many ways in which people make sense of their worlds, gave shape and structure to the lives of individuals and groups. Thinking in this way pushed geographers to reconsider what they meant by landscape, adding to the physical and built environment the spaces and places of domestic life, popular culture, intimacy and sexuality. Doing so encouraged study of the places and spaces that were implicated in less visible and tangible aspects of life, including everyday social practices, like getting dressed, going to work and family life, providing new pathways into study of class, gender and sexuality, and race and ethnicity.

Representation

These concerns led scholars to grapple with questions of representation. In the sense in which it is used here, representation does not mean the simple reflection or reproduction of a known and knowable world, a practice often described by the Greek term 'mimesis'. Instead, representation, drawing on ideas from critical theory in language and literature studies, is recognised to be a much more complicated business. No form of representation is treated as neutral but it is understood as part of the broader exercise of power in a given place at a given time. By taking this approach, we contend with the multiple authors and fragmented meanings inherent in every kind of representation, from textual descriptions in travellers' accounts, fiction, colonial minute-keeping and popular song, to visual depictions, like maps, paintings, advertisements and films. Above all, the politics of culture is brought into focus: how culture is formed and reformed through power relationships, like negotiation and contestation, dominance and subordination. Take, for example, Edward Saïd's influential work on *Orientalism*, which showed how texts and visual images presented people and places of 'the Orient' as irrational, inferior and 'other', often contrasted with the presentation of 'the West' as rational, progressive and modern. This was shown to be part of broader discourses of Western colonialism and imperialism.[16] Saïd unpicked the symbolic meanings embedded in such representations and demonstrated how these relate to broader, 'real world' social, political and economic conditions.

Critical human geography

Not all geographers in the 1980s and 1990s were convinced by the 'cultural' turn their discipline had taken. Some argued for the continued significance of class struggle (simply put, the conflict of interests between workers and the ruling class under capitalism) as the primary explanation of political and economic conditions. Their arguments were strongly influenced by Marxist approaches to understanding urban environments and 'urbanism', and turned on the idea that space is also a commodity which can be produced, and bought and sold. Bringing Karl Marx into analysis of space involved a conceptual leap of faith: even the most committed proponents of this type of spatial analysis acknowledge that Marx and his followers had very little to say about space or place.[17]

Even so, geographers like David Harvey used the theories of Henri Lefebvre to argue that cities, as social, cultural and material entities, were shaped by political and economic arrangements in the past and present, most notably capitalism. The implications of Harvey's approach are clearest in his analysis of the vast public works programme, usually linked to the name of Baron Haussmann (1809–91), which transformed nineteenth-century Paris. He posits that major redevelopment was intended to reshape Paris's urban environment so that it better serviced capital accumulation (the ability to increase assets from investments and profit). Arguing that Haussmann was in cahoots with Parisian banking families, Harvey drew on the evidence of the built environment to make his case, pointing to the strategic development of railways and canals that enhanced the wealth-making potential of elites by ensuring speedier distribution of raw materials and finished goods, along with the process of 'embourgeoisement' (what we might term 'gentrification'), which changed patterns of residence and industry by pushing the latter out of the city centre, to make his case.[18] The useful idea for our purposes is that the material evidence of the urban environment, along with patterns of urban life, could be treated as the material articulation of social, political and economic processes.[19]

Critics of Marxist analyses of urban space have pointed to the lack of interest, especially in Harvey's work, in the particular textures of material life in any given city.[20] Rather than tackle the distinctive impacts of capitalism on urban environments, this work (so it is argued) deals in abstract flows of capital accumulation and 'the power of capital to make, and remake, urban space'.[21] Feminist geographers like Doreen Massey have offered the most powerful critique by drawing attention to the asymmetrical (or uneven) impacts of global capitalism and the extent to which these intersect with other forms of social, political and economic inequality.[22] As Massey writes, 'Social and economic divides are exacerbated by geography', with the global produced locally and the local, globally.[23] It is also worth asking why, in the late twentieth century, place was overshadowed by space as a focus for study in the humanities and social sciences, including history. Its side-lining demonstrates just how power laden the terms of academic discussion can be: where space was treated as abstract, modern, mobile and global, place was labelled particular, traditional, fixed, often feminine and local.[24] It is perhaps no surprise that the most valuable critiques of space, alongside the championing of place, came from feminist and postcolonial geographers.[25] As a result, place has made something of a comeback, typically in dialogue with space, driving work that deals with the multiple, sometimes entangled relationships between places and selves to show that place, like space, is 'always in a state of becoming, always the result of historically contingent processes and social practices'.[26]

Henri Lefebvre's *Production of Space*

Henri Lefebvre's writings about how conditions of economic production and urban space are mutually constitutive – that is, help to form one another – have been hugely influential across the humanities and social sciences.[27] Lefebvre's most useful (albeit densely argued) contribution to debate can be found in his *Production of Space* (1974), where he proposed that urban space is produced through the conversation – or dialectic – between three categories (or a triad) of spatial activities.[28] These are:

- **Spatial practice:** This is how we engage with the world out there, for want of a better expression: how we perceive it and how it shapes our routines. Think, for example, of the routes, networks and patterns of interaction that shape your own experience of where you live. How do you travel between home and the library? Are there different routes by which you can do this? Are there reasons why you might choose one way over another? Are there circumstances that change this? Let us take an example from Lefebvre – post-war high-rise housing – to cement the concept. Its form, scale, materials, location and distribution all shape the lives of people who live in or adjacent to these kinds of complex. We might think about the consequences of verticality, the proximity of other people within a tower block, the relative distance to transportation and other amenities, or even the routine frustration of the lift to the twenty-fifth floor being broken.

- **Spaces of representation:** This refers to how spaces are presented conceptually in the form of maps, plans, policy documents, advertisements, photographs and so forth, which we might think about as discourses – or ideas – about urban space. The important point is that these representations are made by people, such as planners, architects, civil servants and scientists, who have the power to influence what urban environments are actually like – the monuments and buildings that are built, and also how people can behave within those spaces – because they have a closer relationship to the facilities and resources (or means of production, to use the Marxist terminology) that make things happen. Picking up our mid-twentieth-century high-rise housing, we could interrogate what policy makers, urban planners and architects hoped to achieve with these kinds of buildings. Here, we might look to plans, elevations, newspaper editorials, publicity photographs, marketing buzzwords and policy documents to tease out the social, political and economic ideals presented (e.g. modernity, efficiency, rationality, surveillance, alienation and individuation).

- **Representational space:** Lefebvre's third category attempts to capture space as it is lived: that is, the layers of meaning that we all bring to our subjective engagement with wherever we are. These can be emotional, imaginary, sensorial and activated by memory. Think of your favourite coffee shop. Your relationship to this space is shaped by the complex interaction between what it is like (how well lit, how comfortable, the colours of the walls) and your accumulated experiences there: knowing when you are most likely to nab the best place to sit, knowledge of when they serve your favourite cake, treasured memories of a good date. As this example suggests, representational space can be tricky to define in its liveness and immediacy: 'it's rather felt more than thought'.[29] Within Lefebvre's framework, what matters is that in representational space lies the potential for change, as it also includes activities that are potentially anarchic, carnivalesque, underground and subcultural. It is where there is constant negotiation and contestation between the potential for creativity and imagination, and the will of political and economic forces (those with the ability to actively shape representational space) to suppress these conscious and unconscious desires. Indeed, one of Lefebvre's key arguments is that planners, policy makers and their like are constantly attempting to meddle with representational space by ordering and rationalising it. Here, then, to again pick up our example of mid-twentieth-century high-rise housing, we might explore the vertical imaginary evident in fiction, such as the novels of J. G. Ballard, or in films, like *La Haine* (1995), and reflect on the ways in which high-rise living fed into particular forms of representation or symbolism. But we might also ask how residents pushed back through grassroots and community-building activities to reclaim public spaces and campaign for more resources and a better quality of life.

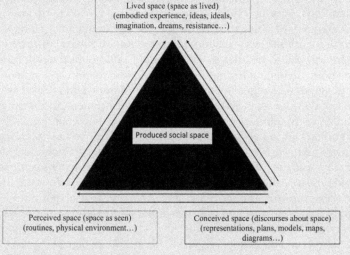

Figure 1.1 Diagram of Henri Lefebvre's spatial 'triad'.

But why might this 'spatial triad' be useful for historians? Above all, Lefebvre's model shows how and why space is not an empty backdrop for other activities but is, instead, created through the conversation – or dialectic – between elements that are material, ideological and subjective. The diagram in Figure 1.1 helps to explain how these interactions work to produce space. Importantly, '[r]elations between the conceived-perceived-lived aren't ever stable and exhibit historically defined attributes and content'.[30] This means that Lefebvre's 'triad' needs to be embedded in specific spatial and historical contexts in order to make sense. When applied to specific examples, Lefebvre's categories are especially useful for negotiating the links between abstract experiences of space and physical and material aspects of the world. They also help us to think through how relationships between space as it is perceived, conceived (or conceptualised) and lived are power laden, pushing us to reflect on how and why space is produced, for whose benefit and, above all, where change can happen.

Historical geography

Historical geography is concerned with 'the geographies of the past and with the influence of the past in shaping the geographies of the present and the future'.[31] Initially, this sub-discipline of human geography combined scrutiny of the physical environment, archival work and cartography in order to reconstruct past environments.[32] Here, scholars argued how the formation and evolution of physical environments were integral to broader social, economic and political developments, including demography, industrialisation, urbanisation and agricultural and agrarian change.[33] While continuing to work with a broad base of material evidence, including the physical environment, historical geography has become ever more outward looking since the mid-1980s. In common with other humanities subjects, scholars became increasingly concerned with issues around representation, drawing on approaches from outside the discipline, including feminist theory, postcolonialism and poststructuralism, most notably the work of Michel Foucault, in the process. Interrogation of power and meaning, as it played out in geographical knowledge and practices in the past, extended 'concerns with questions of class and capital to other axes of domination and identity such as race and gender' to tackle big historical themes such as state formation and nationalism, globalisation and ideas of environmental change and nature.[34]

Foucault: space, power and governmentality

How do we think about power and the city? Perhaps one of the most influential frameworks for urban historians emerged through the far-reaching work of French social theorist, philosopher and historian, Michel Foucault (1926–84). Foucault's large body of research had a profound impact on the ways in which historians examined the connections between urban space, power and identity. It facilitated a shift away from thinking about urban redevelopment in purely structural or physical terms and instead moved towards an approach that analysed the role of the mechanics and infrastructure of the city as fundamentally being about power. Foucault emphasised that power was not top down but infiltrated everyday life and intruded into the minutiae of urban experience, especially within the construction and organisation of the modern city. Foucault's key concepts included:

- **Power:** Underpinning much of his work, Foucault argued that power and language were mutually constructed. Perhaps one of his most famous and influential concepts, Foucault stressed the pervasive power of discourse in producing and classifying 'norms', arguing that nineteenth-century medical and legal discourse constructed and disseminated 'truths' about 'normal' and 'abnormal' bodies. These classifications subsequently influenced the myriad of ways in which urban planners, the police and local government identified and controlled parts of the city associated with those considered subversive, including political insurgents, the poor, migrant groups and criminals.
- **Biopower:** Foucault used this term to explain how the ruling elites manipulated biological features – such as fertility rates – to inform and shape their political strategy that reinforced their control. For instance, the control of poor bodies, including the removal of sewage from overcrowded urban areas, became identified as a form of power and a method of controlling the potentially threatening urban underclass. Foucault used 'the social' to describe the network of social relationships underpinning the power and control of the ruling elite.
- **Governmentality:** A playful term used to encapsulate Foucault's focus on the way in which he perceived some people as allowing themselves to be governed while relying on the concept of 'freedom'. For Foucault, the nineteenth-century city had the illusion of an absent state but, in effect, the state was everywhere. All aspects of urban fabric, from parks, civic institutions, artificial light, to roads and public health initiatives, served to control the urban poor in ways that Foucault saw as

being more insidious and difficult to challenge than more overt power structures.
- **Panopticon:** Foucault used the example of philosopher Jeremy Bentham's eighteenth-century panoptic prison to draw attention to the role of seeing and making visible as a form of power. By the use of invasive surveillance, prisoners were controlled by their knowledge of being watched, which aimed to impose self-discipline. The model inspired other forms of institutional design, particularly the workhouse.

Above all, historians can learn a great deal from how historical geographers have approached 'new imperial histories' since the mid-1990s.[35] This work is underpinned by a key geographical framework: thinking scalarly and paying 'attention to both the specificity of the local and the wider economic, cultural and political processes and institutional structures'.[36] By looking at the connections between places, some of which were at vast distances from each other, historical geographers have shown how relationships between cities, regions and countries were structured and understood by means of geographic practices and knowledge. Writing interconnected, increasingly global historical geographies means following flows of people, natural resources, material culture, trade networks, information, representation and capital between places to explain how these relationships were initiated, structured and policed, and whom they benefited.[37] This approach demands scholarly reflexivity: recognition that geographical knowledge practices, including cartography (or map-making), were implicated in the formation of national and imperial identities.[38] Without due care, we risk reproducing power-laden relationships from the past and omitting particular groups, including women, working classes, people of colour and 'non-Western' subjects, from our studies. Instead, recent scholarship demonstrates that there was no 'one-size-fits-all' model for colonialism or imperialism.

To explore one specific example, Alan Lester shows how nineteenth- and early twentieth-century British colonial identities and discourses were made by means of connections and networks that stretched across the globe, forged by the circulation of government dispatches, maps and visual representations, newspaper reports, letters, people, things and commodities.[39] To take one part of his argument, the biological determinism of discourses about 'inherent racial inequality' were shaped by the networks between colonial settlers in settings as various as the West Indies, South Africa, India and the southern states of the United States, before becoming entrenched in the metropole through journalism, popular music, schooling and disciplines, including geography.[40] Importantly, Lester also shows how circumstances back in the 'metropole' ensured the hardening of racial discourse, with the 'the triumph of settler imagery' aided by domestic social and political concerns, including the perceived threat of increasingly politically organised workers.[41] Critical across this case study is the understanding that relationships between metropole and colony were 'hierarchical but [also] reciprocal' and, most importantly, should be interrogated within the same analytical frame.[42]

Thinking globally and looking for connections and networks also demonstrates the benefits of working with expanded, joined-up geographies – something many historians can be usefully reminded of. This could mean focusing your research on less familiar or, indeed, less Western locations by, say, moving beyond the classic triad of London, Paris or New York in a study of nineteenth-century cities to show how modernity, urbanisation and industrialisation in the West are not the only models. Or it might mean teasing out the sometimes surprising links between places. Caroline Bressey's work on the nineteenth-century periodical *Anti-Caste* offers an exemplary model for historians to follow, placing the tiny village of Street in Somerset at the heart of its national, international and imperial networks. In addition to providing an excellent example of the extent to which the local is always global, Bressey's creative and sensitive use of evidence that includes guest books, correspondence, photographs and printed materials demonstrates the international dimensions of radical political engagement and participation.[43]

CULTURAL HISTORY

Spatial research has been an especially attractive approach for cultural historians, and it is from cultural history that some of the most innovative spatial scholarship has emerged.[44] As a state-of-the-field article at the beginning of this century suggested: 'historians, especially urban historians, have much to gain, and much to offer, by interrogating the proliferation of "spaces" that appear in scholarly literature – mental, political, imaginary, material, and legal space, to name just a few'.[45] In their exploration of the meanings and representations of 'customs, values and a way of life', cultural historians have adopted spatially oriented methodologies to examine the diversity – and contested nature – of human experiences, identities and imaginations.[46] Works of spatially inspired cultural history have been written from almost every conceivable social angle, geography and time period. Cultural historians have, for example, used space as a framework for examining gendered identities and landscapes in medieval England, concepts of 'public' and 'private' spheres in eighteenth-century France and migration patterns in modern South Asia.[47] To take just one early example, a pioneering work by David Rothman, *The Discovery of the Asylum* (1971), explored the site locations, floor plans and façades of prisons, mental hospitals and other early nineteenth-century institutions. In so doing, Rothman uncovered wider cultural attitudes to social control, discipline and institutionalisation.[48]

Cultural historians from the 1970s, often in dialogue with postmodern theorists such as Michel Foucault and Henri Lefebvre, tended to approach space largely as a symbolic or imagined construct, a 'spatial metaphor'. For instance, work on the history of the landscape has typically argued that landscape is a 'concept' which can be 'read' to reveal the politics of production.[49] Frustrated with the use of space principally as a metaphor, historians in the last two decades, since about the year 2000, have been more sensitive to the material reality of spatial experiences. As Riitta Laitinen and Thomas Cohen write in their introduction to a history of early modern streets, 'we have attended to the nature of the street as an urban material entity, as a starting point for studying people in the streets (and near them), highlighting the integral connectivity of the material and the immaterial'.[50] Focusing on a later time period, Leif Jerram's highly engaging book *Streetlife* makes a very convincing case for scrutinising the physical environments – including homes, factories, streets, shops, cinemas and nightclubs – of twentieth-century European cities. In his view, to understand the 'big' events and cultural and political movements of this momentous century we must scrutinise the 'where' of history. In Jerram's own words, 'The physical spaces matter – the layouts of rooms, the relationships of things, the distances between, the temperature, the lines of sight. And the values of the place matter – the ideas it bears, from danger to fun, from sick to healthy, from sacred to profane.'[51]

For some scholars this (slow) move towards the materiality of space has still not gone far enough. As historian Ralph Kingston argued in a 2010 review essay on history and the spatial turn, 'centred on the production of spatial ideas, however, our Spatial Turn has obliterated interest in bricks and mortar. Human beings, we argue, interact *through* space, and only secondarily *in* space.'[52] As you are planning your research project it might be helpful to reflect at various stages on the balance and interactions between the 'material and immaterial' in your own writing. In the final section of this chapter on 'new directions' we will consider the concerted move in the humanities and social sciences to 'rematerialise' urban space.

Cultural history: space and modern identities

The influence of cultural theory reinvigorated the approach of urban historians, encouraging a consideration of urban space as an active agent in shaping and producing behaviour and identity. Bearing this in mind as you approach your project, it is worth considering how cultural historians conceive of the relationship between space and identity as not fixed, but mutually reinforcing and historically specific. Art historian Lynda Nead explains: 'social space is not a passive background to the formation of identity but is part of an active ordering and organising of the social and cultural relations of the city'.[53] Influenced by cultural theoretical approaches, especially the work of Michel de Certeau and Lefevre, historical scholarship has grappled with space as 'dynamic, constructed, and contested. It was where issues of sexuality, race, class, and gender – amongst a myriad of other power/knowledge struggles – were sited, created, and fought out.'[54] These kinds of theoretical frameworks that explain the relationship between space and identity help to historicise the processes that caused and shaped the emergence of modern categories of identity, which many urban historians argue manifested themselves alongside and within the city itself. We can see that there was a dialectical relationship between the organisation of space in the modern era and the forms of social identity that historians of the Western world tend to use as the main organising categories. Understanding this relationship can help us to research and analyse the history of a city not just as a site where things happen but as a key contributor in producing, shaping and influencing key forms of identity and experience through historical case studies and via a range of historical methods. The following exploration of some of the key concepts through which historians have framed and analysed the relationship between space and identity will help you to identify the key conceptual issues that you might address in your own research project:

- **Industrialisation:** One of the most influential and far-reaching forms of social and economic change experienced by modern cities, industrialisation is often identified by historians of the nineteenth century as providing the foundations of modern forms of identity. For instance, Britain experienced significant social and economic change from the mid-eighteenth century, including notable population growth, from a population of 5.8 million in 1751, to 8.7 million in 1801 and 17.9 million in 1851. This shift has been explained by an increase in marriage rates that occurred alongside a rapid period of industrialisation and urbanisation. Manchester, Leeds and Sheffield grew three-fold between 1775 and 1830.[55] These examples are an important reminder of how urban historians must bear in mind that redevelopment occurs hand in hand or is foregrounded by wider social or demographic change. For example, changes caused by rapid industrialisation and urbanisation contributed to new patterns of living and working. Between 1801 and 1841, the population of London doubled, but Manchester's trebled in size and 'acquired almost mythical status as the emblem of a new order of things'.[56] Manchester became the 'shock city' of the Industrial Revolution, attracting visitors from around the world who came to chart the horror and dirt caused by such rapid social and economic change. Alexis de Tocqueville visited Manchester in 1835, famously writing that 'the greatest stream of human industry flows out to fertilise the whole world. From this filthy sewer pure gold flows. Here humanity attains its most complete development and its most brutish; here civilisation works its miracles, and civilised man is turned back into savage.'[57] De Toqueville's description gives some sense of the alarm felt by contemporaries throughout Europe and beyond when they experienced this new urban phenomenon. Yet, as we move on to explore, the impact of industrialisation was profound and contributed to the emergence of modern categories of identity, including class, gender and race. These categories underpin how urban historians have approached the reciprocal relationship between the modern city and power (we will focus on class in more detail presently), which may provide useful frameworks for your own research. Although many of the subsequent examples are drawn from modern British urban history, the insights and methods they offer will help you to think through these key issues in relation to other countries and contexts.
- **Class:** Most urban historians would agree that the modern city was built on capitalism and produced modern class identities. It was no

coincidence that Marx and Engels wrote *The Communist Manifesto* (1848) after spending time in Manchester together. There, they were horrified by the living and working conditions of the armies of industrial workers who had migrated to the city to work in the new factories and warehouses. Their experiences bolstered and shaped their understanding and definition of approaches to class and power – defining those that own the means to production (wealthy industrialists) in comparison to those that did not (workers). The emergence of class as an economic category has buttressed key historical approaches to modern society and is rooted within this model of urbanisation and industrialisation, influencing much historical scholarship. It is certainly difficult to think of how we might explore nineteenth- and twentieth-century cityscapes and those who experienced them without engaging in the language of class, or acknowledging the disparities and inequities caused by variations in economic power.

We can also think about class as a cultural identity, particularly through the emergence of the powerful industrial middle class – the wealthy and powerful industrialists created as a distinct and self-conscious social group in these new cities, such as Manchester, Sheffield and Leeds. As Robert Morris's classic essay of 1983 stated, British towns and cities were 'substantially the creation of their middle class, and in turn provided the theatre within which that middle class sought, extended, expressed and defended its power'.[58] Urban historian Simon Gunn has highlighted the civilising mission of the urban middle class, which was seen as representing 'civility' or 'civilisation' through its associations and institutions, and suggests that this role was true of towns as well as cities. In Derby, for example, the local elite established a Literary and Philosophical Institute (1808), a Mechanics Institute (1825), and in the 1840s a Literary and Scientific Society, a County Natural History Society and the Derby Arboretum. Gunn suggests that this civilising zeal helped to distinguish the urban middle class more clearly and differentiated their identity from the culture and social relations of the surrounding countryside, reflecting a class struggle between old and new forms of power.[59] These strategies were used by the middle classes to assert their collective pride and identity and were a form of power. This framework encourages researchers to think about how power was formed and exerted within the modern city. Patrick Joyce builds on Foucauldian concepts of governmentality and uses the term 'The Rule of Freedom' to explore how the very urban fabric of the Victorian city closely controlled and restricted the behaviour of the working classes, while giving the illusion of freedom. In his argument, 'The city became a place where one watched and was watched: in the public park, the municipal museum, in the public squares of the city, people were led to present themselves in ways that would be "publicly" acceptable, and in presenting themselves to others, these others, in a reciprocal "calculated administration of shame", presented themselves in turn to them as but themselves magnified.'[60] This approach helps us to understand how power can be read through grandiose Victorian civic monuments that were a method to control the unruly and threatening working classes, particularly in the aftermath of important working-class rebellions such as Peterloo in 1819 and Chartism in the 1830s and 1840s. As we shall see in later chapters, historians of urban space and the built environment have at their fingertips an exciting and widespread choice of primary sources and research methods. Gunn and Joyce encourage us to think about how power was created, disseminated and reproduced through the urban fabric and design of the modern city itself. These perspectives may help you to apply new ways of thinking about the relationship between power and the city to novel case studies that help to expose original insights into class identities.

In this way, we can 'read' specific examples of architecture or leisure spaces as examples of how local elites sought to impose control on urban populations. Town halls, for example, became fundamental tools of governmentality – to use Foucault's term to think about how the city itself was used by the local elites to shape behaviour. The urban elites in industrial cities competed to build the largest and most impressive town halls – think of Manchester's neo-Gothic masterpiece by Albert Waterhouse, built in 1868–77; Cuthbert Brodrick's neo-Classical Leeds Town Hall, 1853–58; or the Beaux Arts Glasgow City Chambers by William Young, 1883–88. These buildings were not just about prestige or adverts for commercial wealth. Joyce explains that these intimidating town halls were crucial methods of controlling the working classes: 'the citizen should at all times be able to view this emblem of citizenry, and in turn the citizen should be opened to the view from the town hall. As the view from the town hall was in theory the view of the citizen, the citizen was both seer and seen. The town hall was therefore a sort of omnioptic machine of liberal political reason, virtual governmentality in fact.'[61] Thinking about the position of these town halls – in prominent positions in urban centres that could not be avoided or ignored by the poor who lived and worked in squalid conditions close by – we can see how architecture functioned as an important method of control in the mid-Victorian city. As Figure 1.2. shows, town halls became the centre of performances of elite culture to reinforce the presence and power of the industrial classes. These examples encourage us to reflect on the myriad of ways in which power was expressed and reproduced and remind us that urban inequalities were often purposefully recreated through urban design and architecture. Thinking about how we might 'read' the fabric of urban life – from a town hall to a park, for instance – as a method of controlling certain facets of a city's population might also be extended to more recent case studies and examples. This includes scholarship that looks at post-1945 urban redevelopment and highlights the emergence of new forms of urban space, such as shopping malls, to explain the rise of neoliberalism and the importance of everyday space in reproducing power.[62] These conceptions of power may help us to explore the deep-rooted relationship between the control of urban space and the control of its inhabitants, which so many historians have acknowledged across different historical periods and geographic areas.

Figure 1.2 Leeds Town Hall royal visit 1858, artist unknown.

NEW DIRECTIONS

Rematerialising urban space

There is a tendency in some modern scholarship to universalise: to praise the general and abstract over the precisely located. This is something with a particular bearing on the topic at hand. Studies of urban environments have witnessed the ascendancy of abstract thought at the cost of understanding the role of the physical and material world in social, cultural, political and economic matters.[63] In part, this is a consequence of recent arguments about 'placelessness' and 'non-places', which argue that developments in transport infrastructure and communications technology make all places more and more like one other, precisely because the time and distance between places have been eroded.[64] Chris Otter's survey of recent urban history nails the point, interrogating how and why the past has been dematerialised:

> Although urban sociology, Marxist urban studies, cultural theory and SCOT [Social Construction of Technology] literature provided valuable insights into urban history, they relegated materiality to a limited repertoire of stock roles: background, outcome, medium, obstacle, text, symbol, determinant. The material world became an external environment within which analytically interesting action took place.[65]

Recent histories of science, technology, architecture and the city have reached beyond the discipline, borrowing methods from science and technology studies (often abbreviated to STS), to reassert the significance of the relationship between matter and humans. Most influential is actor–network theory (or ANT), an approach that was developed by Bruno Latour, Michel Callon and John Law at Paris's Centre de Sociologie de l'Innovation in the 1980s. In this first iteration, ANT was a tool for interrogating the social and material construction of scientific and technological knowledge and knowledge practices. ANT is more of a research method, or even a strategy, than an all-encompassing theory. The basic premise of ANT is that abstractions, like 'class', 'capital' or even 'society', are meaningless as categories: they also need explanation. ANT's solution is the description of networked relationships between human and non-human actors. Within this framework, '[n]etworks are rather to be taken literally, as a set of real connections and associations'.[66] An unusual feature of this work is the notion that 'the construction of networks is as much a process of non-humans as it is one of humans', and that humans should not be privileged in analysis, with scholars granting as much agency or influence to the role of things.[67] (That objects can have a mind of their own will come as no surprise to anyone who has ever dealt with a broken phone, key or printer.) Importantly, nothing exists beyond the network. ANT aficionados do not seek additional layers of meaning lying below the surface of reality. Instead, they look to networks made up of people, things and ideas, where all these 'actors' – and their interrelation – are integral to what and, indeed, how something means. The networks are also continually being remade, with the persistence, or durability, of specific networks signalling imbalances in power.

This all sounds very complicated, but one of the features of ANT-led studies is the preoccupation with the tangible and concrete as a way into discussion.[68] In one of his most readable essays, Latour used the curious, double-headed form of a key to a flat in Berlin to collapse the distinction between the social and technological, human and material, and to reveal the ways in which these generate each other.[69] Close study of the form of the 'Berlin key' demonstrates how it was intended to encourage particular behaviours (leaving the street door open during the day, double-locking the same at night). Within his broader argument about the role of the material in shaping social behaviour (and vice versa), the key is framed as a mediator between a 'world of signs' (e.g. spoken or written admonitions to lock the door) and the 'social world' (e.g. where entry into or exit from a building is determined by face-to-face interaction with a porter or concierge).[70] Essentially, this argument is about power: played out in the practices enabled by the lock and key are stories of privacy, access, trust and resistance (in a nice touch, Latour remarks on how Berliners file down their copy of the key to subvert the system).

Although some scholars have found the absence of causal mechanisms a bit hard to swallow (in ANT, the explained and explanation are all one piece), its claims for the significance of the material are useful for our purposes. By scrutinising how scientific and technological knowledge is socially and materially constructed, STS furnishes models for thinking about the relationships between people and 'things', including the built environment. Through its inclusive, non-hierarchical networks, ANT helps to deconstruct the binaries (or ideas made up of two parts) that can confound analysis of space and place, such as social/natural, local/global, internal/external and abstract/material, to steer a more fruitful course between what is termed **agency** (the ability of individuals to act independently) and **structure** (the various arrangements that shape actions or limit choices).[71] This matters to the study of space and place. As Ralph Kingston says, 'For historians of space and place, ANT is of particular importance as it assumes that social relations are both semiotic (made up of signs and symbols) *and* material: they involve not only people and discourse, but also technologies and the physical world.'[72]

The **'black box'**, another tool from STS, also helps to reveal how far the social and technological are crucially linked and mutually constituted. The term is borrowed from cyberneticians, who use the concept 'whenever a piece of machinery or a set of commands is too complex. In its place [cyberneticians] draw a little box about which they need to know nothing but its input and output.'[73] For Latour, 'black-boxing' is 'the way scientific and technical work is made invisible by its own success. When a machine runs efficiently, when a matter of fact is settled, one need focus only on its inputs and outputs and not on its internal complexity. Thus, paradoxically, the more science and technology succeed, the more opaque and obscure they become.'[74] To use the STS terminology, the point at which technology becomes seamless and invisible is termed 'closure'.[75]

The task of the scholar is to open the 'black box', a process guided by the recognition that black boxes are made by means of technological *and* social factors. Two broad approaches to the process of 'un-black-boxing' are especially useful for historians. First, the notion that a technology, whatever it is, has a life cycle. Within this, two 'moments' are worth looking at if we want to establish how something works socially and technologically: when it becomes 'successful' (i.e. invisible and unquestioned) and when it 'fails'.[76] Second, in the process of interrogating the 'success' or 'failure' of a particular technology, we certainly need to grapple with its inner workings – its nuts, bolts, cogs, wires or algorithms. But we also need to pay attention to the huge amount of effort that was invested in bringing different groups of people on board with a technological development, as evidenced in materials including newspaper reports, government papers, statistics, marketing materials and advertisements.

But what does this have to do with urban spaces and built environments? A well-established modernist tradition describes buildings as 'walk-through' machines: 'technological artefacts, made material objects, and humanly constructed physical things'.[77] Jane M. Jacobs,

Stephen Cairns and Ignaz Strebel's article about the Red Road housing estate in Glasgow demonstrates how effectively the idea of the black box can be applied to historical built environments. Focusing on the site's 'birth' (or initial development in the 1960s) and 'death' (or demolition in the early 2000s), the study scrutinises the efforts expended, first, on making Red Road a technological success story and, later, during discussions around its future, how it was resituated as an example of failed high-rise social housing. At each stage, the authors are extremely careful to show that there were multiple perspectives on Red Road, as determined by the relationships of groups or individuals to the site.[78] Ultimately, when analysed through the lens of the black box, Red Road becomes a case study that demonstrates how the social and techno-logical aspects of modernist high-rise housing cannot be separated. This offers an alternative to earlier analysis of the same site that was **technologically determinist** (i.e. our lives are shaped by technological innovations, including the design of buildings) or **socially constructivist** (i.e. humans make buildings what they are).[79] Thinking more broadly about histories of urban spaces and built environments, this approach provides a model for engaging with the 'diverse forces at work in shap-ing and reshaping a housing event like Red Road', as well as suggesting how we can make sense of multiple points in its history, framed here as 'birth' and 'death'.[80] Treated in this way, buildings and built environ-ments emerge as dynamic: the result of complex, changing relationships between materials and technologies, government policy, marketing and many different sorts of people, including residents.

Historians of various kinds are increasingly concerned with matter and materiality; some but not all engage explicitly with the theoret-ical approaches described above. Unsurprisingly, it is historians of science and technology who are especially comfortable with using STS in their work. Engaging with tools from outside history, including STS and environmental studies, has allowed historian of nineteenth- and twentieth-century technology Chris Otter to 'transcend the rather exhausted dichotomies of social-technical and cultural-natural'.[81] Taking as his point of entry resources including electricity, water and meat, Otter shows how 'following' these 'substances' reveals how far the material – its form, circulation, management and distribution – shapes social, cultural, political and economic worlds.[82] To give one example, larger urban populations in the nineteenth-century demanded more water and generated more waste. This spurred comprehensive build-ing of infrastructure, technological developments (e.g. new types of pipe, chemical processing of water), and impacted on the environment (e.g. huge reservoirs located near big cities), home life (e.g. running water, bathrooms) and municipal government. But these networks of materials and technologies also impacted on bodies: 'The cumulative agency of reservoirs, mains, bathrooms and sewage plants makes possible a supply of chemically standardized, objectified, "secularized" water which secures the private hygiene, cleanliness and health that is a foundational dimension of "modern" Western material life and subjectivity.'[83]

GIS and history

In the Introduction we briefly encountered GIS as a cutting-edge approach and methodology of spatial research. As a brief reminder, the use of GIS for historical analysis, or HGIS as it is now known, involves the creation of 'a spatial database that integrates map-based information about the historical location of certain entities (such as census districts, industrial firms, or rivers) with quantitative or qualitative information about those entities (such as population, product, or level of pollution).'[84] This is an approach which uniquely allows for the creation of dynamic visualisations that track change over space and time. There is always a geographic dimension involved in an HGIS project. We might create a visualisation, for example, which shows how levels of voting registration, among different ethnic groups, in a particular geographic area, have changed over decades, or even centuries. HGIS enables the researcher to combine numerous datasets and thus overlay multiple maps showing both physical geographical and human features.

The range of research questions, themes and geographies explored through GIS technology is vast, and expanding all the time. When historians first began to experiment with this technology in the 1980s and 1990s, the focus was largely on the quantitative – subjects such as demography (the study of human populations). Since the year 2000, the field of HGIS has become much more expansive and qualitative in its motivations and interests. Take, for example, the Bomb Sight project. It used data from the Bomb Census Survey, 1940–45, in conjunction with photographs and personal testimony to map and illustrate experiences of the Blitz during the Second World War. The project facilitated an augmented-reality view through mobile phones that 'created a completely new view of the London Blitz, simultaneously showing the overall intensity and scale of the bombings for Greater London, and also allowing users to explore individual street level impacts'.[85] Facilitating users' appreciation of the near proximity of a bomb falling on a specific street and providing some sense of the sheer number of bombs that fell on a particular night, the project helps to retrieve the sensory and emotional experience of the Blitz. Many scholars thus now speak of 'spatial history' rather than 'historical GIS'.[86] To take just one major research centre, the Spatial History Project based at Stanford University, here research collaborations have included projects as varied as the global trade in medicines across the long eighteenth century – spanning South Asia, London and the American colonies; the contribution of Chinese migrants to the construction of America's first transcontinental railroad during the 1860s; and mobility within the Budapest ghetto in 1944.[87]

Crucially, the visualisations created through HGIS – and this term might include maps, charts, tables and other varied visual representations – are not simply illustrations of evidence that might be expressed through other, namely textual means, but are themselves a fundamental way of doing spatial research.[88] HGIS is a time-consuming methodology which requires a high level of technical knowledge and an ability to interpret and contextualise relatively complex visual materials. As pioneers of the field, Ian N. Gregory and Alistair Geddes write, in order to produce new and meaningful historical knowledge, 'Creating a GIS [a database] and analysing the data it contains requires technical GIS skills. Producing new scholarship requires the skills of the historian or other humanities scholar to turn the GIS output into a contribution to our understanding of the past.'[89] It thus comes as no surprise to find that very many historical GIS projects are collaborative endeavours.

IN SUMMARY

Here we have outlined some of the key theories and approaches which have made 'space' a central research concern. In addition, we have begun to consider the different ways in which history as a discipline has been impacted upon by – and engaged in dialogue with – these multiple spatial 'turns'. The next chapter will guide you through the central stages of planning a research project.

NOTES

1   Some excellent examples of books which engage with this theme include:
    K. Lichtert, J. Dumolyn and M. Martens (eds), *Portraits of the City: Representing
    Urban Space in Later Medieval and Early Modern Europe* (Turnhout: Brepolis,
    2014); R. Sweet, *Cities and the Grand Tour: The British in Italy, c. 1690–1820*
    (Cambridge: Cambridge University Press, 2012); Dennis, *Cities in Modernity*.
2   L. Meskell and R. W. Preucel (eds), *A Companion to Social Archaeology*
    (Oxford: Blackwell, 2004), p. 216.
3   J. Seibert, 'Introduction', in E. Robertson *et al.* (eds), *Space and Spatial
    Analysis in Archaeology* (Calgary [Alta.]: University of Calgary Press,
    2006), pp. xiii–xxiv (p. xiii).
4   K. V. Flannery, *The Early Mesoamerican Village* (New York: Academic
    Press, 1976).
5   K. F. Anschuetz, R. H. Wilshusen and C. L. Scheick, 'An archaeol-
    ogy of landscapes: perspectives and directions', *Journal of Archaeological
    Research*, 9:2 (2001), 157–211 (pp. 158–9).
6   C. Y. Tilley, *A Phenomenology of Landscape: Places, Paths and Monuments*
    (Oxford: Berg, 1994), p. 207.
7   M. Johnson, *English Houses 1300–1800: Vernacular Architecture, Social Life*
    (Harlow: Longman, 2010), p. 16.
8   G. Wright, 'Cultural history: Europeans, Americans, and the meaning
    of space', *Journal of the Society of Architectural Historians*, 64:4 (2005),
    436–440 (p. 437).
9   https://historians.org/publications-and-directories/perspectives-on-
    history/january-2014/architectural-history-and-spatial-imagination
    [accessed 20 March 2019].
10 H. Hills, *Invisible City: The Architecture of Devotion in Seventeenth-Century
    Neapolitan Convents* (Oxford: Oxford University Press, 2004); L. Sklair,
    The Icon Project: Architecture, Cities, and Capitalist Globalization (New York:
    Oxford University Press, 2017).
11 J. Agnew and D. N. Livingstone, 'Introduction', in Agnew and
    Livingstone (eds), *The Sage Handbook of Geographical Knowledge* (London:
    Sage, 2011), pp. 1–17 (p. 1).
12 P. Jackson, 'New directions in cultural geography revisited', *Area*, 48:3
    (2016), 367–70 (p. 368).
13 Carl Sauer was the dominant figure in twentieth-century cultural geog-
    raphy in this mode. See the following overview of his legacy: M. Williams,
    '"The Apple of My Eye": Carl Sauer and historical geography', *Journal of
    Historical Geography*, 9:1 (1983), 1–28.

14 P. Jackson, *Maps of Meaning: An Introduction to Cultural Geography* (London: Routledge, 2003 [1989]), pp. 1–8.

15 J. Clarke, S. Hall, T. Jefferson and B. Roberts, 'Subcultures, cultures and class: a theoretical overview', in S. Hall and J. Henderson (eds), *Resistance through Rituals: Youth Subcultures in Post-War Britain* (London: Hutchinson/Centre for Contemporary Cultural Studies, 1976), pp. 9–75 (p. 10).

16 E. Saïd, *Orientalism* (London: Penguin, 2003 [1978]).

17 D. Harvey, 'Space as a keyword', in N. Castree and D. Gregory (eds), *David Harvey: A Critical Reader* (Oxford: Blackwell Books, 2006), pp. 270–93 (pp. 287–8).

18 D. Harvey, *Paris: Capital of Modernity* (London: Routledge, 2003), pp. 1–19. See also the following lucid critique of Harvey's work: S. Zukin, 'David Harvey on cities', in *David Harvey: A Critical Reader*, pp. 102–20 (pp. 112–16).

19 Harvey, *Paris*, p. 19.

20 Zukin, 'David Harvey on cities', p. 103.

21 *Ibid.*, pp. 102–4.

22 See, for example: D. Massey, *Space, Place and Gender* (Cambridge: Polity, 1994); idem., *For Space* (London: Sage, 2005); idem., *World City* (Cambridge: Polity, 2007); M. Wright, 'Differences that matter', in *David Harvey: A Critical Reader*, pp. 80–101.

23 Massey, *World City*, pp. 10, 18–19.

24 Agnew, 'Space and place', p. 319. For a useful genealogy of place, see: T. Cresswell, *Place: An Introduction*, 2nd edn (Oxford: Blackwell, 2015), Chapter 2.

25 See for example: D. Massey, *Space, Place and Gender*; idem., *Power-Geometries and the Politics of Space-Time: Hettner-Lecture 1998* (Heidelberg: Department of Geography, University of Heidelberg, 1999); A. Escobar, 'Culture sits in places: reflections on globalism and subaltern strategies of localization', *Political Geography*, 20:2 (2001), 139–74.

26 A. Pred, 'Place as historically contingent process: structuration and the time-geography of becoming places', *Annals of the Association of American Geographers*, 74:2 (1984), 279–97.

27 Harvey, 'Space as a keyword', pp. 278–9.

28 H. Lefebvre, *The Production of Space*, trans. D. Nicholson-Smith (Oxford: Blackwell, 1991 [1974]).

29 A. Merrifield, 'Henri Lefebvre: a socialist in space', in N. Thrift and M. Crang (eds), *Thinking Space* (London: Routledge, 2000), pp. 167–82 (p. 174).

30 *Ibid.*, p. 175.

31 M. Heffernan, 'Historical geography', *IHR History in Focus: Making History* (2008), https://history.ac.uk/makinghistory/resources/artic les/historical_geography.html#f14 [accessed 15 February 2019].

32 B. Graham and C. Nash, 'Introduction: the making of modern historical geographies', in Graham and Nash (eds), *Modern Historical Geographies* (London: Longman, 2000), pp. 1–10 (p. 3).

33 Heffernan, 'Historical geography'.

34 Nash and Graham, 'Introduction', p. 3.

35 For a helpful overview of the field, particularly the distinctive approach taken by 'new' imperial histories, see: A. Lester, 'Imperial circuits and networks: geographies of the British Empire', *History Compass*, 4:1 (2006), 124–41.

36 Nash and Graham, 'Introduction', p. 1.

37 A few examples: M. Ogborn, *Global Lives: Britain and the World, 1550–1800* (Cambridge: Cambridge University Press, 2008); D. Lambert and A. Lester (eds), *Colonial Lives across the British Empire* (Cambridge: Cambridge University Press, 2006); S. Legg, *Spaces of Colonialism: Delhi's Urban Governmentalities* (Oxford: Blackwell, 2007). See also the following useful overview of the impact of attention to space and place on colonial and imperial histories: A. Lester, 'Spatial concepts and the historical geographies of British colonialism', in A. S. Thompson (ed.), *Writing Imperial Histories* (Manchester: Manchester University Press, 2013), pp. 118–42.

38 For example: F. Driver, *Geography Militant: Cultures of Exploration and Empire* (Oxford: Blackwell, 2001); M. Ogborn, *Indian Ink: Script and Print in the Making of the English East India Company* (Chicago: University of Chicago Press, 2007).

39 A. Lester, *Imperial Networks: Creating Identities in Nineteenth-Century South Africa and Britain* (London: Routledge, 2001).

40 A. Lester, 'Historical geographies of imperialism', in B. J. Graham and C. Nash (eds), *Modern Historical Geographies* (London: Longman, 2000), pp. 100–20 (pp. 112–14). Lester, *Imperial Networks*, p. 8.

41 Lester, 'Historical geographies of imperialism', pp. 114–15.

42 Nash and Graham, 'Introduction', p. 2.

43 Bressey, *Empire, Race and the Politics of Anti-Caste*.

44 Leif Jerram has gone so far as to say that 'the "spatial turn" is an extension of the cultural turn'. See 'Space: a useless category', p. 400.

45 Arnade, Howell and Simons, 'Fertile spaces: the productivity of urban space', p. 515.

46 P. Burke, *What Is Cultural History?* (Cambridge: Polity, 2004).

47 V. Blud *et al.* (eds), *Gender in Medieval Places, Spaces and Thresholds*

(University of London Press, 2019), https://doi.org/10.2307/j. ctv9b2tw8 [accessed January 2020]. See also T. Brennan, 'Taverns in the public sphere in eighteenth-century Paris', *Contemporary Drug Problems*, 32:1 (2005), 29–43; T. Bruslé and A. Varrel, 'Introduction. Places on the move: South Asian migrations through a spatial lens', *South Asia Multidisciplinary Academic Journal*, 6 (2012). Available from: https:// journals.openedition.org/samaj/3439 [accessed March 2020].

48 D. J. Rothman, *The Discovery of the Asylum: Social Order and Disorder in the New Republic* (Boston: Little Brown, 1971).

49 K. Beebe, A. Davis and K. Gleadle, 'Introduction: space, place and gendered identities: feminist history and the spatial turn', *Women's History Review*, 21:4 (2012), 523–32 (p. 524).

50 R. Laitinen and T. Cohen, 'Cultural history of early modern streets – an introduction', *Journal of Early Modern History*, 12:3–4 (2008), 195–204 (p. 197).

51 L. Jerram, *Streetlife: The Untold History of Europe's Twentieth Century* (Oxford: Oxford University Press, 2011), p. 4.

52 Kingston, 'Mind over matter?', p. 114.

53 L. Nead, 'Mapping the self: gender, space and modernity in mid-Victorian London', *Environment and Planning A*, 29:4 (1997), 659–72.

54 Beebe, Davis and Gleadle, 'Space, place and gendered identities', p. 524. See also: S. Gunn and R. J. Morris (eds), *Identities in Space: Contested Terrains in the Western City since 1850* (Aldershot: Ashgate, 2001).

55 H. Barker, '"Smoke cities": northern industrial towns in late Georgian England', *Urban History*, 31:2 (2004), 175–90 (p. 177).

56 A. Kidd, *Manchester* (Edinburgh: Edinburgh University Press, 2002), p. 14.

57 A. de Tocqueville, *Journeys to England and Ireland, 1835*, trans. G. Lawrence and K. P. Mayer, ed. J. P. Mayer (New Haven, CT: Yale University Press, 1958), p. 107.

58 R. J. Morris, 'The middle class and British towns and cities of the industrial revolution, 1780–1870', in D. Fraser and A. Sutcliffe (eds), *The Pursuit of Urban History* (London: Edward Arnold, 1983), p. 287.

59 S. Gunn, *The Public Culture of the Victorian Middle Class: Ritual and Authority in the English Industrial City, 1840–1914* (Manchester: Manchester University Press, 2007).

60 P. Joyce, *The Rule of Freedom: Liberalism and the Modern City* (London: Verso, 2003), p. 148.

61 *Ibid.*, pp. 167–8.

62 S. Wetherell, *Foundations: How the Built Environment Made Twentieth-Century Britain* (Princeton, NJ: Princeton University Press, 2020);

G. Ortolano, *Thatcher's Progress: From Social Democracy to Market Liberalism through an English New Town* (Cambridge, Cambridge University Press, 2019).

63 See also discussion: Agnew, 'Space and place', pp. 317–18.

64 *Ibid.*, p. 318. The French anthropologist Marc Augé's interrogation of 'non-places' has proved especially influential; see: M. Augé, *Non-Places: An Introduction to Supermodernity* (London: Verso, 2009).

65 C. Otter, 'Locating matter: the place of materiality in urban history', in T. Bennett and P. Joyce (eds), *Material Powers: Cultural Studies, History and the Material Turn* (London: Routledge, 2010), pp. 38–59 (pp. 53–4).

66 B. de Munck, 'Re-assembling actor-network theory and urban history', *Urban History*, 44:1 (2017), 111–22 (pp. 117–18).

67 *Ibid.*

68 A classic: B. Latour, 'Mixing humans and nonhumans together: the sociology of a door-closer', *Social Problems*, 35:3 (1988), 298–310.

69 B. Latour, 'The Berlin key or how to do words with things', in P. Graves-Brown (ed.), *Matter, Materiality and Modern Culture* (London: Routledge, 2000), pp. 10–21.

70 *Ibid.*, p. 18.

71 This is a very crude overview; for full analysis, see: T. Gieryn, 'What buildings do', *Theory and Society*, 31:1 (2002), 35–74 (pp. 35–40).

72 Kingston, 'Mind over matter', p. 116.

73 B. Latour quoted in: J. M. Jacobs, S. Cairns and I. Strebel, '"A tall storey … but, a fact just the same": the Red Road high-rise as a Black Box', *Urban Studies*, 44:3 (2007), 609–29 (p. 613).

74 B. Latour, *Pandora's Hope: Essays on the Reality of Science Studies* (Cambridge, MA: Harvard University Press, 1999), p. 304.

75 Gieryn, 'What buildings do', p. 43.

76 Jacobs *et al.*, 'A tall storey …', p. 613.

77 Gieryn, 'What buildings do', p. 41. The best-known statement to this effect was the architect Le Corbusier's aphorism 'la maison est une machine à habiter' ('a house is a machine for living in'): *Vers une Architecture* (Paris: Arthaud, 1977 [1923]), p. 73.

78 Jacobs *et al.*, 'A tall storey …', pp. 614–21.

79 *Ibid.*, pp. 626–7.

80 *Ibid.*, p. 626.

81 Otter, 'Locating matter', p. 59.

82 *Ibid.*, pp. 59–60, 46–55; C. Otter, *The Victorian Eye: A Political History of Light and Vision, 1800–1910* (Chicago: University of Chicago Press, 2008).

83 Otter, 'Locating matter', p. 48.

84   A. K. Knowles, 'Introduction: historical GIS: the spatial turn in social science history', *Social Science History*, 24:3 (2000), 451–70 (p. 452). This was the first dedicated special issue for HGIS.
85   C. Jones and P. Weber, 'The Bomb Sight Project', *The Bulletin of the Society of Cartographers*, 41:1–2 (2013), 3–10 (p. 7), http://bombsight. org/#15/51.5050/-0.0900 [accessed January 2020].
86   I. N. Gregory and A. Geddes, 'Introduction: from historical GIS to spatial humanities: deepening scholarship and broadening technology', in Gregory and Geddes (eds), *Towards Spatial Humanities: Historical GIS and Spatial History* (Bloomington, IN: Indiana University Press, 2014), pp. ix–xix (p. ix).
87   http://web.stanford.edu/group/spatialhistory/cgi-bin/site/index. php [accessed December 2019].
88   R. White, 'What is spatial history?', White paper published online. Stanford University Spatial History Lab, Stanford, CA. (2010). https:// web.stanford.edu/group/spatialhistory/media/images/publication/ what%20is%20spatial%20history%20pub%20020110.pdf   [accessed September 2021].
89   Gregory and Geddes, 'Introduction: from historical GIS to spatial humanities', p. xii.

RECOMMENDED READING

T. Cresswell, *Place: An Introduction*, 2nd edn (Oxford: Blackwell, 2015).
I. N. Gregory and A. Geddes (eds), *Towards Spatial Humanities: Historical GIS and Spatial History* (Bloomington, IN: Indiana University Press, 2014), especially Chapter 8, 'Further reading: from historical GIS to spatial humanities: an evolving literature', pp. 186–202.
D. Harvey, 'Space as a keyword', in N. Castree and D. Gregory (eds), *David Harvey: A Critical Reader* (Oxford: Blackwell Books, 2006), pp. 270–93.
R. Laitinen and T. V. Cohen, *Cultural History of Early Modern European Streets* (Leiden: Brill, 2009).
D. Massey, *For Space* (London: Sage, 2005).
A. Mayne and T. Murray (eds), *The Archaeology of Urban Landscapes: Explorations in Slumland* (Cambridge: Cambridge University Press, 2001).
N. Thrift and M. Crang (eds), *Thinking Space* (London: Routledge, 2000).

✵ 2 ✵

PLANNING A RESEARCH PROJECT

INTRODUCTION

In Chapter 1 we examined some of the central theories of and diverse disciplinary approaches to spatial research. In this chapter we turn our attention to the formulation of research questions and the development of your spatial research project. We begin with a consideration of first steps in the research process. We suggest several possible starting points for thinking through and designing your project, divided here into the broad parameters of location or building type, theme or concept and body of evidence. Each 'route' into a research project is exemplified by a concrete case study. The remainder of the chapter provides some wide-ranging advice for formulating useful research questions. Chapter 3 will follow on from this discussion by investigating the application of suitable methodologies to your evidence and research plans.

FIRST STEPS: THE OUTLINES OF A RESEARCH PROJECT

The process of planning and structuring a research project is unique to each historian. Nevertheless, in the formulation of your ideas and research strategies there are a number of broad routes into spatial research. This would apply whether you are writing an extended essay or dissertation, a book chapter, journal article or monograph, or, indeed, planning a lecture, talk or exhibition. We suggest several such routes here. These paths are not mutually exclusive, nor are they meant to be prescriptive. First, you might take a particular location or building type as your starting point. Second, a particular theme, concept or theory might be your way into a spatial research project. Third, a body of sources might be the initial spring of inspiration for carrying out a project based on place or space.

WHEN THE LOCATION OR BUILDING TYPE IS YOUR STARTING POINT

For many historians engaged in spatial research, the motivation to explore the built environment and wider themes of place, meaning and belonging comes from direct viewing or experience of historic, or indeed relatively contemporary, buildings and landscapes. In our everyday lives as urban inhabitants, and on our travels and holidays to new towns and cities, we constantly encounter different built spaces, of various eras or ages, including domestic residences, commercial sites, institutional buildings – like banks or embassies – sacred locations, schools and universities, and many others besides. Focusing on a specific place, whether city, unit of urban space (e.g. square, market) or building, can be the most straightforward way into a spatial research project. Research projects that start with a location often track changes in the built environment. In these instances, you may find yourself exploring how and why your location was transformed over time, as well as how unusual this rate or type of change was. Often such enquiries link to questions of power and agency, leading you to investigate who was in charge, who benefited from the transformation of the urban fabric and how far change was resisted.

With this research, one of your first jobs is to work out the *scale* of place you will engage with: a single building, a complex (like the Forbidden City in Beijing), street(s), a quarter, a city, a region? Is this feasible within practical constraints, such as the time you have to complete your project or the evidence you can access? While choosing a location, you will also need to engage with what has already been written by other scholars. Getting a handle on what, or indeed where, has been written about already will help you to identify gaps. Doing so is essential in an original research project, where it is expected that you will demonstrate your contribution to knowledge. The originality of your project will be assured through the combination of time period, place and/or theme and your grasp of what has already been written. To offer one example, while a great deal has been said on the subject of coffeehouses in seventeenth- and eighteenth-century London, cafes in Paris during the same period have received much less attention.[1]

While reviewing the secondary literature, you will also establish available evidence and reflect hard on its limitations. Chapter 4 goes into more detail about how and where to find sources, but the following questions are good places to begin. Are you planning to write about an extant built environment that you can visit, walk around and look closely at? Is this location accessible to the public? If not, from whom will you need to get permission? Will you have the time and resources to visit it during your research? May fragments of your location be found in museums or even incorporated into other buildings? Where built environments no longer survive, can you find enough information elsewhere? Can you uncover any possible surviving documentary evidence for the building in local or national archives? Are there representations (e.g. drawings, prints, paintings, photographs, film footage, maps, plans, models, representations on three-dimensional objects) that you can use to build up a picture of your location? Are there descriptions in printed books, pamphlets, newspapers or printed legislation? Are there references to your built environment in manuscript sources (e.g. royal or municipal records, deeds, leases, diaries, letters, churchwardens' accounts, visitation records)? What does this visual and textual evidence reveal about your location? Just as importantly, what does it not tell you? Close study of surviving material, visual and textual evidence will also help you to establish the physical properties of a given location. This is an essential dimension of any study of the built environment and, depending on your evidence, may include attention to size, materials, costs, processes of production and construction, design and style.

But your investigation will need you to push beyond describing what a location was like, to engage with wider social, cultural, political, economic and religious matters. A good way of doing this is to ask about the relationship between 'your' location and the people who used it. 'Use' here is a broad category, extending from those with the social, economic and political power to influence the form of a variety of built environments, from palaces to asylums to corporate campuses, and to shape the behaviours of residents, workers, out-of-towners and passers-by.[2] But it must also encompass the actions of ordinary city dwellers who resisted attempts to regulate their behaviour. Here, we might think about the people in seventeenth-century Rome who attached anonymous criticisms of the authorities to the talking statue 'Pasquino' to voice their discontent during times of hardship, famine and war.[3] Or we could look to the rent strike in Glasgow in 1915. Working-class women successfully resisted a proposed 25 per cent rent increase by exploitative landlords at a time of hardship, refusing to let bailiffs evict those in arrears and leading a mass march in support of rent strikers who were taken to court.[4]

Most often, you will begin this part of your enquiry by working out who were the main players involved. Who was associated with your location? Did they own it? Were they residents or did they use it in some other way? Did they make the rules that governed its use? Were they involved in its design, manufacture, reconstruction or deconstruction? Or were they responsible for its representation? Often linked are questions that look at how a given environment was regulated. What activities or practices happened in your location? How were these managed or controlled? Was anything completely forbidden? How did this change? Indeed, many of these enquiries are keenly spatial. When we probe questions around access, we might ask who was allowed where, what behaviours were permitted, what role the built environment played in this and, most tantalisingly, how and when people pushed back. Broadly, this is to ask how far specific environments played a part in the operation of power. But this power was not shared equally. For this reason, it is always critical to consider whose body are you imagining this history through, its sensorial and experiential dimensions, and broader social, cultural and political contexts.

Once you have a clearer sense of what your location was like and who 'used' it, you can then move out from its specifics to place it in the broader context of other environments, including what was built near it. Comparing, contrasting and contextualising will help to make more sense of your location. You will be better placed to evaluate how 'typical' (or not) it was of a particular time or place. Thinking about your location in relation to other sites can bring fresh perspectives. You might explore linked sites/buildings in other places, the relationships between associated groups of people and the 'mechanisms' (e.g. architectural and building style, funding, family relationships, professional networks, governance and jurisdiction, trade) that tell us how these locations were crucially linked. Where was joined to where? Who to whom? How did this change, and what does this tell us? Or you may choose to investigate a type or category of place (e.g. public baths). From here, your study could look at the distribution of a particular type of location and how this changed over time.

Your motivation for undertaking a research project centred on space or place might thus be interest in a particular location or building type. You might choose to use a specific church of medieval origin as your point of entry, but in order to make wider claims about society, politics and culture it will be necessary to consider other buildings of a similar type. The next step would be to investigate if there are churches in nearby towns, cities or counties built at a similar time. Can you make comparisons between their structure, design and materiality? Did they have similar numbers and types of parishioners? Did these parishioners have comparable regulations regarding access to and use of the building? Having conducted a wider survey of comparable building types, you might be in a stronger position to make analyses and conclusions about political, social and gender relations. To deepen your spatial investigation of location or building type still further you could consider connections and networks between your sites of analysis. In other words, you might examine the relationships between places of a similar type. Some of the richest historical research on sacred sites, such as churches, has considered the movement of people, commerce, goods – sacred and profane – between religious spaces. For example, Eamon Duffy's landmark study of religious culture and belief in fifteenth- and sixteenth-century England, *The Stripping of the Altars*, is rooted in a rich analysis of the relationships between communities, sites of religious significance and sacred material cultures. Duffy's compelling argument about the deep-rooted commitment of many English men and women to the Catholic Church on the eve of the English Reformation is based on a close reading of material cultures and more traditional archival materials (such as churchwardens' accounts).[5]

Of course, research focused on building types can also be carried out on very contemporary structures, for example evangelical Protestant 'megachurches'. These have become an increasingly familiar sight from the 1980s onwards in the British, American and Australian 'post-suburban environment – the sprawling, freeway-laced landscape'.[6] Intriguingly, super-sized megachurches on the fringes of large metropolitan centres (usually with congregations of over 2,000 people) are often indistinguishable externally from commercial sites like shopping centres and nightclubs; many megachurches have in fact been established in abandoned commercial sites like bingo halls and warehouses.[7] The relationship between 'sacred' and 'profane' or 'commercial' space is clearly very different in this contemporary context, as compared to medieval churches and their wider hinterlands.[8] Nevertheless, the research *process* of making comparisons between buildings of a similar type – examinations of floor plans, designs and interior structures, and thinking about questions of access, hierarchies and multifunctional use – would be very similar. A 2008 study of the Australian charismatic megachurch Hillsong found that its deconstructed architecture and ritual mirrored the ideal individual spiritual encounter with the divine. At Hillsong 'the interior layout of the church auditorium is literally an open space (akin to a giant version of a theatrical black box), without the foregrounding of any of the massive permanent and semi-permanent structures of the traditional cathedral'. The result of this open layout is 'to induct the individual worshiper ... into a personal experience of a spiritual space that transcends the concretely physical'.[9]

Case study:
starting with a location or building type

The Gulag system in Soviet Russia

The Gulag was the system of forced labour detention in the Soviet Union. The word itself is a Russian acronym for the Main Administration for Correctional-Labour Camps, established in 1930, although the Soviet institution of correctional-labour camps originated in 1919. Between 1929 and Stalin's death in 1953, approximately 18 million people were sentenced to time in the Gulag's camps and prisons. Those sent to the camps included 'ordinary' criminals as well as those deemed politically dangerous by the state. And although not 'death camps', akin to those in Nazi-occupied wartime Europe, conditions in the Gulag system were often atrocious and brutal: at least 1.6 million people died as a result of their incarceration.[10] The purpose of the camps is evident from the name: correction and labour. Labour played an important role in Soviet penal theory as a means of 're-educating' offenders, allowing them to appreciate the benefits and the dignity of comradely work in order to be rehabilitated into Soviet society. Those sentenced to the camps were given finite sentences, because – in theory at least – they were supposed to return.[11] However, the benefits of labour for the Soviet state went beyond the rehabilitation of offenders. The Gulag was an immensely important component of the Stalinist system, a regime characterised in large part by the forcible modernisation of the relatively backward and underutilised expanses of what was the largest country in the world.

Individual prisons, camps and settlements, and the broader Gulag system/network, raise many interesting research questions for historians interested in space. During the Stalin era, the camps of the Gulag became a central component of the furious-paced industrialisation of the country. Those camps located at the remote extremities of the land were explicitly understood by the authorities as means of 'reclaiming' the 'margins'.[12] One such camp, described in detail by the historian Steven Barnes, was Karlag in the Karaganda region of Kazakhstan. One of the largest and longest-lasting of the Gulag camps, Karlag became the 'central institution' of the region. Primarily an agricultural camp, the enormity of its space is conveyed by its size: 300 kilometres from north to south, and 200 from east to west.[13]

In examining the Gulag system through a spatial lens, we might begin with an individual camp, such as Karlag. We could ask what the design of this camp tells us about Soviet political culture. To what extent did its spatial and social organisation reflect the hierarchy of Soviet society more broadly? Extending our analysis outwards, to consider the wider Gulag network, we might reflect upon what the development of the Gulag system tells us about perceptions of space and territory in the Soviet Union. We should bear in mind that the Gulag system was not composed of isolated sites, but consisted of a highly complex network of people, goods and transport routes – indeed the forced labour of the camps physically created a number of major transport routes, such as the White Sea–Baltic Sea Canal, dug by over 100,000 prisoners.

Questions which you might ask

- How did the built environment of the Gulag reflect attitudes towards criminality in twentieth-century Russia?
- What does the close physical location between prison buildings and residential buildings – many were located side by side in cities – tell us about the relationship between Gulag and 'non-Gulag' society and political culture?[14]
- To what extent did the development of the Gulag system impact upon urbanisation in Soviet society?

WHEN THE THEME OR CONCEPT IS YOUR STARTING POINT

Extended research projects can emerge from undergraduate and postgraduate taught courses that focus on a particular period, place or theme, where a dissertation often functions as a 'capstone' piece of work that concludes a course of study. Where other written assignments require you to synthesise, analyse and communicate historical ideas and arguments, longer forms of academic writing also demand that you demonstrate the ability to generate original research that is rigorous, critical and shows its significance. Themes and concepts with a spatial dimension can help you to do this.

To take an example that cuts across histories and theories of urban space, you might use ideas about what made somewhere 'public' as a starting point. This concept, which is fundamentally spatial, is often interrogated through comparison with ideas of 'privacy' or 'inaccessibility'. But how might we start a project about 'public' space in a historical context or, indeed, use any other key theme or concept to begin? In common with most academic research, your first job will involve defining your terms. To extend our example, definitions of what constituted 'public' (and opposite – 'private') are geographically and historically situated. One route through the topic and into an original research project could involve asking what 'public' meant to a particular identity group in a particular place at a particular time. This invariably raises the question of whether 'public' is the 'right' word. Labelling some categories of place – the street, say, or home – as definitively 'public' or 'private' is not especially helpful. It is instead much more useful to look at what different sorts of people did in them – their spatial practices, which were invariably informed by social convention, custom, expectations and the physical environment. In place of clear-cut oppositions between 'public' and 'private' spaces and, indeed, lives, this approach tends to reveal continuities, overlaps and the multiple meanings that spaces held at any one time.[15] Care with terminology is especially important for medieval and early modern projects. Could an alternative term, like 'accessibility', prove more useful? Or, to think socially and politically, what characteristics make a group a 'public' as opposed to, say, an 'audience' in the early modern city, or 'consumers' in the twenty-first-century city?[16]

Exploring the relationships between 'public' and 'private' can push us to think about the relationship between different sorts of people within cities and, above all, between people and authorities in specific places at particular times. How were spaces made public? Who was involved? What were they doing? Theoretical categories and positions will help to shape your thinking. Indeed, a feature of histories of urban spaces and built environments is their combination of theoretical writing, often from outside the discipline of history, with empirical research. Ideas about 'public', 'the public' or 'publicness' might lead to engagement with the 'public sphere' (a concept that emerges in the work of the German sociologist Jürgen Habermas), or benefit from approaches taken in feminist writing, queer studies, postcolonial and critical race theories.

Your review of existing primary and secondary literature on a particular place or period will help to identify the gaps in a topic. Are you surprised that something has not been discussed? Are there issues flagged by historians or buried in footnotes that remain unexplored? Are there time periods or geographies where your theme or concept has not been interrogated? Could a specific theoretical slant help you to do this? Or can you use a named individual or type of person (e.g. sixteenth-century working woman, eighteenth-century constable, twenty-first-century activist) to shed fresh perspectives on your topic? This phase of work is also critical for the identification of primary sources. Studies of urban space and the built environment demand that you work across a range of source materials, including archival manuscripts, printed texts, an array of visual and material sources and, where it survives, the built environment. Note down episodes, buildings and built environments and practices that are relevant to your study. Follow up references in the footnotes and bibliographies of published work. Read texts from adjacent disciplines, such as archaeology, anthropology, cultural studies and sociology. All of this activity will sharpen the parameters of your research project.

Once your primary evidence is gathered, you can build up a clearer picture of its 'textures': what it comments on, by and for whom it was produced, what it does not tell you and, above all, where the power lies. Irrespective of your particular focus, you will find yourself address-ing two linked questions. First, what does your source material tell you about how urban environments were meant to be used? Second, what do your sources tell you about how these spaces were *actually* used? Let us return to our 'public' example. In this instance, sources like printed regulations and proclamations, archival records of policing and sur-veillance, such as court records, will flesh out expected behaviours in accessible urban spaces like markets, streets, squares, shops or cafes. What barriers to entry or restrictions on activity existed? How far were these applied and enforced? Or you might start with signs of resistance and non-compliance by amassing evidence of riots, protests, petition-ing and occupation of/within specific urban environments. Equally, rather than beginning with a focus on a particular space or place, you could choose instead to explore the topic through categories of events that took place outside and were witnessed by socially diverse publics, like rituals, celebrations or judicial punishment, as documented in government papers, commercial printed sources (e.g. newspapers, pamphlets, visual representations) and eye-witness accounts captured in diaries and letters. Or you could explore how far the activity of making spaces public and people into publics was actually played out through modes of representation, dissemination and communication, like print, telecommunications and digital technology. Deployment of less frequently used source types (e.g. material culture) can provide an effective way of finessing your thinking and justifying the originality of your study.

Through this process, your broad interest in a topic will be focused by relevant primary, secondary and theoretical literature and well-thought-through definitions. Once you have a good handle on the available evidence and relevant scholarly literatures, you will also be able to ask more finely honed questions and, in tandem, identify the best means of answering them (see Chapter 3 for discussion on methodology).

Case study:
starting with a period and theme or concept

Women in the city

Historians are always looking for ways to challenge our assumptions about the past. Spatial histories are one way of doing this, as is clear from a rich seam of work that interrogates relationships between gender and urban space. Take, for example, the different ways that historians have explored the visibility and mobility of women within urban environments. This broad theme has led to fresh perspectives on topics as varied as the theory and practice of patriarchy, domesticity, the impacts of modernity and industrialisation, honour, reputation and status, economic opportunity and political participation.[17]

Historian Danielle van den Heuvel zeroes in on the key spatial question asked across this work, 'Who "owns" the street?'[18] This prompts study of who could move freely in the city and where; who could not; whose behaviour was policed and how; and what this meant socially, culturally and politically. It also means engaging with the less tangible aspects of being a woman in the past – experiences that are not always explicitly stated in primary sources. Were some places 'no-go' areas because being there put a woman in physical danger? Or would her presence in some parts of the city lead to gossip and disgrace? Was there a temporal dimension to this? Were some places legitimate during the day and out of bounds at night? Importantly, looking at women in urban environments overturns the notion that 'street life' and 'public life' were solely accessible to men, an idea informed by preoccupation with the figure of the masculine *flâneur* in the nineteenth- and early twentieth-century city.[19] But, as van den Heuvel also suggests, 'The idea of the flaneur and the male dominance of the city streets remains a key feature in many of the debates on the nature of historical and contemporary cities.'[20]

Attending to the detail and complexity of 'lived' experiences has helped historians to reinscribe women into histories of the early modern city. Significantly for our purposes, this work has been driven by engagement with a much broader range of sources, including spatial and material evidence. In terms of your own project, you might contrast 'theories' of patriarchy, as found in laws, legislation and prescriptive literature (texts advising girls and women how to behave), with broader evidence of how different sorts of women were present in and moved around cities. This approach might be helped by using a particular body of sources as your point of entry, such as judicial records, diaries, letters, literature, visual sources and material culture, in order to shed light on the ordinary lives of early modern women. Take, for example, Laura Gowing's essay, 'The Freedom of the Streets', which uses literary texts, prescriptive literature and testimony from defamation cases to prove the complexity of the spatial practices and landscapes women negotiated in early modern London.[21] Working across sources in this way allows us to scrutinise the differences between what was expected of women, the evidence of how early modern women lived their lives and how this was interpreted by contemporaries. At the crux of this work is rigorous attention to the specificity and complexity of 'lived' experiences and the ways in which these were informed by spatial practices. It is worth remembering, as Gowing argues, that the latter 'always involved an interplay between the concrete and imaginary'.[22]

The presence of women in urban environments in later periods was no less contested. The notion of 'separate spheres' has been used to argue for the emergence of increasingly defined concepts of

masculinity and femininity in the late eighteenth century. In Leonore
Davidoff and Catherine Hall's landmark *Family Fortunes: Men and
Women of the English Middle Class, 1780–1850,* these gendered roles had
pronounced spatial dimensions. Davidoff and Hall used prescriptive
literature, including novels such as *Coelebs in Search of a Wife* by the
influential Evangelical writer Hannah More, to explore how ideas
about space and place informed tropes like the middle-class 'angel in
the house'. Emphasis on the distinctive spaces and spatial practices of
men and women was used to explain the construction of urban space
as explicitly masculine, associated with work, politics, amusement and
danger, in comparison to the feminine domestic sphere of family,
morality and safety.[23]

But no conceptual model is universally applicable – something
that is worth remembering when developing your own project. While
'separate spheres' remains an important framework for analysing the
relationship between gender and space, there have been important
critiques of the assumptions underpinning this work.[24] Looking
back to the early modern period, scholars have pushed against the
idea that there was a 'Golden Age' of freedom for working- and
middle-class women in the premodern city, before their activities
became increasingly restricted to the 'separate sphere' of the home
in the eighteenth and nineteenth centuries.[25] Other studies reveal
how deft use of comparison, between groups of women or different
cities, can complicate theoretical models. In place of the 'angel in
the home', Hannah Barker's research on small businesses in the
late eighteenth and early nineteenth centuries shines a light on
the commercial lives of middle-class women in northern England.[26]
She uses trade directories (detailed lists of businesses and trades,
their owners and locations), alongside advertisements in the local
press, to emphasise that middling-sort women were at the heart of
commercial life in the towns and emerging cities of Leeds, Sheffield
and Manchester.

Barker's work also reminds us to take heed of the intersections –
or relationships – between identity categories. The ability to move
around, to be seen and to work was not only determined by gender,
but informed by social status, age, race and ethnicity as well.[27]
Much research on working-class women in cities focuses on their
marginalisation and the sexual danger they experienced. Judith
Walkowitz's seminal *City of Dreadful Delight* uses novels, print culture
and songs to tease out the meaning of female experience in the

late-Victorian city.[28] Through an examination of public scandals and spectacle, such as the Jack the Ripper murders, Walkowitz mobilises Foucauldian ideas about discourse and sexuality to chart how middle-class men increasingly maintained their power and privileged access within urban space. Her approach is especially useful for the new insights it afforded into the relationships between gender, media and urban space. The area of Whitechapel became associated with danger and sexual misadventure because of the media coverage of the Ripper murders, which in turn shaped how people perceived and behaved in that area.

Across these examples, attending to the variety of experiences of women – and men and non-binary people – in cities in the past also transforms how we define key spatial terms. Most notably, showing the presence of men in the home and women in 'open spaces' in the city reveals the inadequacy of using 'public' and 'private' as distinct and separate concepts. Instead, thinking spatially, using a broad evidence base and, where possible, harnessing the latest digital humanities tools shows that the connections between 'inside' and 'outside', 'feminine' and 'masculine', 'private' and 'public' were fluid, multiple and always under negotiation within any given space and at any given time.[29]

Questions which you might ask

Research questions that respond to the theme of gender and space in the early modern and modern city include:

- To what extent was the presence and mobility of women determined by time of day?
- How significant was social order, or class, in determining women's presence in the city? What about other key factors of identity, such as race, age and religion?
- What does the comparative visibility of early modern women in the streets of seventeenth-century Rome and Amsterdam tell us about the perception and practice of 'respectability' in both cities?
- How did new forms of transportation impact on the mobility of women in early twentieth-century cities?
- In what ways did women contribute to the structure and organisation of the built environment?

WHEN A BODY OF SOURCES IS YOUR STARTING POINT

Another way into a spatially oriented research project is through a particular body of primary sources. We have already considered the possibility of focusing on a specific location, or a 'type' of built space, but your attention may have been drawn to spatial questions and issues through a particular collection of material, documentary or visual evidence. These sources might include (but in no way is this list expansive) material cultures, maps, plans, paintings and photographs. Many (spatial) histories have their origins in a curiosity about a particular material or visual source, and object-based research frequently leads us in unexpected and exciting directions.

If your route into spatial research is through a particular object or visual source, you might first consider the design of the artefact, the materials from which it was made, and check for marks of ownership or use. Do you think it served a specific social, economic or political purpose? Is it possible to locate the object in a particular historical era or geography? Can you find any similar examples? Building up a wider collection of material evidence or, in other words, a source base, will be important for broadening your analysis and asking searching questions about its creation, use and circulation. A preliminary search of online museum catalogues might help in the identification of similar types of artefacts, related designs or materials (we suggest some especially useful sites in Chapter 4). Consulting works of secondary historical scholarship will also be essential. Specialist catalogues of artefacts – such as connoisseur guides for porcelain, silver and many other material and object types – could also be useful. Once you have undertaken some basic preliminary research, wherever possible, conversations with museum curators and conservators will be an invaluable way of deepening your understanding of the materials and techniques involved in production, and the social contexts within which the object operated.

The use of objects in historical research, spatial or otherwise, is a rewarding and challenging exercise. A number of excellent research handbooks are in print, including one in this particular research guide series, specifically providing guidance on writing histories in dialogue with, and through, material cultures.[30] Our relatively modest aim here is to flag two particular features pertaining to research with material cultures which are worth bearing in mind as you begin to plan your project. First, as historians, we must be aware that extant objects in archives, galleries and private collections are highly selective specimens. By this we mean that their very survival and preservation throughout their 'social lives' has depended on a whole host of decisions about their social, political, economic, emotional and indeed aesthetic worth. We are very rarely privy to these value judgements about what is worth preserving (and most things that have survived are relatively elite objects). Moreover, there is the related and equally thorny issue of the way in which things are stored and displayed according to culturally specific hierarchies of value. Display in contemporary cultural institutions profoundly shapes our interpretation and understanding of the people that made, used and valued things.

Second, we should remain mindful that objects are highly mobile sources – much more so than people or buildings – and this peripatetic feature clearly has implications for how we write histories of place and space, particularly global histories. The value and meanings of an object shift over geographies as well as time periods. Glenn Adamson and Giorgio Riello have written about a suit of Japanese armour gifted by the emperor of Japan to King James I of England in 1613, and on display in the Tower of London. This spectacular gift was in the style of fifteenth-century Dō-maru display armour, crafted by Iwai Yozaemon of Nambu. Adamson and Riello bring out the challenges for us, as twenty-first-century and largely decontextualised viewers, in interpreting this artefact. They write: 'Needless to say, this single artefact represents an important episode in the relationship between England and Japan [...] But one should also ask what this object might hide or erase from view. Clearly it was a token of friendship, but one should not fall into the misleading impression that it signalled the start of a process, that of the diplomatic relationship between England and Japan.' We are primed as modern viewers to perceive 'exotic' objects (undoubtedly a very problematic and value-laden word) as representations of dramatic first encounters between different cultural, political and ethnic groups. And yet, as Adamson and Riello stress, at the root of this gift exchange was commercial advantage. 'The armour is therefore not symbolic of a surprising encounter, but is a token of "understanding" between people willing for their own reasons to open up their borders to each other's commodities.' This object is not in fact telling a story, despite our somewhat romantic first impressions, of 'interaction taking place against the odds'.[31] The use of objects for spatial research requires us to be as critically aware and rigorous as we would be with any body of evidence.

Case study:
starting with a body of sources

Objects and sacred geographies

At some point in the eighteenth century, a (now unrecorded) artisan or craft workshop produced a small, tin-glazed earthenware bowl (Figure 2.1). It measures just 3.9 cm in height and 10.9 cm in diameter. Brightly decorated in blue, sage-green, yellow, orange and brown glaze, this bowl depicts the Madonna of Loreto and her shrine, the Holy House. This imagery would have been familiar to contemporaries. Legend has it that angels transported the Virgin's home from Nazareth to Loreto (a hilltop town in what is now central Italy, on the Adriatic coast). This location, on which a church was built in c. 1500 to protect the Virgin's shrine, became one of the most visited pilgrimage sites in

Figure 2.1 Maiolica pilgrim's souvenir bowl, painted with polychrome with the Virgin holding the Christ Child in front of Santa Casa.

early modern Europe. An inscription across the bottom of the bowl in purple manganese (a metallic substance) reads: 'CON. POL[VERE]. DI. S. CASA' ('With dust of the Holy House'). This inscription gives us an important clue as to the object's making and social value – it was manufactured by mixing dust from the sacred site at Loreto with clay and holy water. We can imagine that a pilgrim purchased this bowl and brought it back to their home as a significant memento of their visit to the Holy House. It was perhaps used to hold holy water during private devotions in the domestic environment.[32]

This intriguing object could be interpreted in multiple ways by a historian interested in issues of place and space. Its movement from the sacred site of Loreto to a new domestic environment tells us about the journeys undertaken by religious devotees in early modern Europe. It is a material souvenir of pilgrimage; and many other such mementos, made from a variety of materials and depicting a great range of holy figures and environments, survive in private and museum collections across the world. They are testament to the profound social, emotional and spiritual experience of pilgrimage (which could often involve expeditions across vast swathes of territory) and the large international market of sacred material cultures. In other words, they tell us about the huge networks of people and material goods in the medieval and early modern eras across geographical space. We might also place this object in a more conceptual framework. Its imagery shows a sacred site – the Holy House at Loreto. It thus gives us an insight into the sacred imaginary (or geographies) of early modern believers. As we have already seen, place and space are not simply physical sites or locations but could also be concepts projected in minds and imaginations.

Here we have foregrounded an eighteenth-century example, but representations of sacred landscapes are also part of a rich modern and contemporary material culture and imaginary of pilgrimage, which continue to open up intriguing research avenues on space and place. Multimedia representations, including prints and photographs of the Hajj and its sacred landscapes, for example, have been hugely significant to individuals and Muslim communities. These images can work to connect a community to each other and to its landscapes, as well as 'vertically with higher beings and the cosmos' and 'temporally with the past, present and future'.[33] To take another example, we can look at ambitious Catholic architectural projects such as the Basilique du Sacré-Coeur de Montmartre in Paris (1875–1914) and the 1930s

cathedral designed by Sir Edwin Lutyens for the archdiocese of
Liverpool but left unfinished. Such ventures relied on comprehensive
fundraising campaigns to finance grandiose projects, using a
proliferation of images of the planned cathedral to attract financial
donations and to foster a link between urban space and religiosity,
even as the cathedral area remained a building site. In Liverpool, these
images ranged from cathedral-branded and illustrated cigarette packets
to a film, unfortunately now lost, which apparently depicted Lutyens'
design superimposed over the city's other buildings.[34] There is still
much we do not know about the relationship between spirituality, visual
culture and urban space. Twentieth- and twenty-first-century collections
of postcards (such as that in Figure 2.2, depicting the Catholic shrine
in Lourdes, France, where the Virgin Mary was believed to have
appeared to a local girl named Bernadette Soubirous), films, calendars,
signboards and posters could be a very fruitful route into research
projects on space, communities and the sacred.

Figure 2.2 Postcard from Notre-Dame de Lourdes, depicting pilgrims
praying at the Grotto of Massabielle, c. 1904–8.

FORMULATING RESEARCH QUESTIONS

The quality of your research project will be determined by the quality of your research questions, so it is advisable to spend some time getting them right. Think of your questions as a series of tools that are there to help you get the most out of your evidence and argument. The sorts of questions you ask will be determined by the nature of your project. This is especially pertinent in studies of urban space and the built environment, which are by their nature multidisciplinary. Different kinds of scholar will approach the same topic from a variety of perspectives. Take, for example, the impact of celebrations on cities: while an art historian may privilege the aesthetic qualities of an event, such as contributions made by famous painters and sculptors, an anthropologist would scrutinise what the same occasion tells us about the relationships between particular groups within a community.

Research projects, such as the ones discussed in this book take the basic question posed by historians: how and why did that happen then? – but add in 'where' as another essential criterion. Thinking spatially pushes historians beyond their comfort zones, from a primary focus on time, temporality and chronology, to embracing space, place and, as suggested by the examples discussed above, material culture. Most projects, whether dissertation, essay or book, ask two or three main questions. Nested within these are sub-questions that scaffold your research project and will help you to communicate your ideas and arguments to your readers. Research questions are also there to provide a framework that ensures your project is fulfilling the expectations of original research: that it is sufficiently evidenced, critical (rather than merely descriptive) and addresses a properly justified gap in knowledge. In a nutshell, your questions should make you ask 'so what?' at every stage of the research process, from framing your project to writing it up. The following broad lines of enquiry may be helpful when framing your study.

- Why is this project significant? To whom is it significant?
- How and why are your chosen case studies meaningful? How do they allow us to understand a particular time or place better?
- What does your study tell us about change over time or the interaction between different sorts of people?
- What new light does your study throw on key historical categories like power, gender, race and ethnicity, identity and class?

- How far does your project make us think differently? In what ways does it extend debate in a particular area?
- How does your methodology – in this instance a focus on space and place – shift how a topic is understood?

As historians, when we ask questions about space and place we are always bringing another dimension to our thinking. The following questions, with their emphasis on what goes where, in relation to whom and what, may also be useful.

- **Scale:** What units of place does the study engage with (e.g. house, street, quarter, city, region)? Why? What other units of place were related, either spatially or because of other social, cultural, economic or political reasons?
- **Networks:** Where was joined to where? Who was being brought into contact with whom? How new were these relationships? What was being exchanged? How did this happen? How did this change? What does this reveal?
- **Distribution:** Where were some types of place? How dense (or scattered) were these places/positions? Did this change? How? Why?
- **Power:** Who had the power to shape the built environment? Who was allowed where? What activities were permitted, and where? What role did the form of the built environment play in this? How and when did other sorts of people push back?
- **Agency:** Whose body are you imagining this history through? Where was this situated? What do we know about the sensorial and experiential dimensions of this?
- **Durability:** What stayed where? How long for? What does this tell us about power and agency? What were the benefits/opportunities of not enduring?
- **Transformation:** How did the built environment change? Was this unusual? Who was in charge? Who benefited? How far was change resisted?

In the context of our 'public' case study, this might mean asking what makes somewhere 'public'. What social and cultural 'values' were ascribed to this publicness and how did this change over time? Whom or what did these ideas benefit?

DEVISING A RESEARCH SCHEDULE

The essence of good project management is working back from your final deadline to make sure you have left enough time to complete each phase of work. It is no good spending five months on your secondary reading if you have only six months to complete your project! In planning your research schedule, be realistic about other commitments you have during the time you plan to write and research.

But what are the jobs that you need to factor in? Almost your first piece of work is to scope the existing secondary literature on your topic. It is only once you have completed this work that you will have a sufficiently detailed knowledge of where there are significant gaps in your topic. This is essential for ensuring that your project is a genuine contribution to our understanding of the past. From here, you can frame your research questions (see previous section of this chapter), think about methodologies for addressing them (Chapter 3) and identify primary sources (Chapter 4). Build flexibility into your schedule: even the best-planned research projects can go awry. Some aspects of the project – for example, locating and making sense of your primary sources – can take much longer than expected, especially if you are unfamiliar with this kind of work.

Producing a significant piece of research is a useful moment to reflect on how you work most effectively. This can be as simple as establishing the time of day when you are most productive and focused and using these hours to push on with complex tasks. But do also reflect on what has pulled you off track in previous assignments. Do you need to leave more time for honing your research questions and planning at the beginning? Would more time for writing and redrafting improve the final presentation of your dissertation? Could you ask a friend or family member to read your drafts and check that they make sense?

IN SUMMARY

In this chapter, we have discussed some of the key steps you should take in order to plan your research project successfully. We also presented some of the most important theoretical approaches that spatial historians often make use of in their research. Our overview of some of the most influential frameworks will help you to apply relevant conceptual approaches to your own research questions and body of sources. Our next chapter will help you to formulate one of the most crucial aspects of an original piece of research, developing a methodology.

NOTES

1 See discussion: B. Cowan, 'English coffeehouses and French salons. Rethinking Habermas, gender and sociability in early modern French and British historiography', in A. Vanhaelen and J. P. Ward (eds), *Making Space Public in Early Modern Europe: Performance, Geography, Privacy* (London: Routledge, 2013), pp. 41–53 (p. 44).

2 For example: J. Hamlett, *At Home in the Institution: Material Life in Asylums, Lodging Houses and Schools in Victorian and Edwardian England* (London: Palgrave Macmillan, 2015).

3 R. M. San Juan, *Rome: A City out of Print* (Minneapolis: University of Minnesota Press, 2001), pp. 1–22.

4 For the rent strike in a wider context of women's citizenship, see E. Breitenbach and V. Wright, 'Women as active citizens: Glasgow and Edinburgh c. 1918–1939', *Women's History Review*, 23:3 (2014), 401–20.

5 E. Duffy, *The Stripping of the Altars: Traditional Religion in England, 1400–1580*, 2nd edn (New Haven, CT; London: Yale University Press, 2005).

6 J. Wilford, *Sacred Subdivisions: The Postsuburban Transformation of American Evangelism* (New York: New York University Press, 2012), p. 4.

7 K. Karnes *et al.*, 'Mighty fortresses: explaining the spatial distribution of American megachurches', *Journal for the Scientific Study of Religion*, 46:2 (2007), 261–8 (pp. 262–3).

8 Wilford, *Sacred Subdivisions*, p. 4, 'Sacred place achieves its power precisely because it is sharply bounded and removed from everyday life. But these new evangelical performances blend the sacred and secular so that the secular becomes only the *potential* for the sacred, not its opposite.'

9 R. Goh, 'Hillsong and "megachurch" practice: semiotics, spatial logic and the embodiment of contemporary Evangelical Protestantism', *Material Religion*, 4:3 (2008), 284–304 (p. 293).

10 S. A. Barnes, *Death and Redemption: The Gulag and the Shaping of Soviet Society* (Princeton, NJ: Princeton University Press, 2011), p. 1.

11 This is a central argument in Barnes, *Death and Redemption*. For a general overview of Soviet penal policy, see for example P. H. Solomon, Jr, 'Soviet penal policy, 1917–1934: a reinterpretation', *Slavic Review*, 39:2 (1980), 195–217.

12 Barnes, *Death and Redemption*, p. 29.

13 *Ibid.*, p. 31.

14 O. Khlevniuk, 'The Gulag and the non-Gulag as one interrelated whole', *Kritika*, 16:3 (2015), 479–98.

15 See the very useful discussion in: D. van den Heuvel, 'Gender in the streets of the premodern city', *Journal of Urban History*, 45:4 (2019), 693–710.

16 See for example: R. Darnton, *Poetry and the Police: Communication Networks in Eighteenth-century Paris* (Cambridge, MA: Belknap Press of Harvard University Press, 2010).

17 For a good overview of recent work in this area: van den Heuvel, 'Gender in the streets'.

18 *Ibid.*, p. 693.

19 For the presence of women in the nineteenth- and twentieth-century city, see: E. Wilson, *The Sphinx in the City: Urban Life, the Control of Disorder and Women* (London: Virago, 1991); J. Walkowitz, *City of Dreadful Delight: Narratives of Sexual Danger in Late-Victorian London* (London: Virago, 1992).

20 van den Heuvel, 'Gender in the streets', p. 694.

21 L. Gowing, '"The freedom of the streets": women and social space, 1560–1640', in P. Griffiths and M. Jenner (eds), *Londinopolis: Essays in the Cultural and Social History of Early Modern London* (Manchester: Manchester University Press, 2000), pp. 130–53.

22 *Ibid.*, p. 147.

23 L. Davidoff and C. Hall, *Family Fortunes: Men and Women of the English Middle Class, 1780–1850* (London: Hutchinson, 1987).

24 See particularly, A. Vickery, 'Golden age to separate spheres? A review of the categories and chronology of English women's history', *The Historical Journal*, 36:2 (1993), 383–414.

25 Gowing, 'The freedom of the streets', p. 133; Vickery, 'Golden age to separate spheres?'

26 H. Barker, *The Business of Women: Female Enterprise and Urban Development in Northern England 1760–1830* (Oxford: Oxford University Press, 2006), p. 42.

27 R. B. Shoemaker, 'Gendered spaces: patterns of mobility and perceptions of London's geography, 1660–1750', in J. F. Merritt (ed.), *Imagining Early Modern London: Perceptions and Portrayals of the City from Stow to Strype, 1598–1720* (Cambridge: Cambridge University Press, 2007), pp. 144–65.

28 Walkowitz, *City of Dreadful Delight*.

29 For recent use of digital humanities tools to map presences, absences,

mobilities and flows within the early modern built environments, see: van den Heuvel, 'Gender in the streets', p. 704.

30 L. Hannan and S. Longair, *History through Material Culture* (Manchester: Manchester University Press, 2017).

31 G. Adamson and G. Riello, 'Global objects: contention and entanglement', in M. Berg (ed.), *Writing the History of the Global: Challenges for the Twenty-first Century* (Oxford: Oxford University Press, 2013), pp. 177–93 (pp. 179–83).

32 V. Avery, M. Calaresu and M. Laven (eds), *Treasured Possessions: From the Renaissance to the Enlightenment* (London: Philip Wilson, 2015), p. 255.

33 J. Campo, 'Visualizing the Hajj: representations of a changing sacred landscape past and present', in E. Tagliacozzo and S. Toorawa (eds), *The Hajj: Pilgrimage in Islam* (Cambridge: Cambridge University Press, 2016), pp. 269–87.

34 C. Wildman, *Urban Transformation and Modernity in Liverpool and Manchester, 1918–1939* (London: Bloomsbury, 2016), pp. 167–89.

RECOMMENDED READING

L. J. Hare, J. Wells and B. E. Baker, *Essential Skills for Historians: A Practical Guide to Researching the Past* (London: Bloomsbury, 2019).

L. Jordanova, *History in Practice*, 2nd edn (London: Bloomsbury, 2006).

T. Loughran (ed.), *A Practical Guide to Studying History: Skills and Approaches* (London: Bloomsbury, 2017).

✥ 3 ✥

DEVELOPING A
METHODOLOGY

INTRODUCTION

There are many different ways of doing a research project. With these multiple possibilities in mind, the key job of the methodology section is to convince your reader that you have selected the right 'tools' for the job. 'Tools' in the context of historical research include research questions, review of relevant literatures, specific approaches (e.g. oral history) and theoretical frameworks (e.g. looking at a topic through a feminist lens). In your project, the methodology will do two main jobs: first, it will set out your approach – the tools you have decided to use – and second, it will explain why this is appropriate for the matter at hand.

But how do you know if you are on the right track? First and foremost, your discussion of methodology – what you are doing and why – should be clearly grounded in your firm grip on existing relevant scholarship. This is why the literature review is one of the first major pieces of work to be undertaken in any research project. Producing a critical survey of what other scholars have already written about (and how) means that you will know what has already been done, where existing published research falls short and, most importantly, where there are opportunities for new work, and fresh questions and perspectives. From here, you will be able to demonstrate that your methodological choices are informed and properly thought through and will support you to produce work that is rigorous, critically engaged and creative.

Methodological decisions are determined by your questions, the nature of available evidence and, more practically, how much time you have. In choosing your methods you will need to think about how you will gather, process and analyse or explain your 'data'. There are two broad categories of historical methodology, quantitative and qualitative, with many projects using some combination of the two. Quantitative

research projects deal with large datasets, such as significant quanti-
ties of economic and demographic information (e.g. population distribution in Edo and surrounding areas between 1500 and 1750, or
unemployment statistics in the United Kingdom [UK], 1970–92), in
a standardised way. To aid this, data is often organised in the form of
databases and interrogated using quantitative, statistical and computer
tools, such as the GIS discussed in the Introduction and Chapter 1.
Qualitative research is no less rigorous or empirical, but brings a more
interpretative approach to a smaller body of sources or exemplary case
studies. Here, the emphasis is not on counting numerically, but on how
and what these cases meant to a particular group of people and why they
are useful for inferring something about a place or moment in the past.
In excavating meaning, historians taking a qualitative approach might
interrogate concepts, characteristics, symbols, phenomena, metaphors,
experiences and the mechanics of representation, grounding each in a
keen understanding of historical contexts. How far your study is quantitative or qualitative will be informed by what you want to find out and,
perhaps, by your own skill set as a historian. Take, for example, a project
that seeks to understand the impact of new transport infrastructure on
people's lives. A quantitative approach would allow you to gather huge
amounts of statistical information about where people lived within a
region, to map this over time and discern whether we can see any new
patterns of residency and labour that could be attributed to changes
in transportation. By contrast, a qualitative approach to the same topic
could use representations drawn from visual and literary culture to tease
out how everyday experiences or inner lives were transformed by the
same technological changes.

It is worth spending time to choose the 'right' methods, as these
decisions will ensure that originality is part of the 'DNA' of your project.
You might select a mode of analysis drawn from history or an adjacent
discipline – for example, close object analysis drawn from art history –
that has not been used before to think about a topic. Or you may find
that application of a theoretical lens, like ANT discussed in Chapter 1,
may help you to say something new about your data. A sound methodology discussion will also explain the potential drawbacks of your choices
and how you intend to address these. Typically, this will mean telling
your reader what you have decided to sacrifice in your project and why
this is justifiable. This process can be complicated by the interdisciplinary nature of spatial projects: you may find yourself using theories and
approaches from multiple disciplines. It matters, then, that you have a

clear idea of your project's questions and headline aims. At every step, your choice of approach or theory should help, rather than hinder, this work.

In this chapter we consider four broad methodologies pertaining to spatial research, and have chosen historiographical case studies to exemplify each approach. Our discussion of spatial methodologies begins with personal testimony and tracing personal experiences and routes through urban space. We then turn to consider the built environment as a key focus for historical research. Networks – the connections between people, places, things and ideas – are the next approach to come under scrutiny. Finally, we reflect upon representations of space (in print, photography and the novel) as a medium for and way into spatial research. The organisation of the chapter is deliberate: by starting from the social and embodied experiences of a person in the past, before moving outwards to the built environment, the networks within which these two sit and, finally, the production and circulation of representations, we hope to reiterate the spatial dimensions of each approach.

PERSONAL TESTIMONY: TRACING SUBJECTIVE EXPERIENCES OF URBAN SPACE

Historians interested in analysing urban experience, particularly of marginalised groups, have often turned to forms of personal testimony in place of records produced by the dominant culture. Personal testimony refers to a range of sources, including letters, diaries, memoirs and autobiographies, and oral histories, that give access to intimate aspects of the past to locate how individuals thought about and experienced the world around them. As Penny Summerfield's *Histories of the Self* explains, 'We too might wish that we could travel through time as well as across space, to visit such a home, or an eighteenth-century penal colony, or a nineteenth-century migrant ship, or even a Nazi concentration camp, in order to experience what life was like there, albeit briefly. Personal narratives give us that imagined opportunity.'[1] Personal testimony emerged as part of the move towards 'history from below' in the 1970s and has been crucial in 'humanising, democratising and diversifying history'.[2]

As a methodological approach, personal testimony has changed how we conceive of histories of the built environment, moving away from a focus on urban infrastructure and redevelopment and towards a focus on experience and identity. For instance, Gemma Romain's life-history approach to Patrick Nelson as 'a queer black Jamaican man' explores sexuality, class and race. Romain uses letters to chart Nelson's engagement with queer Black spaces in interwar London, noting that 'Patrick's letters during 1938 and 1939 place him firmly within queer socializing of the avant-garde and within the worlds of Bloomsbury and Chelsea, through work, relationships and home.' Yet Romain's analysis of his correspondence points to the enduring implications of class divisions, despite the opportunities he experienced, such as in 1938 when Patrick was living in Chelsea. 'It appears he was seeking work in domestic service and also working as an artist model. Work was hard to find and during this time Patrick wrote about the stresses of seeking to find employment.'[3] This use of letters illuminates the contradictions and challenges around understanding the relationship between identity and space, and is a helpful framework. You may wish to build on this in your own research, especially in considering the complexities and variations in individuals' ability to move between different social, cultural and economic worlds.

Personal testimony in focus: reading the diary of Samuel Pepys spatially

Source materials such as diaries, journals, chronicles and letters have been employed by historians across a wide chronological spectrum to elucidate urban experiences and identities. For early modern historians, the diary of naval official Samuel Pepys has been one of the richest sources for tracing urban life and movements through England's metropolis. To take one day in the diary: on 11 April 1662 Pepys travelled from his home on Seething Lane in the City of London 'by water to Deptford' to view some boats that were to be dispatched to Portugal. That same morning, he journeyed further east to Greenwich, 'and had a fine pleasant walk to Woolwich' with a navy captain. Pepys then caught a boat back to Greenwich, had (another) walk in Greenwich Park with a professional associate, before making his way back to London for 'dinner at the Globe' with friends. Later that evening Pepys went to talk to merchants at the Royal Exchange, before going home 'to bed very weary'.[4] Such a journey across the metropolis and its environs (and back again) by foot, coach and boat was not unusual. Pepys's diary (1660–69) reveals that he often traversed the city in a single day, or even afternoon, as he carried out professional tasks, made sociable calls and sought news and entertainment.

Pepys's diary is exceptionally rich in social, political and cultural detail. As well as describing major political events of the 1660s, he recorded human relations in vivid depth (including interactions with his wife, kin, servants, city merchants, retailers, craftsmen, Navy Office colleagues and lovers, and sexual conquests). His diary also describes the built environment of London in great detail – including the traumatic destruction of the city in the Great Fire of 1666. Such is the richness of this source that it offers a multiplicity of routes into explorations of urban space and place. Of course, the author never intended for his manuscripts to be read in this way. But by reading such sources 'against the grain' we can make imaginative use of their evidence. Here are outlined two different spatial approaches to Pepys's diary, adopted by historians with distinct research questions and methodologies in mind. The first considers social networks; the second explores mercantile and print exchanges.

In a chapter on 'Social networks in Restoration London: the evidence from Samuel Pepys's diary', the London historian Ian Archer applies a combined quantitative and qualitative approach to this intriguing source.[5] As a consequence, Archer is able to make some very interesting observations about the spatial and social dynamics of Pepys's metropolitan life and identity. Taking the 'diary of Samuel Pepys as a guide to his social relations', Archer counted and categorised (according to social order) the 'people with whom he dined, supped or drank in two sample years, 1660 and 1666'.[6] As well as hosting visitors in his home, Pepys very often frequented taverns, alehouses and coffee houses to socialise, negotiate deals with merchants and gather news and gossip. Using this methodology, we are able to get a sense of the 'topography of Pepys's social transactions' by considering 'the location of the places in London and Westminster at which he ate, drank and shopped'. Archer finds that Pepys 'divided his time between the City and Westminster, but concentrated his visits on certain locations within those areas. Pepys rarely ventured into the less fashionable northern, eastern and southern suburbs.' Ultimately, 'Pepys's social life was therefore "bi-polar", with social transactions focused on both the West End and on the commercial heart of the old city.'[7] Further, while Pepys ate, drank and shopped across a broad metropolitan area, he tended to focus his sociability and custom on particular commercial sites. And thus, contrary to the stereotype of the growing anonymous city, we find that there were particular taverns and coffee houses in which 'he was likely to find people of his acquaintance'.[8]

Our second example of reading Pepys's diary through a spatial lens is historian Joseph Monteyne's study of metropolitan print and knowledge networks. At the opening of his monograph, *The Printed Image in Early Modern London: Urban Space, Visual Representation, and Social Exchange*, Monteyne takes us on a walk with Pepys through the streets of Restoration London. We have already seen that this diarist and civil servant was a keen frequenter of coffee houses. These were new social spaces in which print and news were avidly exchanged and discussed. Here Monteyne traces Pepys's engagement with coffee houses as a means of thinking about 'the intersection between spatial practices, print culture, and the formation of urban identities within the metropolis'. Monteyne interprets Pepys's increasing visitation of coffee houses as a valuable barometer of new patterns of knowledge exchange and mercantile sociability. Monteyne's qualitative reading of this urban source thus shows us how 'the geography of mercantile exchange seems to shift as the speech of the market floor [at sites such as the Royal and New Exchange] is precluded and extended by the coffee-house'.[9]

These examples show us how a close reading of personal testimony, such as Samuel Pepys's diary, allows us to trace personal routes through the city. It is possible to quantify and even map the frequency with which particular urban sites (including inns, brothels, playhouses, workshops, dockyards and many others) are visited, thus building up a picture of social, political, cultural and emotional lives and networks. The detail provided about urban sites and interpersonal relations gives us a sense of professional, sociable and often highly personal activities and geographies. Ultimately, what emerges from a reading of Pepys's diary through a 'spatial lens' is a highly individualised 'mental map' of London. If we were to compare Pepys's spatial experiences to those of his contemporaries, using similar sources (and this would be a worthwhile exercise), we would undoubtedly uncover different spatial impressions.

This methodology – of tracing everyday movements and spatial impressions through broadly autobiographical sources – is not without its limitations and challenges. As hinted at above, the highly personal nature of the sources means that we are inevitably interpreting a singular viewpoint. Moreover, journals and diaries are notoriously selective sources, so we are almost certainly getting a rather partial overview (many sites and persons visited might go unrecorded, for instance). The nature of these sources, which require full literacy (an ability to both read and write) to produce, means that we are also inevitably viewing the city through a gendered (male) and socially exclusive prism. What about the social geographies and 'mental maps' of women, children and socially marginalised groups (in other words, the majority of the urban population in early modern and modern Europe)?

Personal testimony in focus: oral histories and 'everyday' spatial practices

For historians of the modern world, oral history, particularly, is seen as a critical tool for uncovering the experiences of those who remain 'hidden' from history. Emerging in the 1960s and 1970s, oral history maintains an emancipatory ethos and is especially valuable in giving ordinary individuals their place in history. But there has been a shift away from using the approach to retrieve information, and towards an emphasis on the construction of narratives to explore how and why individuals remember their life stories. For instance, historians of race have typically used oral history as a methodology to chart the experiences of migrant groups or ethnic minority communities, who often remain excluded from or stigmatised within more formal local government records, sociological surveys, the media and police records. The shift owes much to the important early work of social anthropologists, such as Pnina Werbner, in developing the use of life histories to challenge stereotypes about migrant experience.[10] This methodology remains influential; one of the key aims of the Ahmed Iqbal Ullah Race Relations Resource Centre in Manchester – named in honour of the Bangladeshi school boy who, aged thirteen, was murdered by a fellow pupil in the playground of a local high school – is to undertake oral histories from the city's Black and ethnic minority communities as an approach to anti-racism. Other significant initiatives include Wolverhampton's Black and Ethnic Minority Experience and London's Chinese Oral History Project, which reflect the ongoing importance of oral history in shaping and contributing to counter-archives and community histories. It is always worth contacting local archives to see what plans are in development, and considering volunteering to assist in these valuable schemes, especially as a way to support the ongoing importance of oral history as a tool of activism and for challenging inequalities.

An insightful example of the value of using oral history can be found in Joanna Herbert's study of migration, ethnicity and gender. It uses a mix of existing oral history archives and life-history interviews undertaken by Herbert with members of the South Asian diaspora to bring to light meaningful and complex, yet often overlooked, spatial immigrant experiences. Herbert draws attention both to explicit and more insidious forms of racism, and to the ambivalence or reluctance reported by her respondents in describing seeing coarse or intimidating behaviour as racist. One illuminating interview recounted the experience of harassment by a neighbour:

> We had a little garden and he used to put his dog over deliberately to come and mess in our garden and come and mess the vegetables up. It was only a small garden but yeah he would throw the dog over and mother couldn't really do anything about it because she was a woman on her own with three kids ... I think that was racism ... It was just him, 'cause he used to row with his wife as well, there'd be pots and pans flying between the two of them and I never thought it was a racial act. I just thought that's the way he is, a bit of a lunatic and when he's not fighting with his wife, he's having a go at us.[11]

Herbert's approach provides a useful insight into how hostility and discrimination may occur through contested spaces and reminds researchers taking a spatial approach to the past to be cautious in presuming that we should focus on major commercial or civic spaces in order to understand migrant experience. Rather, this example stresses the value in exploring the small, liminal and incidental spaces – in this case a garden – where individuals may have been subjected to racism that would just not appear in more formal archival records. Perhaps one of the most valuable aspects of oral history is the way it can take the researcher into privatised or hidden spaces, facilitating new ways that we conceive of and explore spatial experiences. Thinking carefully about the kinds of spaces you wish to explore and considering the voices that you want to hear through your research is crucial as you develop your methodology.

Alongside the history of race and immigration, the history of women and feminism also remain closely linked with the use of oral history as a tool to recover women's experiences, which are so often overlooked in traditional historical sources. Studies integrated women's voices into historical scholarship and, in doing so, transformed our understanding of key moments of historical change.[12] For example, the over-focus of official archival records on the formalised spaces of politics and the workplace has contributed to the persistent silencing of women's experiences in the past. Yet, as with all oral histories, the retrieval of women's historical experiences cannot be separated from the influence of memory and culture on the production and narration of life stories. You may find that Summerfield's *Reconstructing Women's Wartime Lives* provides a valuable framework for understanding how women interviewees framed their life narratives in relation to the often contradictory wartime narratives of femininity and wartime citizenship. It shows that women narrated their wartime experiences in relation to 'heroic' stories about wartime service or 'stoic' responses to duties that they were keen to relinquish when war ended. Building on Graham Dawson's theories of subjectivity and 'composure', meaning the cultural practice of establishing an acceptable self through these stories, Summerfield emphasises that 'since discourses tend to be multiple, contradictory and fractured, the narrator must also find words for what discourses marginalise or omit'.[13] In spatial histories, this approach has especially been fruitful in thinking about women's mobility, including in powerful scholarship on their role as migrant workers.[14] In your own research, it might be helpful to consider the intersections of gender and ethnicity, alongside religious belief, race, age, life cycle, region and class, for instance, and how an individual's movement across spatial boundaries may necessitate the reshaping and renegotiation of selfhood through the process of creating their own life stories.

As we saw earlier, one of the most productive insights that oral history methodologies provide for spatial historians is the ability to uncover the experiences of privatised, domestic and less accessible spaces. Subsequently, oral history has been used effectively to chart women's experiences of the home, which remains central to spatialised accounts of women's experiences. Histories of interwar housing, such as Madeline McKenna's work on Liverpool's council estates, use interviews with women to explore what might be presented as a dramatic move from 'slum' to suburb and the profound impact on living standards:

Compared with the old houses they were a dream to keep clean and then having running hot water, well, that was wonderful, especially for the women with young kiddoes. All my life, till we came here (Larkhill Estate, 1922) I had to go down a yard to the toilet, you can imagine the difference it made having the toilet next to your bedroom, especially in winter, you felt like the Queen.[15]

McKenna's interviews not only recorded women speaking about their experiences within domestic space, as linked to their roles as wives, mothers and homemakers, but also allowed women to identify and report on the relatively mundane innovations that transformed their worlds. These are precisely the details that are often neglected by other historical sources and, therefore, shape and influence the kind of history that is written. At the same time, one consequential issue relating to the application of oral histories is that of nostalgia, which is often cited as a motivation for individuals to record their life histories at a moment when they feel emotionally secure enough to revisit traumatic or exciting moments in their own pasts.[16] This conceptualisation of nostalgia can be useful to help analyse spatial experiences in the past and remind us that for some interviewees, like McKenna's, the everyday life we may take for granted – having hot running water and an inside toilet – was perhaps the most notable and transformational spatial experience of their lives.

THE BUILT ENVIRONMENT AS YOUR SUBJECT

Another approach to urban place and space is a close focus on the built environment – by which we mean our human-made surroundings. Here we begin by outlining the methodology adopted by two historians who engage in a very close observation and examination of the urban material fabric, before exploring how we might uncover how built environments were emotionally and imaginatively meaningful to people in the past. We should bear in mind that in all instances of historians taking the built environment as a research focus the aim is not simply to describe architectural, material or decorative features – although this may certainly be part of the research process – but, rather, to draw out and critically analyse broader themes of political, social, economic, cultural and even emotional relations.

Bernard Herman's late-1990s article on 'Slave and servant housing in Charleston, 1770–1820' was one of the first pieces of scholarship to consider the built environment of slavery in antebellum cities and towns of the United States.[17] Specifically, Herman was interested in the built fabric of enslaved African Americans' environment and their lived experiences, rather than in an exclusive focus on the architecture of the white populace. By undertaking a thorough examination of surviving houses in Charleston, South Carolina, Herman identified a typical spatial arrangement of these built environments, and in so doing made significant conclusions about racial and social relations in these urban communities. Crucially, Herman found that:

> In Charleston the dwelling represented only one element in an ensem-ble of buildings that included kitchen, washhouse, quarters, privies, stables, work yards, gardens, and a variety of other structures […] Through the usage of everyday life and work, the urban lot with all its attendant buildings (and not just the principal dwelling) defined the Charleston town house.[18]

In other words, white urban inhabitants and African American enslaved people frequently occupied the same properties. The material con-ditions of their existence were very different, however. While white slave-owners often lived in considerable material comfort, the evidence from surviving properties gives an indication of the discomfort and everyday aggravations experienced by the enslaved. Herman found the kitchens in which African Americans laboured 'floored with heavy slate pavers, a practice that enhanced maintenance, but further blackened an already dark interior and exhausted the legs of those who stood and crouched on those hard surfaces'. In the upper-storey quarters in which slaves often slept, windows 'were shuttered, but often left unglazed, leaving the occupants in summer prey to mosquitoes […] in winter, loose-fitting shutters offered little protection from the cold and damp'.[19] By looking at the existing built environment in dialogue with other surviving archival materials such as plans, inventories and court records, Herman discovered that many of these Charleston buildings were undergoing change over time. Towards the end of the eighteenth century a new type of slave quarters became more popular among white slave-owners. The removal of fireplaces at the back of rear walls enabled a better view for masters from upper-storey windows of enslaved labour in the yard below. The new placement of a stairway 'with its own exter-nal entry between the work rooms' also resulted in 'the architectural segmentation and regulation of domestic spaces where servants often worked out of the sight and hearing of their masters'.[20]

Notably, Herman's work made innovative use of the built environ-ment of eighteenth-century Charleston alongside other primary sources, including building plans. A more recent article by Catherine W. Bishir, 'Urban slavery at work: the Bellamy Mansion Compound, Wilmington, North Carolina', also examined an extant house, including its slave quarters, that was deeply implicated in the politics of the late antebellum era.[21] Bishir examined the evidence of the built environment in dialogue with historic photos, building plans and the textual memoirs of the white, slave-owning Bellamy family. Like Herman, Bishir found that the built space both reflected and directly informed the lived experience of slavery. She writes of the Bellamy Mansion Compound (constructed between 1859 and 1861): 'Not only was the imposing complex meant to display the slavery-based wealth and stature of the Bellamy family; it was carefully planned to control and integrate as conveniently and discreetly as possible the work of domestic slaves in the daily operation of the household.'[22] What is most striking about Bishir's work is the way in which she brings to light the hugely significant role of Black enslaved people not just in negotiating the built environment but in physically shaping and constructing it. Highly skilled slave artisans, including carpenters, plasterers and stonemasons, among others, played a central role in the building and decoration of Bellamy Mansion. Indeed, in the mid-1990s, during a renovation project on the house, the initials of enslaved plasterer William Benjamin Gould were discovered on the back of ornamental plaster mouldings. This mark of professional and personal identity had been embedded within the structure of the slaveowners' house since its construction.[23]

As the example from Bishir's research demonstrates, we cannot understand the meaning and significance of the built environment without a consideration of how individuals and groups shaped, challenged or reinforced the material world around them. Yet one challenge that may present itself when you are developing your own methodology relates to the proliferation of writings and images that created a fantastical or imagined urban space. One famous example is located in Seth Koven's *Slumming: Sexual and Social Politics in Victorian London*, which uses visual sources and guidebooks to trace the practice of 'slumming'. This is defined as the practice of middle-class men and women visiting 'slum' areas of London as a form of liberation and experimentation, including in sexual terms, with the desire to 'rescue' the poor often intersecting with attempts to sexually exploit and eroticise them. Koven's study reveals the ways in which the 'slum' was an imagined space onto which the fantasies of the dominant middle class were imposed. That is not to say that the urban poor did not experience harsh living conditions, but that contemporary observers infused their understandings of the working classes and their lives with socially loaded and eugenicist beliefs that 'othered' them.[24]

Bearing this influential case study in mind, we need to ask how we might analyse imagined spaces such as the nineteenth-century 'slum' that existed primarily as a product of the thoughts and prejudices of Victorian urban explorers and philanthropists. How do we understand the experience of these urban spaces that occupied both a marginalised and central role in shaping the built environment, without sensationalising the plight of their inhabitants? Returning to the constructive insights offered by personal testimony, one approach might be to compare visual and more formal representations of the built environment with the perspectives of everyday interactions within 'sensationalised' urban spaces. For example, interwar suburban houses have been typified as dull and lonely for new inhabitants, through methodologies that focus on the analysis of adverts for new homes and the associated 'labour-saving devices', social surveys and local council handbooks and promotional materials. Historians of suburbs, such as Peter Scott and Judy Giles, suggest that the pressure to live up to the image of the 'suburban dream', combined with the isolation that many women experienced, led to the creation of a new category of mental ill-health, 'suburban neurosis', to describe the anxiety and loneliness caused by life on the new estates.[25]

However, returning to McKenna's oral history interviews, we can see that some inhabitants' perspectives on their interactions within the micro-spaces of the new suburbs jarred with or undermined these more official interpretations. For instance, rather than acknowledging loneliness, many women reported enjoying the new, privatised culture of domesticity afforded by the new estates. One interviewee, who had moved to Liverpool's working-class estate of Norris Green in 1929, recalled that 'people were neighbourly but they liked to keep to themselves. My next-door neighbour came from the rough part of town where they kept their doors open all the time. She didn't like me keeping my door closed, but you had to. You didn't want people getting to know all your business, you know, too familiar like.'[26] The interview hints at the potential tensions between neighbours who might have had different wants and expectations of suburban life, evidenced here by distinctive attitudes to opening or closing doors, but it also suggests that the presumptions around what inhabitants wanted or found difficult about the new estates may not have reflected the 'official' view. It is a useful reminder also of the power of everyday interactions – and the refusal of such – and the value of exploring micro-spaces as contested sites in understanding how individuals and communities shaped the urban environment that they occupied.

Built environment in focus: the preservation of contested spaces

It is important to think about how certain spaces remain contested, shaping attitudes towards their preservation and the communication of their histories in the present. To take a valuable example, we can address the important and current issues around the disputed preservation of imperial and post-imperial spaces. For instance, we can read the formation and manifestation of imperial power through the physical and spatial arrangements that characterised urban redevelopment in colonised lands, through the spectacle of imperial exhibitions and through the challenges and tensions around how these spaces should be preserved – or not.

A useful starting point for such issues might be through the influential framework offered by Timothy Mitchell's *Colonising Egypt* (1988) and its explanation of colonisation within spatial terms. Drawing comparisons with French administrators' rebuilding of villages in Algeria, Mitchell suggested that colonisers emphasised conformity in order to reinforce colonial control: 'resulting in an ordered countryside of containers and contained ... the new methods of spatial order also worked by producing and codifying a visible hierarchy. The distinction was to be made ... between four different ranks of housing. Besides the model house for the ordinary peasant, there were dwellings for the well-to-do, for the rich, and for foreigners.'[27] Mitchell used Foucauldian theories relating to power and governance to demonstrate how colonial structures of power relied on the careful reorganisation of space to control the colonised, inhibit protest and rebellion movements and reinforce the authority of the colonisers. You may want to think about how this approach could be applied to different colonised or postcolonial spaces, perhaps to bring new insights into the relationship between imperial power and the built environment and the ongoing issues around how to approach the heritage of these spaces.

There are very live debates about how imperial sites should be treated, revealing how the built environment can become a particularly emotive and highly symbolic site for the renegotiation of power in the postcolonial city. To take a well-known case, India's New Delhi has emerged in scholarship as the quintessential example of a colonial city. Anthony King's influential *Colonial Urban Development* (1976) used Delhi to explain how the colonial city typically had four distinct zones: (1) Old Delhi, built in the seventeenth century and characterised by its dense population and narrow streets; (2) New Delhi, with its wide roads built for cars, low population density, symbolic buildings and ceremonial spaces; (3) the military camp; (4) the unplanned shanty town, home to rural migrants. King suggests that the colonial city was planned more comprehensively than the Western city, since it represented the imposition of the dominant power onto subjects. Delhi illustrates 'how the power structure inherent in the dominance–dependence relationship of colonialism influenced urban development'.[28]

The decision to build New Delhi, about five kilometres south of Delhi city centre, as the new capital of India in 1911 aimed to consolidate imperial power, as the existing capital, Calcutta (now Kolkata), was the centre of nationalist movements and anticolonial uprisings. Designed by Sir Edwin Lutyens, the most prominent English architect of the early twentieth century, the comprehensive urban redevelopment plan aimed to build a monumental cityscape that reinforced the power and authority of the British Empire with clearly zoned administrative and residential areas. Officially opened in 1931, Lutyens' design produced a garden-city pattern based on a series of hexagons characterised by wide, tree-lined boulevards, deliberately contrasting with the narrow and crowded streets of Old Delhi. His landmark Viceroy's House, now Rashtrapati Bhawan (built 1913–30), dominated the landscape and combined classical architecture with features of Indian design. The design reflected Lutyens' well-known rejection of Hindu architecture, although he reluctantly incorporated some elements of Indian tradition, including the distinctive dome inspired by the Buddhist Stupa at Sanchi.[29] New Delhi has come to symbolise imperial tyranny: Jawaharlal Nehru, the first prime minister of an independent India, described it as a 'symbol of British power, with all its ostentation and wastefulness.' Much has fallen into disrepair, despite attempts made by preservation and heritage practitioners to maintain Lutyens' key buildings, perhaps reflecting the ongoing challenges of confronting the West's colonial legacy and acknowledging the imperial past. This example is a useful reminder of how the choices around the preservation or restoration of the built environment are often political and can tell researchers a great deal about contemporary power dynamics. Important current discussions around the repatriation of artefacts housed in Western museums, the presence of statues of individuals linked to colonialism and the relationship between some English National Trust properties and the profiteers of historic slavery are timely reminders of the ongoing and complex debates around the built environment, heritage and history.[30] These kinds of questions and issues may frame your decisions with regard to choosing and analysing the spatial and material organisation of built space in your own research projects.

NETWORKS

Looking at networks will move your study beyond the scrutiny of an individual site or place. A network-focused project, with its emphasis on connections, interactions, intersections and points of contact, brings us closest to the definition of space with which we began in the Introduction, and for this reason offers historians a useful framework for thinking spatially.[31] The importance of networks to spatial studies should be evident from what you have read of this book so far. Many of the theories and disciplinary approaches that we have already looked at – from historical geography to ANT – foreground the connections and relationships between people and places.

Historians who put networks centre stage do so in order to interrogate the social, cultural, political and economic reasons why some people and places were connected in the past. This work operates at different geographical scales. But, irrespective of whether your study is micro or macro in its ambition, a network-led approach will require you to think about how and from where you gather data and, in turn, how you propose to make sense of it. Taking a micro-historical approach, you might decide to tease out connections between people and places that are local, even intimate, in their horizons – as in the studies of Samuel Pepys's social and spatial networks in early modern London discussed earlier.[32] In recent work in this vein, historians employ data-driven approaches to make sense of sizable data samples spread across multiple institutions and, in some cases, countries.[33] Networks themselves can be the explicit focus of a research project. This is most apparent in work on infrastructure for communications, transportation, trade, production and supply, and provision of resources (e.g. water, electricity), which looks at how these developments resulted in new conceptualisations of place and space.[34] Think, again, of the nineteenth-century metropolitan railways with which we began this book: innovations in transportation resulted in new connections between places and, in doing so, pushed back the boundaries of what – or, more properly, where – constituted cities such as London and Paris.

How connections fostered new ideas about space and place is most apparent in the recent turn towards global history. Here, you might

trace the flow of people, ideas, information, capital, materials and commodities across the world. In addition to proving the many ways in
which the local was global, and the global local, this joined-up and
global approach to history reveals the power-laden character of networks, bringing into focus questions of who has benefited from 'cultural
exchanges that criss-crossed the globe'.[35] But, crucially, global networks
were also reciprocal: each interconnected point was transformed by
being part of a network. As geographer Miles Ogborn argues for the
period between c. 1500 and c. 1800, 'different areas of the globe were
tied together into a new set of relationships, which changed what was
grown, made and consumed in each part of the world'.[36] Choosing a
strand of activity, an individual or group, or an object, may help you to
structure a project with global dimensions. Historians increasingly combine approaches from microhistory and global history to study a particular individual, event, place or object as a way into understanding the
global connections and dimensions that were part of lives in the past.[37]

Networks in focus: lived experience of diasporas in early twentieth-century Paris

Networks are central to Michael Goebel's radical rethinking of anticolonial nationalism in the early twentieth century.[38] Placing Paris in
its global and imperial contexts, he argues that 'Paris and other nerve
centres of African and Asian diasporas were fruitful terrain for incu-
bating anticolonial nationalism because they condensed global inequalities in a pressure cooker.'[39] This means that Goebel can approach
nations and nationalism in non-European contexts, not as ideas that
were spread by means of 'intellectual diffusion', but as ideals forged
through lived experience of migration, colonialism, imperialism and
bigotry. It matters that many future global leaders who promoted anticolonial nationalism, from Ho Chi Minh to Messali Hadj, were part of
diasporic communities in interwar Paris, where they had the opportunity to organise within communities, and also – and this is a critical
part of Goebel's argument – to engage in cross-community exchanges
and activism and to share and compare experiences of discrimination. For these reasons, 'Paris became a practical school of curtailed
citizenship.'[40]

Let us look at two of Goebel's methodological shifts in more detail,
as this may help you to ensure the originality of your project. First,

Goebel brings together the concerns of different disciplines, which is one way that historians can ask new questions and produce fresh insights. In his article 'The Capital of Men without a Country' he takes a subject that is usually dealt with by one type of scholar – political and intellectual historians asking 'the old question of how sovereign nation-states spread and became the global gold standard for territorial political organisation' – and shows what happens when this is addressed through the concerns and techniques of social history. In the case of Goebel's study, this means taking seriously the lived experiences of African and Asian diasporic groups and showing that these were shaped by Paris as a particular place. From the quantitative headlines of migrant populations in interwar Paris, Goebel explores the entangled experiences of people from North Africa, West Africa, China and Vietnam and demonstrates how the day-to-day realities of life in Paris, including cross-national associations, underpinned the emergence of anticolonial nationalism. Arguing that '[e]thnic origin and migratory networks contoured the settlement and employment patterns of Africans and Asians in interwar Paris', Goebel demonstrates the social and spatial specificity of migrant experiences and discrimination by mapping patterns of residency and employment, and showing the significance of gathering places (e.g. cafes, restaurants), mutual aid associations, student clubs and community newspapers.[41] 'Everyday' lived discrimination, from low wages to racist social legislation, as experienced by colonial subjects in the metropole, is shown to politicise groups and individuals.

Goebel's second key methodological innovation is his selection of sources. To move beyond the geographical limits of previous analyses of his topic, he deliberately works across French government archives. As he sets out at the beginning of the article, separate government institutions monitored different diasporic groups: 'Whereas surveillance of the political activities of Chinese, Indians, Moroccans, and Tunisians in France fell chiefly into the remit of the Foreign Ministry, Algerians were assigned to the Interior Ministry, and the Vietnamese and pan-African movements were a matter for the Colonial Ministry.'[42] As Goebel acknowledges, working across multiple archives in this way is enabled by developments in digital technology and archival practices: 'The greater leniency regarding the photographing of archival records, the simplification of digitization and optical character recognition (OCR) software have all helped overcome the methodological nationalism that once characterized both French intelligence gathering and historical scholarship.'[43] Working across this evidence base, and harnessing digital technology, reveals previously unseen networks that extend between and across community groups. The quantity and accumulation of these networks across space and over time offer further proof of the social experience of migration and reiterate the article's reinterpretation of anticolonial nationalism and post-1945 decolonisation.

REPRESENTATION

Representation is used here in its broadest sense to encompass the depiction, description and reflection of space and place in visual and material culture, literature and time-based media, including film. Most obviously, there is a rich seam of evidence specifically linked to and generated by urban built environments in the form of designs, plans, maps, diagrams and promotional materials, many of which relate to buildings or environments that no longer exist – something we will discuss in greater detail in Chapter 4. Irrespective of what form they take, representations of urban space and built environments fall into two broad, sometimes overlapping, categories: places that existed in some physical form and imagined or imaginary environments. Clearly, there are forms of representation that straddle this line, such as designs for speculative architectural projects, like the experimental architectural studio Archigram's proposition for a Walking City, or unbuilt urban plans, like Sir Christopher Wren's radical proposition for how to rebuild London after the Great Fire.[44] As we have already touched on, asking questions of representation(s) from the past is about more than working out whether something was successful in mimetic terms and managed to replicate a known or knowable world.[45] Instead, historians often focus on the representational strategies used in a source or, more often, group of sources in order to ask questions about the exercise of power and agency at a given time. When undertaking this work it is your job to understand the contexts of representation, to puzzle out its purpose and establish whose perspectives were 'centred' or emphasised. What was a particular representation or representational strategy trying to do, and why? How was it made, and by whom? Whose perspective does it show, and how? How typical or unusual was this? Whose perspectives are not included? What does all of this tell us about the time and place in which it was made?

To answer these kinds of questions, we could take our lead from work that looks at the production of representations, from printed texts and images to paintings, photographs and film, and shows how these practices were rooted in, and transformed, urban contexts and subjectivities. The interplay between practices of building and architecture, and representations of urban space and built environments, provides one route into discussion of representation. Architectural historian Mario Carpo does this by looking at how printing impacted on the theory and practice of architecture across early modern Europe.[46] Or you might think about how new patterns of urban life and emotional experiences were shaped by practices of representation. A nice example is architectural historian Elizabeth McKellar's work on London's suburbs, which demonstrates that a combination of commercial leisure opportunities, printed – often illustrated – guidebooks and the practice of drawing changed how eighteenth-century Londoners thought and felt about the city's peripheral areas.[47] Recent work by scholars of architecture, design and media brings these issues right up to date. Here we might think of design historian Jessica Kelly's work on architecture and mass media in 1930s Britain. In one article she uses the interconnected and overlapping personnel and activities of the *Architectural Review*, Modern Architecture Research Group (or MARS Group), BBC and Penguin Books to interrogate the cultivation of a sympathetic, non-specialist, middle-class audience for modern art and design within the broader landscape of interwar 'public culture'.[48] Or we could look to Scott McQuire's work, which explores how the presence of electronic screens in contemporary city centres across the globe 'reconstitutes static buildings into active information surfaces'. In McQuire's argument, this brings the domestic technology of television outside, blurring the relationship between 'public' and 'private' spaces in the twenty-first-century city.[49]

Representation in focus: an early modern printed topographical view of Rome

Let us analyse another example in order to understand in more detail the methods used to explain an early modern printed image. Elena Napolitano's study of the seventeenth-century printmaker Israel Silvestre's 'Profile of the City of Rome' (1687) (Figure 3.1) uncovers the political motivations that informed how urban environments were used, enhanced and represented in print.[50] Indeed, Napolitano shows

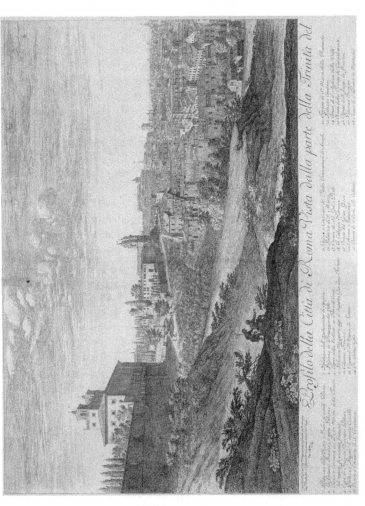

Figure 3.1 Panel of Israel Silvestre's *Profile of the City of Rome Viewed from the Trinità dei Monti*, 1687.

that Silvestre's huge printed panorama makes sense *only* in the context of French political ambitions and the shifting balance of power in seventeenth-century Europe.[51]

Napolitano's approach provides a useful model for historians, who are often more comfortable with textual evidence. One of the many pitfalls of moving from textual to visual and, indeed, material sources is the temptation to treat representations from the past as if they were uncomplicated reflections of what was there. Instead, Napolitano demonstrates how necessary it is to work across different kinds of evidence – in this case, diplomatic, ceremonial, architectural and representational – while showing sensitivity to the purposes of each type. At the study's core is the idea that European territorial and dynastic ambitions were projected onto the Pincian Hill as both a physical *and* imagined place. At its base was Piazza de Spagna, home to the Spanish embassy; at its summit, Trinità dei Monti, under French patronage from 1494. This already contested geography was intensified by the ceremonies, celebrations and architectural enhancements by which different European powers sought to put their stamp on this site.[52] Napolitano treats these activities as evidence of French attempts to 'concretize [their] pre-eminence over the hillside, branding the area as a royal territory' – something that provoked Spanish and papal opposition.[53] Setting up the idea of multiple projections of power, with each seeking to enlist stakeholders, from French ex-patriots to local Romans, allows Napolitano to frame the Pincian Hill as a site of debate: 'a point of contact, contestation and association amongst disparate interests'.[54]

Only once this broader context is established can Napolitano consider in detail the political strategies at work in Silvestre's 'Profile'. Close analysis of the panorama, in the context of other contemporary representations of Rome, reveals how politically motivated Silvestre's representational choices were. This part of the argument turns on teasing out what the 'Profile' does and, more crucially, does not show, and what this tells us about Franco-papal diplomacy. Through close analysis, contextualisation of production and well-chosen points of comparison, Napolitano explains that the 'Profile' was the product of multiple 'traditions' of printed views, all of which say different things about the spatial dimensions of power. Silvestre's panorama is compared with contemporary printed views of Rome, such as the 1665 panoramic view created by Giovanni Termini and engraved by Hendrick Van Cleef.[55] Chosen because of its similarity in size and format to Silvestre's print and its appeal to a similar group of wealthy collectors, Van Cleef's production was part of a tradition of views of Rome that promoted the papacy by showcasing major building projects and urban improvements initiated by a series of sixteenth- and seventeenth-century popes.[56] In deliberate contrast, Silvestre's 'Profile' filtered out recent papal improvements made to Rome. Instead, his view was based on drawings made during a visit to the city nearly forty years beforehand, in the 1640s. This means that major building projects from the reign of Pope Alexander VII, evident in other contemporary views of Rome, were excluded.[57] Silvestre also made some telling additions that boosted French prestige and further diminished the papacy. A closer look at the 'Profile' reveals Bernini's botched tower on St Peter's, an embarrassing failure dismantled in 1642, and a French royal escutcheon, which is added to the façade of Trinità dei Monti. The latter was put in place only in 1668, long after Silvestre's visit to the city.[58]

Representation in focus: photographs

Photography emerged alongside the modern city and, arguably, technological developments in capturing images cannot be separated from the visual experience – or spectacle – of the urban landscape. As with earlier printed images, we must not use photographs as value-free depictions of cities. For philosopher Roland Barthes, writing in *Camera Lucida*, photography actually increased the gap between 'image' and 'reality'. For him, photographs create a certainty about the past that did not exist, rooted in the existence of the image and what it purports to show, and he offers an important reflection on how we as historians should question and analyse photographs to challenge these kinds of assumptions.[59] An essential text for any student grappling with photographs as historical evidence (or indeed the practice of history, full stop) is visual and historical anthropologist Elizabeth Edwards' *Photographs and the Practice of History: A Short Primer*, which explores these (and other) productive tensions in more depth than we can cover here.[60]

The perception, use and understanding of photographs also have explicit relevance to histories of urban space. Art historian Lynda Nead's study of still photography and film in late nineteenth-century London shows how the availability and technological development of commercial film and photographic equipment, such as hand-held cameras that took 'instantaneous' photographs, captured everyday life to an unprecedented extent, changing how people saw themselves and perceived their city.[61] Nead's analysis of Victorian photographs and films of London reminds us how and why historians should reflect critically on urban images. Nead argues that they

> do so much more than show us images of the city, or what places, things, and people actually looked like ... They convey the social topography of the period and the changing patterns of observation and visibility in the urban context ... The new photographic practices forced a reassessment of social behaviour in the streets and of individual rights to a private self within public space.[62]

Nead was one of the first historians to advance the use of photographs as a way to think about the framing and representation of urban space and to link this to changing technologies in order to analyse key historical processes relating to power, the self and modernity.

Caroline Bressey's pioneering research on London uses photographic archives to expose new historical geographies. She demonstrates that photographs are especially necessary as tools to locate the 'biographies of "people of colour" that it would otherwise be very difficult, if not impossible, to trace'.[63] Through her work with photographs contained in the archives of the City of London Asylum, Bressey also reminds us to pay careful attention to the genre and contexts of evidence. Noting that many of the images do not stress the colour of the skin belonging to those in the pictures, she explains that 'the photographs are not records of an individual's exotic otherness, but part of their medical record'.[64] These records, in common with the census, birth and marriage certificates, had no dedicated 'space' for capturing information about subjects' race and ethnicity.[19] Bressey uses these sources to argue for the need for a diverse but integrated approach to the social history of the East End of London that challenges the presumption we might have about othering those whom we see in these images. This method illuminates the value of using photographic images to think about urban experience, while stressing the importance of not using them as static images that merely emphasise difference. Her surfacing of the discrepancies between textual and visual records also offers a powerful challenge to historians not to presume the whiteness of the people documented in archival sources. As she writes: 'What we can no longer assume is that everyone in the archive who is not allocated another colour is White. The imagined Whiteness of our national archives is one of the most blatant examples of the Whitening of Britishness.'[21]

Photographs have also been used by urban historians of the later twentieth century. Impactful recent analyses of key moments of urban disorder illuminate the importance of visual sources in drawing attention to the entanglement of the market and the state in the production, dissemination and interpretation of photographs of urban space. Take, for example, Erika Hanna's comparison of the distinctive ways that photographs, including images produced by amateurs, press photographers, the army and police, were mobilised as evidence at the Scarman Tribunal (1969–72) and Widgery Tribunal (February–March 1972), which investigated early episodes in the 'Troubles' in Northern Ireland. Hanna's close attention to the contexts in which the photographs were produced (including where they were taken), circulated and interpreted by a range of contemporaries provides a model for us to follow. Through comparison of the distinctive and contingent processes by which state narratives about the 'Troubles' were forged, Hanna reveals 'the complex and contingent processes through which images of violence were produced, how they were used to make sense of civil disorder, and the problems and possibilities they contain for historians'.[65] Shirin Hirsch and David Swanson are equally attentive to the production and dissemination of photographic images: in this case forty-six photographs showing the disorder in Moss Side, Manchester, published in the *Manchester Evening News* between 7 and 9 July 1981.[66] Through quantitative and qualitative image analysis, Hirsch and Swanson highlight the social, political and material dimensions of press photography. Especially interesting for our purposes is the prominence of damaged and destroyed buildings in the published photographs. Hirsch and Swanson deftly link this presentation of the urban environment to longer histories of urban protest's vilification as 'mindless' attacks on the values and virtues of English capitalism.[67] Like Bressey, they also alert us to the importance of working across source types, arguing that 'photography of the 1981 riots allows acknowledgement of "race" when in contemporary written accounts its existence is denied'.[68]

The photograph in Figure 3.2, similar to those used by Hanna, Hirsch and Swanson, attests to the complexity of spatial information captured by photographs. One of a series taken by local photographer Kim Aldis during the Brixton, London disturbances of 1981, it fixes the existence of competing spatial 'regimes' within the same place – in this instance, the intersection of Coldharbour Lane and Atlantic Road. Note, for example, the contrast between the line of police with riot shields in front of the Atlantic pub on the corner and the people, including a woman laden with shopping bags, seeming to go around their ordinary business

Figure 3.2 Photograph by local photographer Kim Aldis showing riot police at the intersection of Coldharbour Lane and Atlantic Road in Brixton, London, in April 1981.

in the midst of this threatening presence. These discordant details resonate with the 'excess' of information Edwards attributes to photographs, far beyond the intentions of even the most exacting photographer.[69] In the context of spatial histories, these 'excesses' encompass details of place, spatial relationships and presences not registered in earlier forms of image-making, such as the printed topographical view by Silvestre that we considered earlier in this chapter. Such unintentional traces form the evidential base of a recent study by historian of technology Tiina Männistö-Funk. She combines quantitative and qualitative analysis of thousands of 'street photos' taken in Helsinki between 1890 and 1989 to explore urban spatial practices. In doing so, Männistö-Funk tackles a historiographical double bind: the comparative absence of women in urban histories and oversight of pedestrian 'socio-technologies' in histories of transport and urban mobilities. By using 'street photographs' to assert 'everyday practices and phenomena of walking', her study usefully complicates understanding of the presence (or absence) of women in cities, stretching well beyond the figure of the *flâneur* and 'the idea of the city as labyrinth of sexual danger'.[70]

Representation in focus: novels

Cultural historians interested in the modern city have also turned to literature, particularly novels, to chart contemporary descriptions, responses to and representations of the urban landscape. Novels from the mid-nineteenth century may well chart the social problems and squalor of the industrial city, for instance, but they can also reveal the varied impact of the urban environment on the senses. Elizabeth Gaskell's *Mary Barton* (1848), for example, depicts the visual spectacle of Manchester's shopping streets as a way to emphasise the city's stark social divisions:

> It is a pretty sight to walk through a street with lighted shops; the gas is so brilliant, the display of goods so much more vividly shown than by day, and of all shops a druggist's looks the most like the tales of our childhood, from Aladdin's garden of enchanted fruits to the charming Rosamond with her purple jar. No such associations had Barton; yet he felt the contrast between the well-filled, well-lighted shops and the dim gloomy cellar, and it made him moody that such contrasts should exist.[71]

Novels can also reveal how the city and its new forms of culture might have caused a dramatic experience for all the senses. Émile Zola's *The Ladies' Paradise* (1883) famously depicted the development of the modern department store in late nineteenth-century Paris run by the innovative retailer Octave Mouret. The novel gives some sense of the noise, smells and sights associated with this new form of commercial retail culture:

> In the yellow light streaming down into the silk hall, ladies had taken off their gloves to feel the Paris Delight on which they commented in whispers. And there was no longer any mistaking the noises which came from outside, the rolling of cabs, the banging of carriage-doors, all the increasing tumult of a growing crowd. Mouret felt that his machine was again setting to work beneath him, getting up steam and reviving to activity, from the pay-desks where gold was jingling, and the tables where messengers were hurriedly packing up goods, to the delivery-room in the basement, which was quickly filling with the parcels sent down to it, its subterranean rumble seeming to shake the whole house.[72]

Extracts like the above illuminate sensory experience and remind us that the city was never just about what contemporaries saw, but also about what they heard, smelt and touched. Novels might be one resource to help historians to examine these meaningful, yet often under-explored, elements of urban life.

Novels may also help to chart the perspectives of those who might otherwise be assumed to be marginal or victimised figures within the urban landscape. As novels represented an artistic method for middle- and upper-class women, for example, they can provide a valuable insight into how such women saw the city in ways that can challenge the stereotypes about gender and urban experience. For instance, twenty-three-year-old Lucy Snowe's seemingly unencumbered movement around the City of London, as depicted in Charlotte Brontë's *Villette* (1853), provides an account of adventure, freedom and urban exploration that is not usually associated with women in cities during the mid-nineteenth century:

> Elation and pleasure were in my heart: to walk alone in London seemed of itself an adventure ... Prodigious was the amount of life I lived that morning ... I went wandering whither chance might lead, in a still ecstasy of freedom and enjoyment; and I got – I know not how – I got into the heart of city life. I saw and felt London at last: I got into the Strand; I went up Cornhill; I mixed with the life passing along; I dared the perils of crossings. To do this, and to do it utterly alone, gave me, perhaps an irrational, but a real pleasure.[73]

The novel points to the elation and excitement experienced by Snowe as she walks freely around the City, associated with the male worlds of finance and capitalism. It offers a different perspective from the prescriptive literature issued to women at this time that reinforced their roles within domestic space. As fiction, we cannot say it is 'truth', but it is a reflection of the world around them as interpreted by the author – arguably as much as any other historical source.

IN SUMMARY

In this chapter we have outlined a handful of possible routes, and presented a number of exemplary case studies, relating to spatial research. As we stressed at the outset, the methodological pathways presented here are not exhaustive. Your research questions, source materials, particular skill set and period focus will shape the methodology for your project. In the next chapter we consider how you might go about locating primary evidence.

NOTES

1   P. Summerfield, *Histories of the Self: Personal Narratives and Historical Practice* (London: Routledge, 2018), p. 2.

2   *Ibid.*, p. 6.

3   G. Romain, *Race, Sexuality and Identity in Britain and Jamaica: The Biography of Patrick Nelson, 1916–1963* (London: Bloomsbury, 2017), pp. 94–6.

4   *The Diary of Samuel Pepys: A Selection*, ed. R. Latham (London: Penguin, 2003), pp. 189–90.

5   I. W. Archer, 'Social networks in Restoration London: the evidence from Samuel Pepys's diary', in A. Shepard and P. Withington (eds), *Communities in Early Modern England: Networks, Place, Rhetoric* (Manchester: Manchester University Press, 2000), pp. 76–94.

6   *Ibid.*, p. 77.

7   *Ibid.*, p. 79.

8   *Ibid.*, p. 81.

9   J. Monteyne, *The Printed Image in Early Modern London: Urban Space, Visual Representation, and Social Exchange* (Aldershot: Ashgate, 2007), pp. 1–3.

10 P. Werbner, 'From rags to riches: Manchester Pakistanis in the textile trade', *New Community*, 8 (1980), 84–95. See also: A. Thomson, 'Moving stories: oral history and migration studies', *Oral History*, 71:1 (1999), 24–37.

11 J. Herbert, *Negotiating Boundaries of the City: Migration, Ethnicity, and Gender in Britain* (Aldershot: Ashgate, 2008), p. 115.

12 S. Geiger, 'What's so feminist about women's oral history?', *Journal of Women's History*, 2:1 (1990), 169–82 (p. 170); J. Sangster, 'Telling our stories: feminist debates and the use of oral history', *Women's History Review*, 3:1 (1994), 5–28.

13 P. Summerfield, *Reconstructing Women's Wartime Lives* (Manchester: Manchester University Press, 1998), p. 17.

14 L. Ryan, 'Moving spaces and changing places: Irish women's memories of emigration to Britain in the 1930s', *Journal of Ethnic and Migration Studies*, 29:1 (2003), 67–82; L. McDowell, *Migrant Women's Voices: Talking about Life and Work in the UK since 1945* (London: Bloomsbury, 2016); B. Hazley, *Life History and the Irish Migrant Experience in Post-War England* (Manchester: Manchester University Press, 2020).

15   M. McKenna, 'The suburbanization of the working-class population of Liverpool between the wars', *Social History*, 16:2 (1991), 173–89 (p. 177).

16   F. Houghton, *The Veterans' Tale: British Military Memoirs of the Second World War* (Cambridge: Cambridge University Press, 2019), p. 40.

17   B. L. Herman, 'Slave and servant housing in Charleston, 1770–1820', *Historical Archaeology*, 33:3 (1999), 88–101.

18   *Ibid.*, p. 91.

19   *Ibid.*, p. 97.

20   *Ibid.*, p. 93.

21   C. W. Bishir, 'Urban slavery at work: the Bellamy Mansion Compound, Wilmington, North Carolina', *Buildings & Landscapes: Journal of the Vernacular Architecture Forum*, 17:2 (2010), 13–32.

22   *Ibid.*, p. 19.

23   *Ibid.*, pp. 13–14, 28–9.

24   S. Koven, *Slumming: Sexual and Social Politics in Victorian London* (Princeton, NJ: Princeton University Press, 2004).

25   P. Scott, *The Making of the Modern British Home: The Suburban Semi and Family Life between the Wars* (Oxford: Oxford University Press, 2013), pp. 138–40; J. Giles, *Women, Identity and Private Life in Britain, 1900 – 50* (Basingstoke: Palgrave Macmillan, 1995), pp. 78–85.

26   M. McKenna, 'The Development of Suburban Council Housing Estates in Liverpool between the Wars', Appendix 13, Interview Number 15 (PhD thesis, University of Liverpool, 1986), p. 442.

27   T. Mitchell, *Colonising Egypt* (Cambridge: Cambridge University Press, 1988), p. 45.

28   A. King, *Colonial Urban Development* (London: Routledge and Kegan Paul, 1976), p. xiii, as quoted in J. Ridley, 'Edwin Lutyens, New Delhi, and the architecture of imperialism', *The Journal of Imperial and Commonwealth History*, 26:2 (1998), 67–83 (p. 68).

29   Ridley, 'Edwin Lutyens', p. 81.

30   See C. Fowler, *Green Unpleasant Land: Creative Responses to Rural England's Colonial Connections* (Leeds: Peepal Tree Press, 2020); D. Hicks, *The Brutish Museums: The Benin Bronzes, Colonial Violence and Cultural Restitution* (London: Pluto Press, 2020).

31   Refer back to our definitions of 'site', 'place' and 'space' outlined in the Introduction.

32   For application of this framework, alongside discussion of the challenges it raises, see the following useful review essay: C. Wetherell, 'Historical social network analysis', *International Review of Social History*, 43:S6 (1998), 125–44.

33   See, for example, the Mapping the Republic of Letters project at

Stanford University, which uses digital methods to reassemble and interpret international correspondence networks in the early modern period: 'About the Project', Mapping the Republic of Letters, http://republicofletters.stanford.edu/ [accessed January 2021].

34 For an example of this approach, see: V. Taylor and F. Trentmann, 'Liquid politics: water and the politics of everyday life in the modern city', *Past & Present*, 211:1 (2011), 200–41.

35 C. Hall, 'Histories, empires and the postcolonial moment', in I. Chambers and L. Curti (eds), *The Post-colonial Question: Common Skies, Divided Horizons* (London: Routledge, 1996), pp. 65–77 (p. 76).

36 M. Ogborn, 'Historical geographies of globalisation, c. 1500–1800', in B. J. Graham and C. Nash (eds), *Modern Historical Geographies* (London: Longman, 2000), pp. 43–69 (p. 43).

37 An article demonstrating this approach: J. P. Ghobrial, 'The secret life of Elias of Babylon and the uses of global microhistory', *Past & Present*, 222:1 (2014), 51–93. See also the excellent special journal edition exploring the methodology of 'global microhistory': J. P. Ghobrail (ed.), *Global History and Microhistory, Past and Present*, Supplement 14 (2019).

38 M. Goebel, '"The capital of the men without a country": migrants and anticolonialism in interwar Paris', *American Historical Review*, 121:5 (2016), 1444–67.

39 *Ibid.*, p. 1465.

40 *Ibid.*, p. 1456.

41 *Ibid.*, p. 1452.

42 *Ibid.*, p. 1447.

43 *Ibid.*

44 D. Crompton (ed.), *Archigram: The Book* (London: Circa, 2018); M. Hebbert, 'The long after-life of Christopher Wren's short-lived London plan of 1666', *Planning Perspectives* (2018), 1–22.

45 See our discussion of 'representation(s)' in Chapter 1.

46 M. Carpo, *Architecture in the Age of Printing: Orality, Writing, Typography, and Printed Images in the History of Architectural Theory* (Cambridge, MA: MIT Press, 2001), esp. Chapter 4.

47 E. McKellar, 'Tales of two cities: architecture, print and early guide-books to Paris and London', *Humanities*, 2:3 (2013), 328–50.

48 J. Kelly, '"To Fan the Ardour of the Layman": *The Architectural Review*, the MARS Group and the cultivation of middle class audiences for modernism in Britain, 1933–1940', *Journal of Design History*, 29:4 (2016), 350–65.

49 S. McQuire, 'Rethinking media events: large screens, public space broadcasting and beyond', *New Media & Society*, 12:4 (2010), 567–82 (p. 571).

50 E. Napolitano, '"Exposed to everyone's eyes": the urban prospect and the publicity of representation in Israel Silvestre's *Profile of the City of Rome*, 1687', in A. Vanhaelen and J. P. Ward (eds), *Making Space Public in Early Modern Europe: Performance, Geography, Privacy* (London: Routledge, 2013), pp. 151–72.

51 *Ibid.*, p. 152.

52 *Ibid.*, pp. 151–7.

53 *Ibid.*, p. 152.

54 *Ibid.*, p. 152, 156.

55 *Ibid.*, p. 161.

56 *Ibid.*, p. 161–3.

57 *Ibid.*, p. 160–2.

58 *Ibid.*, p. 166.

59 R. Barthes, *Camera Lucida: Reflections on Photography*, trans. R. Howard (London: Cape, 1982).

60 E. Edwards, *Photographs and the Practice of History: A Short Primer* (London: Bloomsbury, 2022).

61 L. Nead, 'Animating the everyday: London on camera circa 1900', *Journal of British Studies*, 43:1 (2004), 65–90.

62 *Ibid.*, p. 69.

63 C. Bressey, 'The city of others: photographs from the City of London Asylum Archive', *Interdisciplinary Studies in the Long Nineteenth Century*, 19:13 (2011), 1–15 (p. 3).

64 *Ibid.*, p. 6.

65 E. Hanna, 'Photographs and "truth" during the Northern Ireland Troubles, 1969–72', *Journal of British Studies*, 54:2 (2015), 457–80 (p. 458).

66 S. Hirsch and D. Swanson, 'Photojournalism and the Moss Side Riots of 1981: narrowly selective transparency', *History Workshop Journal*, 89 (2020), 221–45 (p. 227).

67 *Ibid.*, pp. 222, 228–30.

68 *Ibid.*, p. 222.

69 Edwards, *Photographs and the Practice of History*, pp. 21–3, 44–6, 49–53.

70 Tiina Männistö-Funk, 'The gender of walking: female pedestrians in street photographs 1890–1989', *Urban History*, 48:2 (2019), 1–21.

71 E. Gaskell, *Mary Barton* (London, 1848), pp. 47–8.

72 É. Zola, *The Ladies Paradise*, trans. F. Belmont (London: Tinsley Bros., 1883), Chapter 4, n.p.

73 C. Brontë, *Villette* (London, 1853), Chapter 6, n.p.

RECOMMENDED READING

S. Berger, H. Feldner and K. Passmore, *Writing History: Theory and Practice*, 2nd edn (London: Bloomsbury, 2010).

E. Edwards, *Photographs and the Practice of History: A Short Primer* (London: Bloomsbury, 2022).

B. Graham and C. Nash (eds), *Modern Historical Geographies* (London: Longman, 2000).

S. Gunn and L. Faire (eds), *Research Methods for History*, 2nd edn (Edinburgh: Edinburgh University Press, 2016).

T. Loughran (ed.), *A Practical Guide to Studying History: Skills and Approaches* (London: Bloomsbury, 2017).

D. A. Ritchie, *Doing Oral History*, 3rd edn (Oxford: Oxford University Press, 2015).

M. Tamm and P. Burke (eds), *Debating New Approaches to History* (London: Bloomsbury, 2018).

❖ 4 ❖

LOCATING PRIMARY SOURCES

INTRODUCTION

This chapter, the first of two to consider the central role of primary sources in your research project, looks at the categories of sources most often used by historians of urban space and the built environment: buildings, archival evidence, visual representations and objects. Dividing the material in this way results in slightly artificial distinctions. A strong theme across this chapter, and the book as a whole, is the extent to which doing spatial history demands that you use a variety of source types and engage in interdisciplinary research practices. Your project may, for example, require you to combine oral histories, visual materials, like maps and plans, and surviving fragments of the built environment. Each category of evidence comes with its own strengths and limitations, questions and research practices – something we will focus on in Chapter 5. Read together, Chapters 4 and 5 demonstrate how evidence and its analysis can provide alternative ways into your project. Coming across an exciting series of documents, in whatever form, or applying a less well-thumbed method to your evidence can act as a catalyst for the development of your research. For these reasons, it is really important that you allow enough time to locate and analyse sources, alongside scoping existing secondary literatures on your topic and fine-tuning your research questions. The texture of the evidence you decide to work with will inform the questions you ask, and vice versa.

Some of the specifics of the advice offered are geared towards students undertaking research in Britain, reflecting the primary market for this book, as well as our own expertise. But, where possible, we have framed the text so that our general advice is applicable to other local, national and international contexts. More significantly, building on Chapter 3's emphasis on networks, our discussions are rooted in an approach to history that takes seriously the reciprocal and mutually defining relationships between sometimes geographically distant places, and the extent to which these need to be understood within the same analytical frame.[1] Other, more generic advice can be applied to a wide variety of historical periods and geographical locations. First, every collection or archive has its own history. Some aspects of the formation and development of these institutions reflects broader historical currents – for example, the perceived role of royal and national archives in the emergence of the modern state, or the contribution of collections-management practices to the development of modern academic disciplines.[2] But each will also come with its own idiosyncrasies, complexities, silences and biases. With this in mind, finding out as much as you can about the classification systems, collecting policies, histories, shifting agendas and current and historical 'blind spots' of any collection or archive you work with will pay dividends. Second, and thinking strategically, some starting points are the same, irrespective of your subject, chronology and geography. It is worth keeping in mind the kind of historical study that you wish to produce. Think back to the broad spatial-methodological routes outlined in Chapter 3; these will determine the kind of evidence you need to work with, as will the following useful questions.

- What type/level of evidence is most appropriate for the kind of history you want to do? Is your study going to be qualitative, quantitative or a combination of the two? For example, the level of detail/ texture of evidence needed for a seventeenth-century microhistory focused on a person or building is very different from a twentieth-century 'big data' project looking at how people circulated in urban environments.
- Does your project need to be comparative in order to draw out what is most meaningful about your source material?
- Are you planning to trace networks? Will this require you to visit or access materials from archives/collections that are at some distance from one another?
- Can you read the languages your sources are in? Can you read the handwriting? If not, will you have the time and other resources (e.g. funding) that will allow you to access relevant training?
- Do you need to use special software to keep track of your dataset? Will you be able to acquire this?
- What are the practical implications of each decision you make?

Once you establish the loose parameters of your study – the type of history you are doing, your broad theme – working through the following bullet points and questions will also help you to uncover the right sources for your project.

- **Literature review:** Have you combed the footnotes, endnotes and bibliographies of any useful secondary texts that you have read? Are there any tantalising references you could follow up? Are particular archives and collections mentioned frequently? Can you access these online or in person?
- **Talk to supervisors/lecturers/peers:** Have they come across materials that could be useful in your project? Do they have experience of working with institutions/source types that you plan to use? This is especially useful if you plan to work with private collections and papers, undertake research in other countries and/or use archives and collections for which there is no up-to-date catalogue or hand-list.
- **Identify specialist societies, collections and archives:** Are there local history centres, city museums, local/national archaeological surveys, local history societies or specialist groups in the place you have chosen to focus on? Have they produced print and/or online publications? Can you contact an archivist/curator/society member with focused questions about your project? Can you visit in person? (Note: Although it is very important to build good relationships with professionals in archives, collections and specialist societies, they cannot do your research for you!)

Ultimately, primary research of any kind requires patience and forbearance. Looking and not immediately finding what you want is part of the business of doing history. Archives will also throw up many questions and lines of enquiry which you were not anticipating. But following some of the strategies outlined in this chapter should help to ensure that your journey through archives and collections is rewarding.

THE BUILT ENVIRONMENT

The vast majority of historic buildings have not survived the vicissitudes of time. Across the centuries, urban built environments have been destroyed by fire, flood and natural disasters, such as earthquakes; most destructive of all, though, have been warfare and conflict, and purposeful demolition. In all cities, decayed and 'unfashionable' build-ings have been removed over time to make way for new developments and industries. As architectural historian Carl R. Lounsbury has written:

> Like their makers, buildings change over time. Their parts and mate-rials wear out, break, rot, rust, or decay. Structures are refurbished or reconfigured to meet new demands or the latest fashions and are often recycled to serve entirely new functions. Old sweatshops and schools are gutted to accommodate luxury condominiums; medieval churches are converted into art galleries. Most buildings have brief tenures before they are destroyed or fall into ruin [...] Only a very small number of them [buildings] survived for much longer periods to give an historical dimension to the landscape.[3]

Survival rates of buildings vary hugely. As we might anticipate, historic grand buildings and institutional structures, commissioned and inhab-ited by the wealthy and politically influential, are much more likely to survive than the housing of ordinary people (buildings which are often referred to as 'vernacular architecture', typically made by regional craft-speople from locally sourced materials).

If the building or structure which is the focus of your study is extant – even only partially – then the built environment will evidently be a key source material. Ease of access to the site will depend upon the type of building under scrutiny. In advance of your visit, you will need to ascer-tain ownership. Is the building privately owned, under state or local council ownership, or managed by a religious, heritage or charitable trust (for example English Heritage, or Churches Conservation Trust)? Once you have established who has jurisdiction over the site, you will need to contact the relevant owner or authority, outlining the nature of your project and, if appropriate, your university affiliation. At this stage it might help to get a letter of introduction from your academic supervisor or tutor – this would be useful for access to specialist archives and libraries too.

Your ability to personally view the exterior and/or explore the inte-rior of the building will depend upon its state of repair. You might be refused entry to a dilapidated building on health and safety grounds. If a research trip to a historic building has been arranged, make sure that you check in advance with the owner or relevant authority whether par-ticular footwear or safety clothing is needed. We will discuss in the next chapter some of the methods and techniques by which you might get the most out of your research trip to a built environment; but it is worth setting out some broad observations at the planning stage.

When viewing a historic building you should remain mindful that all structures change over time. Most of us who have visited a curated country house have had the peculiar sensation of arriving at medieval or early modern exterior walls, and yet entering into eighteenth-, nineteenth- or twentieth-century interiors. These changes might be subtle, or explicit. Transformations could take the form of new materials, adaptations to layout, the insertion of new windows, doors or storeys – or indeed their removal. Interior decoration will almost certainly have physically deteriorated over time or will have been changed very significantly from the intentions of the original owners or founders. This is where additional primary sources, beyond the surviving fabric, can be very helpful – including visual representations like maps and plans, photographs, and archival materials, like inventories.

If we take the spatial and material organisation of a built space to have significant implications as to its users' social, political, economic and even emotional lives, then such changes matter to us as historians. But observation of material and structural alterations does not make research of the historic built environment futile, far from it. In fact, observation and analysis of the accretive character of buildings is central to our study of historic structures. Cultural archaeologist Kate Giles has encouraged researchers to think of buildings as 'palimpsests' (writing surfaces which have been repeatedly effaced and overwritten). Like many medieval manuscripts, surviving historic buildings are composed of multiple physical and symbolic layers; it is our role as researchers to uncover the multilayered record of use and meanings.[4] To be clear, our objective as historians is not to try to recreate a 'pristine' state of original building but, rather, to explore and understand motivations for changes and adaptations. Why did later generations feel that it was necessary to knock down walls, or to cover over painted wood panelling with imported wallpaper? How do we interpret the installation of glass windows, or the storage and reorganisation of object collections in display cabinets? Changes to materials, designs and display are all signals of broader shifts in understanding about themes as diverse as gender roles in the family or the relationship between humans and the environment. In other words, when exploring the historic built environment, pay attention to continuities and to change. Building conservators or archaeologists may be able to help you ascertain if such adaptations were typical for buildings of that date, or unusual.

Additional online resources

There are a huge variety of online or digitised resources, both textual and visual, which might be useful in further contextualising the inhabitants, functions, designs and meanings of the building under scrutiny:

- The National Heritage List for England. A register of all nationally protected historic buildings and sites.
  https://historicengland.org.uk/listing/the-list/
- Victoria County History (VCH). Encyclopaedic histories of each English county – including themes such as landscape and the built environment.
  www.british-history.ac.uk/search?query=VCH
- Historic England Archive. A useful search tool for photographs, plans and drawings of buildings and historic sites, held in the Historic England Archive (Swindon).
  https://archive.historicengland.org.uk
- The Royal Institution of British Architects (RIBA) Collections – a vast collection of architectural books, periodicals, drawings, objects, and photographs.
  www.architecture.com/about/riba-library-and-collections

ARCHIVES

Archives are intrinsically spatial. Each object in an archive, irrespective of what it is, is defined by its context and relationships – to other objects within the archive, and to the people and institutions that created and used it. The work of professional archivists is informed by the recognition that such contexts and relationships are meaningful. This underpins research into the provenance – that is, information about the creation and prior ownership – of collections, as well as emphasis in archival best practice on keeping archives in their original order.[5] In many cases, however, some or all information about ownership and original order has gone astray. While it is not always possible, one stage of your research may involve tracking down provenance or reassembling archives by identifying component parts within single or across multiple collecting institutions.

Let us return to the example of a research project centred on a particular building or building type. It will be essential to establish further context relating to its design, construction, ownership, contents and uses. You could begin by visiting the local archive in the geographical area where the building is (or was) situated. Borough and county archives may contain useful materials such as title deeds and estate papers which will flesh out your understanding of the historic ownership of the building. Local record offices may also hold historic electoral registers (kept annually from 1832) which could enable you to trace a building's occupants over time. We should be mindful, though, that these records will not give us a holistic social picture – for example, women did not appear on the registers until 1918. If you are very fortunate, an inventory may survive relating to a building under consideration. Probate inventories are documents listing the possessions of a person at the time of their death. In the UK the vast majority of surviving inventories date from after 1529 (when the requirement to compose them was laid down in law). Survival rates for these documents vary quite widely across different regions of the country.[6] In recording the goods and chattels of an individual, and their values, these records can often tell us a great deal about the material and spatial environment – they are typically structured according to the rooms of a house or institution. As we read inventories, we are thus taken room by room through a house, gaining insights into the spatial organisation of the building and the particular material contents of each room.

Depending upon the type of building and its functions and ownership, your research might also take you to national archival collections, such as The National Archives (TNA) at Kew or the British Library. At these institutions you might find visual sources relating to your building, such as maps, plans, architectural designs or photographs. For instance, TNA holds a very large collection of architectural drawings, particularly focused on the eighteenth to twentieth centuries, and largely relating to major civil engineering projects, municipal buildings and public works.

Having a working knowledge of how and why archives were put together, their many functions and longer histories will also help you to uncover useful sources for your project. This is time-consuming work, which will require you to think contextually and track down multiple lines of enquiry. The example of a researcher looking for historic maps at TNA demonstrates the value of reflecting on which government department or court might have created or collected maps, in what way and for what purpose. Maps are spread across TNA's collections, showing local, regional, national and international geographical areas. But they are very rarely searchable by place name or geography. Instead, some, like a town map of Thamesmead produced in 1968, are part of the records of the government department or court that created or acquired them – in this case the Department of the Environment – and can be better understood in the context of supporting texts and broader information we may have about a given office or office-holder.[7] Others were extracted from a series of documents and stored with other similar materials, primarily as a preservation measure. For example, researchers looking for a 'Plan of a Town and Township of Ten Miles Square' near Quebec (dated 1789) will find a 'dummy' page within the archival series, in this case the Colonial Office papers, preserving the original location of the map, which has been extracted and stored elsewhere.[8]

Both of these examples reiterate how vital it is to understand why an archival 'document' was made – whether map, inventory, traffic code or improvement act – *and* (as far as this is discernible) its history once it became part of an archive or collection. This is especially important for spatial histories and studies of the built environment, where you may find yourself negotiating extensive series of documents that relate to the social, cultural, political, economic and religious dimensions of urban life. This information exists because individuals and groups were made responsible for monitoring, surveying, managing and capturing some aspects of urban life, from crime and traffic regulation, to building codes, sanitation and public health, which may be relevant to your project. The conventions of this record keeping, and the number and type of personnel who were involved, were determined by specific contexts of where and when your study is situated. Knowing as much as you can about the practical details of a given archive and the people and processes involved in generating the materials therein can help you to get the most out of this strand of work. By its very nature, and as discussed in greater detail in Chapter 5, archival material is *always* selective.

Moreover, in past decades, time and money have been invested in large-scale digitisation and cataloguing projects. Many national, municipal and local archives have websites containing useful information. TNA includes invaluable information about many of its collections, with special guides to searching for historic maps, architectural drawings and land tax and ownership. Even archives without substantial online presences have, most likely, produced printed catalogues, calendars, guides and hand-lists. But printed publications, websites and online documents are by no means comprehensive and should not become a substitute for visiting the archive.[9] It is only on site that you will be able to consult older manuscript catalogues or card catalogues or, more importantly, speak to knowledgeable staff.

There is a broader point here: as historians, we must begin by thinking laterally or, more precisely, contextually, because at the start of a project we rarely know what we are going to find or, indeed, what we are looking for in the first place. Having the following points at the back of your mind may prove useful.

- What broader circumstances mattered to the design and making, ownership, governance, regulation, surveillance, survey, mapping of a building, site or place at a given time? (Delete as applicable.)
- Who was involved in looking after places or spatial practices in the past in the city/town you have chosen to focus on? What kinds of records did these individuals/institutions keep? Where else were their actions documented?
- Where might something relevant to your project still exist in material form?
- Where might buildings, sites, places or spatial practices be documented incidentally? Take, for example, the records kept by the Old Bailey, London's principal criminal court, which are fully digitised for the period 1674 to 1913 and full of brilliant evidence of spatial management, even where this is not the explicit focus of testimony.[10]

Thinking in terms of geographical scales may also be productive. Materials in many local, municipal and national archives were generated by a range of administrative, organisational, legislative and judicial activities. These tend to be geographically and administratively defined, although such jurisdictions changed over time, underlining the importance of establishing the histories, collecting policies and purposes of any archives that you work with.

- **Buildings:** As we have seen, documentation generated by very specific sites, such as individual buildings, included deeds, leases, inventories (including probate) and records tied to associated people (from census to trial records). In most cases, this material will be spread across a range of archives, including local, municipal and, in some cases, national institutions.
- **Professional, corporate and business archives** contain the papers of 'spatial specialists', such as architects and urban developers. Specialist and professional institutions, like the RIBA and the Victoria and Albert Museum's (V&A) Archive of Art and Design, have extensive

holdings of records of architectural studios, design firms and individual practitioners.

- **Local and regional archives and history centres** preserve evidence of geographically delineated governance and administration, including records that relate to crime, public health, poverty, housing and urban improvement. Personal papers, such as correspondence, account books and, in some cases, journals and diaries, are a rich seam of evidence and may also be found in local, regional and state archives and libraries. **National and state archives**, like TNA and the National Archives Scotland, are the place of deposit of records of central government and the courts. These are your first port of call (but by no means your last) for evidence of activities managed by state departments and ministries and, in the case of medieval and early modern studies, projects that fell within the remit of the royal household. Let us take as an example a hypothetical study of Thamesmead, a new riverside town in south-east London, planned in 1965–66, partially built in the late 1960s and early 1970s and probably best known for its iconic appearance in the 1971 film adaptation of *A Clockwork Orange*.[11] While the London Metropolitan Archives (LMA) holds detailed records of the Greater London Council's planning, construction and subsequent review of the site, documents relating to the involvement of state departments are kept by TNA.

- **Archives**, however seemingly local, are nearly always home to materials generated in, representing or connected to other parts of the region, country and, indeed, world. This is why it is important to take a **networked approach** to archives. Reflecting London's global and colonial histories, the distribution lists of Bogle-L'Overture Publications, established by the Guyanese-born publishers and activists Jessica and Eric Huntley, reveal this London-based company's expansive networks in Africa, the Caribbean and the Americas.[12] This example, drawn from a supposedly local archive, emphasises how histories, experiences and identities were shaped by global links and contexts, and local and national archives were shaped by asymmetrical, reciprocal networks between places. Diplomatic correspondence and memoranda, records of war and conflict, missionary papers and business records, detailing colonial and imperial interests, all speak to the necessity of putting Britain and other Western European nations at the heart of often unequal and exploitative social, political and economic networks. This approach pays dividends when working with the records kept by specific colonial-era offices and institutions, like the East India Company, Foreign Office, Colonial Office and their predecessors, which encompassed expansive geographical terrains and were intended to circulate information about and between 'colony' and 'metropole'.[13] Take, for example, an early twentieth-century map of Cairo in TNA's collection. It was owned by the Foreign Office and originally sent in one of Lord Kitchener's dispatches from Egypt, presumably during his stint as British Agent and Consul General.[14] In lordly fashion, someone has used blue pencil to mark suitable sites for diplomatic residences. In this case, having a rough idea that government departments commissioned, created or used maps has led us to this interesting object. But, as with other types of evidence, even with an advanced digitised catalogue, these materials are often 'hidden' within larger documents.

Crime records

One of the key archival routes into researching the built environment and urban space is through crime records. The Old Bailey Online, established by historians Clive Emsley, Tim Hitchcock and Robert Shoemaker, is a searchable, digitised collection of all surviving editions of London's Old Bailey Proceedings from 1674 to 1913. Containing nearly 200,000 criminal trials, it has revolutionised how historians have been able to trace the rate, location, nature and punishment of a range of crimes and has shifted emphasis away from the notorious criminal cases to everyday forms of criminality. However, partly by implication of this wonderful resource, London has remained central to the history of criminal history because of the quality of the archival material, and has been used effectively to explore the intersections of gender and class in the modern city. For instance, influential work on London, along with other important metropoles such as Paris and New York, has focused on women's criminality particularly by using crime records and accompanying news reports to look at shoplifting as a method of exploring and understanding wider class-based attitudes and anxieties towards women's presence in commercialised spaces. An example is research by Tammy Whitlock and Elaine Abelson, which argues that middle-class shoplifters were treated far more leniently than poorer thieves and shows that the emergence of kleptomania as a category of women's mental weakness was used by affluent women to defend themselves when accused of shop theft and that they convincingly drew on language about their perceived vulnerability within urban space.[15] We can see that these class differences in accounts of shoplifting persisted into the twentieth century, as the reportage of the *Manchester Guardian* illustrates. In

1925, a laundress convicted of stealing a packet of envelopes, a purse, a pack of playing cards and a small tape measure worth eight shillings from Lewis's was sentenced to a month in prison. The newspaper reported that the Chairman of the court had 'said the case was a very bad one, and there was no excuse for (her) conduct, which appeared to have been deliberate'.[16] In contrast, in 1927 a 'well connected' woman received a £5 fine for stealing a dress, hat and umbrella worth £8. The *Manchester Guardian*'s coverage of the offence noted that her defence claimed that 'her act was inexplicable, except that her friends believed that her mental balance had been upset by her recent delicate state of health'.[17] These distinctive approaches to convicted women emphasise how crucial influencing factors like class – alongside gender and race – were in shaping the perception of offenders and their crimes, because they were seen as being related to their right – or lack thereof – to inhabit particular spaces. These examples are a helpful reminder of how crime records can help researchers to consider how spatial experience was shaped by social identity, was contested, and the manifest inequalities within the built environment.[18]

Outside of London, the Quarter Sessions were local courts held quarterly, usually before a justice of the peace, judge or recorder. They were dissolved in 1972. They dealt with a range of judicial matters including theft, violence and sexual offences, but cases were often less serious than those heard by the Assize courts. Archived records from the Quarter Sessions or Assizes vary significantly in size, depending on localised practices as well the sheer chance that such material could survive over world wars, changes in local government and the restructuring of criminal justice systems. The value of using local crime records is that they may provide alternative perspectives than metropolitan records, illuminate different spaces and cover various types of offences. Crime archives can also help to chart the processes and patterns of immigration and uncover the experiences of migrants in different spaces. In Britain, the Alien Registers required immigrants to report to the police from 1914 onwards, and immigrants received a certificate on payment of a registration fee. TNA has digitised 600 registration cards from 1918 to 1957 which give the personal details and employment history of a small sample of immigrants who registered in the London area. Many record offices and local police archives have kept their Alien Registers, and these not only help to understand more about who immigrated into Britain but also help us to understand who was defined as an 'alien' and why. For instance, the British Nationality and Status of Aliens Act 1914 decreed that any British woman who married an 'alien' lost her British citizenship, and reflected the impact of the First World War in narrowing definitions of Britishness. Crime records can also be used to understand police harassment toward ethnic minorities and the latter's treatment within the urban landscape. Historians of crime have also developed more innovative and creative methodologies, particularly because crime archives often provide an overly strong focus on offences by men, and privilege violent crimes or property offences, often against businesses. Eloise Moss's history of burglary turned to business insurance records to chart the rise in fear of domestic burglary and the relationship to privatised domestic space, so as to assess a wider shift towards a 'risk society' from the late nineteenth century.[19] Records relating to criminal activity can tell urban historians about much more than just criminal offences that occurred in the past, therefore. One area that is worth further exploration is to consider how these types of sources can illuminate the various ways in which certain spaces were invested with meanings of risk, danger and safety, as well as to retrieve the experience of those individuals who were more heavily scrutinised within the urban landscape.

VISUAL SOURCES

A multitude of representations of urban built environments from across all periods and geographies exist: from paintings, technical drawings, sketches and printed views, to maps of all shapes and sizes, photographs and digital renderings, not to mention the depiction of urban spaces on things, from textiles to handheld objects (see, for example, the bowl discussed in Chapter 2, Figure 2.1) to wallpaper. This material, in its many forms, can be enormously useful for historians undertaking spatial projects. When looking for visual sources, do reflect on whether materials were commissioned or created by specific individuals, offices or institutions or were collected after having been made. Most obviously, and as touched on above, visual sources can relate to specific buildings, sites and places within the built environment. Some of these objects – and it is always useful to think of representations as things – were produced as part of a design and construction process (e.g. designs, plans, elevations). Others depicted, mapped or surveyed extant built environments (e.g. prints, drawings, paintings, maps, photographs). Still more visual sources provide an incidental or tangential representation of a known place, or propose an imagined urban vista, as in the late nineteenth-century card, designed to be given away with packets of cigarettes, which imagined the city in the year 2000

Aero-Cab Station

Figure 4.1 Cigarette card, designed by Jean-Marc Côté c.1900, imagining France in the year 2000.

(Figure 4.1). Interestingly, this last example exists only as a prototype and was not put into production.

Seeking only to establish the veracity (or not) of a particular depiction can limit the horizons of your study. More constructive are histories that combine close object analysis with the exploration of social, cultural, political and economic dimensions of image-making. In each case, it is worth remembering, visual forms were shaped by the available technologies, and the social and cultural conventions and expectations around their use – something we will discuss in greater detail in Chapter 5. Irrespective of form and purpose, visual sources provide insight into how place and space were perceived, theorised, managed, regulated and resisted. From this perspective, John Britton's *Topographical Survey of the Borough of St Marylebone*, a large and impressive display map commemorating the borough's incorporation into London following the Reform Act 1832, offers a window into the spatial practices of the past. In this instance, it also suggests the concerns of what Lefebvre would term 'spatial specialists'. Geographer Stephen Daniels uses close attention to the map's 'context, production, marketing and meaning' to show how it marks a 'significant moment in political cartography', as well as embodying a complex articulation of Britton's personal and professional relationship to Marylebone, where he was a long-term resident, and his 'reformist' political aspirations for the area.[20]

One of the most valuable suites of primary sources for urban and spatial historians are historical maps, plans and architectural sketches, even for projects that remained unfinished or were never undertaken. Most public libraries provide access to historical maps of cities and towns that are useful for charting the growth and changes in the city, and which can be used to chart wider social and cultural changes. There are also some useful online collections, such as the University of Manchester's Old Maps of Manchester web resource; comparison of its holdings from the late eighteenth to mid-nineteenth centuries gives some sense of the city's relatively sudden and dramatic growth. Plans are often also widely available, and many have been digitised or are available as bound publications. These plans differ from maps because many of the ideas were never put into action, and they reflect a moment of imagination and ambition on the part of planners, architects and local governments. For instance, see the City of Manchester Plan 1945, digitised by the University of Manchester following support from the Manchester Statistical Society's Campion Fund. As we shall see in Chapter 5, however, these plans are very useful in thinking about local government, civic pride and the relationship between planning and broader social and political change. Although many of the plans were not implemented, they may still have influenced urban experience and the way in which inhabitants thought about their city, or shaped other programmes of urban redevelopment, which warrants historical interrogation.

The full variety of visual material relevant to spatial histories is rarely found in a single archive, collection or specialist research organisation. Instead, you may find yourself working across a range of institutions. Each institution will have its own collecting policies (current and historic), history and strengths in particular areas. It is only by doing your research that you will build up a sense of what these are and how they may impact on your work. Let us think through another hypothetical study: the links between a series of urban parks in nineteenth-century England and North America. The development of publicly accessible green spaces was one of the ways in which big cities sought to address some of the challenges posed by accelerated urbanisation, particularly rapid expansions in population size and density.[21] In England, these concerns prompted the establishment of the Select Committee on Public Walks (1833), which had a remit to 'consider the best means of securing open spaces in the immediate vicinity of populous towns, as public walks calculated to promote the health and comfort of the inhabitants'.[22] This national call to action was taken up locally, resulting in the planning and development of a series of urban parks that included Victoria Park in East London (opened 1845) and Birkenhead Park in Merseyside (opened 1847), the latter being the world's first publicly funded park.[23] These projects were rooted in earlier initiatives. Birkenhead Park's appearance owed a great debt to Regent's Park, developed in London in the 1810s and 1820s.[24] But even more so, Birkenhead's committee drew on Regent's Park's novel funding model. This relied on the speculative development of private residences and, in particular, the 'proximate principal' that enabled higher prices to be charged for properties close to large green spaces.[25] Locally situated debates about how best to nurture urban green spaces also had global reach. Birkenhead Park was a significant influence on New York's Central Park, which adopted Joseph Paxton's design for a circulation system that separated pedestrians and carriage traffic.[26] Central Park is also a useful reminder that concern for the health and well-being of city dwellers was not without prejudice. Its development in the 1850s resulted in the displacement of Black New Yorkers, including those who lived in Seneca Village, one of the first and largest of the free Black Communities in pre-emancipation New York. This thriving neighbourhood was completely destroyed to make way for the park.[27]

Visual sources relating to the development, maintenance and marketing of the parks are spread across the main types of archive, professional and specialist societies and collecting institutions that may prove useful for your study. These include:

- **National archives**, such as TNA, mostly preserve records generated by government and state departments and central courts. Visual materials, such as maps, plans, architectural designs and drawings, and photographs relating to historic urban environments, can be found within the archival series, including materials produced as part of the process of designing and constructing buildings and urban built environments. Relevant to our parks example is a series of early nineteenth-century proposals for what would become Regent's Park, including some by the project's architect, John Nash. These are part of the Crown Estate's papers, reflecting the history of the area as royal parkland.[28] More whimsical, perhaps, is Decimus Burton's 1826 plan, drawn in ink on handmade paper, for a garden promenade for the

Zoological Society – now better known as London Zoo – which is also in TNA.[29]

- Similarly, **local and regional archives** contain visual evidence, including maps, plans, designs and photographs, and tend to be more geographically specific in their holdings. As with national archives, these are typically found within series of documents and, likewise, their presence may not be apparent in printed or online catalogues. To reprise our hypothetical parks study, the LMA is home to textual and visual evidence of Victoria Park's development, including a wide range of plans, designs and sketches for the site.[30] Or we could look at the visual materials in the care of Wirral Archives Services that relate to Birkenhead Park, including a plan and section of a bridge for the lower lake signed by the project's lead designer, Joseph Paxton.[31] In both cases, the archives hold the papers of the local and municipal authorities with oversight of the projects.

- **National and local museums and galleries** look after a wide spectrum of prints, designs, drawings and marketing materials that show specific locations, buildings and built environments and, in some cases, plans for unrealised projects. Institutions with holdings in art and design may include visual and material cultures that are relevant to your study. For our parks study, for example, we might consider the silver commemorative mug, now in the collection of the V&A, shown in Figure 4.2. It is decorated with a picture of the Crystal Palace – the building for which Paxton, designer of Birkenhead Park, is best known, which housed the Great Exhibition in Hyde Park in 1851.[32] Smith & Nicholson, the company who made the mug, also showed presentation silver at the Great Exhibition.[33]

- **Professional and specialist societies** (such as the RIBA) also have significant holdings in drawings, prints, specialist periodicals and publications and architectural models. For example, the RIBA holds drawings from a later stage in Regent's Park's history in the form of plans and photographs of the London Central Mosque, which opened next to the park's Hanover Gate in 1977.[34] These include competition designs for unexecuted versions of the building.[35]

- **University and national deposit libraries** (such as the British Library and National Library of Scotland) contain a wide range of relevant materials for your study, including maps, prints, drawings, photographs, books and pamphlets. The beautifully coloured map in Figure 4.3a is in the collection of the New York Public Library and is accessible to remote researchers as part of the institution's

Figure 4.2 Smith & Nicolson, commemorative mug, London hallmarks for 1851–52.

extensive digitised resources. It was printed in lithograph for the city's Department of Public Parks in about 1873, the year the park was virtually completed.[36] The inscription at the bottom reveals that the map includes unusually detailed information about the position of the '642 species and varieties of hardy trees and shrubs ... 361 perennial and alpine plants ... and 551 [plants] in the nursery and exotic collection' located throughout the park. It can usefully be compared with an earlier printed map from 1859 (Figure 4.3b), also in the New York Public Library's collection, which shows the roads and pathways that were still under construction. In addition, **specialist libraries of art and design** (such as the National Art Library at the V&A) have extensive holdings in publications relating to art, architecture, design and the decorative arts. In all cases, it is worth learning what is in a library's special collections, which can be especially strong in early printed materials, manuscripts (including the letters and papers of well-known practitioners), maps, designs and drawings, artists' books and historical periodicals.

- A range of visual materials, including maps, historical prints and drawings, and photographs, underpin the work of **local, regional and national surveys of archaeological sites and historic built environments** (e.g. Survey of London, Historic England, Historic Environment Scotland). Relevant materials are held in the archives and library collections of these specialist public bodies; reports about specific buildings and locations, produced by in-house and freelance researchers, are comprehensively illustrated. The 2007 conservation area appraisal and management plan for Birkenhead Park, commissioned by Wirral Council, provides guidance for the area's future protection and development. It also includes historical and contemporary maps, drawings and prints, along with detailed analysis of the built fabric, which could prove useful for historians.[37]

- National, regional and local surveys, libraries and archives are also home to **large collections of historical photographs of buildings and urban environments**. To give you a sense of the scale: the RIBA's collections include 1.5 million photographs from the earliest days of photography, while Historic England's archive includes over 9 million photographs documenting the historic built environment. These resources evidence what places looked like in the past; more importantly, they also tell us about the ways in which photography has fundamentally transformed how historic urban environments were perceived, preserved and understood.[38]

As for all primary sources, you will need to be mindful of the implications of survival rates, especially for medieval and early modern material. Objects in museums, archives and library special collections are rarely representative of the sorts of things that most people owned in the past. Undeniably magnificent, large-format, expensively produced maps and panoramas, such as the view of late seventeenth-century Rome by Israel Silvestre that we considered in Chapter 3 (Figure 3.1), were regarded as exceptional at the time when they were made, and were looked after accordingly. Less costly representations of early modern Rome, like a woodcut of the obelisk in Piazza Navona from the title page of a 1651 pamphlet, can be even rarer. In this instance, this fragile pamphlet survives because it was slipped between the pages of a seventeenth-century cardinal's diary, now preserved in the Archivo di Stato, Rome.[39] Accidents of survival are not just a concern for early modern historians. Categories of visual sources from the nineteenth and twentieth centuries can be just as fugitive. Take, for instance, the V&A's Jobbing Printing Collection,

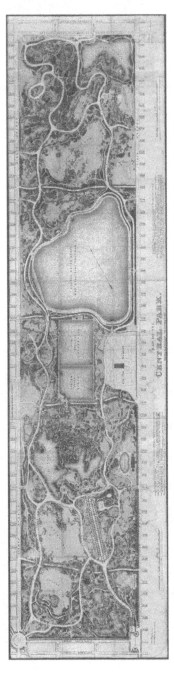

Figure 4.3a Otto Sibeth (cartographer), John Bogart (engineer), Calvert Vaux (architect), map of the Central Park, New York, c. 1873.

Figure 4.3b Calvert Vaux (architect), Frederick Law Olmstead (architect), W. H. Grand (engineer), map of the Central Park, New York with details of roads and pathways under construction, January 1859.

named after the trade term for smaller-scale printing jobs than books or newspapers. Begun in 1936 as an 'open reference collection of commercial typography', it was intended to provide students with examples of good contemporary practice. With samples requested from high-profile companies, designers and artists across Europe and America, its c. 6,000 objects are rare examples of the sorts of printed things that are abundant in our own lives, including leaflets, catalogues, labels and magazine covers, alongside printing samples, advertisement proofs and lettering artwork.[40]

OBJECTS

Objects may be a useful primary source material for your research project on urban space. We saw in previous chapters how material cultures, and human interactions with objects, can be central to how we build up a meaningful understanding of social, cultural and political spaces (and many other types of space besides). Your interest in material cultures might take a variety of forms. A researcher could be looking for specific moveable objects known to have been within a particular building (for example, paintings catalogued in a historic collection). Alternatively, your search for material cultures might be related to broad 'types' of objects associated with specialised spaces (for instance, early drug jars, or pharmacy jars, if researching early modern grocers' shops, apothecaries' shops or hospitals). A project on urban spaces might also profitably consider building fixtures, such as surviving doors, window frames, flooring, or shop signs and building façades, which have often been removed from their original built environment to new display or storage contexts.

Material cultures suitable for analysis might be found in museums, galleries and curated houses and palaces. Innumerable historic objects also, of course, exist in private collections.[41] Where you look for your material source base will depend on the nature of your project. For example, a historian interested in spaces of experiment might consult museums focused on the histories of science and technology. By contrast, a researcher exploring elite domestic spaces might examine collections focused on decorative arts and design. The advantages of modern technology mean that it is relatively easy to quickly scope material collections; though, as we will see, there is no substitute for personally visiting objects in museum stores.

When using historic material culture as a primary source, and in searching through collections, you should bear in mind that you are only ever seeing a small snapshot of any given culture and era. The vast majority of material cultures (from all eras of human history) have not survived. As with built environments, the material cultures of social elites (made from more exclusive materials and by esteemed makers) are more likely to have endured than everyday things owned by ordinary people. The reasons why certain things have survived and others have perished or been recycled might be down to chance, the specific collections policies of museums and the materiality of particular objects (wooden things rot much more easily than other materials, for example). As historian Karen Harvey has written:

> An object may have been collected by a museum because it was thought to exemplify the very best in design, an object may have survived because the ceramic material did not deteriorate in the conditions in which it was later found by an archaeologist, and a building may have survived because of local geo-political factors leading to its preservation.[42]

Ultimately, there are a wide range of factors as to why certain things have survived and others have not. Once you have begun to select your object(s) for analysis it might be worth reflecting upon these contexts.

Broadly speaking, your search for material evidence might begin with museum or gallery catalogues. Catalogues itemise the objects within a particular collection. They usually provide basic information relating to the object: its dimensions, materials, design, significant symbolism and markings. If the maker(s) are known, they will also be noted. Any conservation work undertaken since the object entered the museum should also be recorded here. Catalogue entries will often provide details relating to the object's provenance, that is, where the object originated from, its donor and how it came to be part of the collection. This is linked to the object's accession number – a detailed discussion of which can be found in Leonie Hannan and Sarah Longair's research guide *History through Material Culture*. Examination of the origins and provenance of objects has become especially urgent and politically charged in the wake of the recent movement to decolonise museums (and cultural institutions more broadly). Undoubtedly still a work in progress, the movement to decolonise has encouraged what scholar and journalist Sarah Jilani describes as an upfront engagement with 'the colonial histories of Western museums, the narratives surrounding people of colour that such histories perpetuate' and, crucially, a deep interrogation of the circumstances in which material cultures were acquired, ideally 'repatriating objects where feasible, especially if they were plundered from peoples for whom they sustain cultural value'.[43]

Customarily, museum and gallery catalogues were written on cards, and later printed, but, increasingly, heritage institutions, on a local, national and international level, are also making their collections accessible through online databases. In making use of digital catalogues a researcher should, however, remain mindful that such resources are rarely comprehensive; these databases very rarely include all the objects within a particular museum, gallery or heritage site. Ideally, you would visit the specialist collection to consult the written card catalogue or internal institutional online database. This will give you a more holistic understanding of the entire collection.

Online catalogues operate at various levels of sophistication, but most will allow you to search for a particular type of object, material or maker. You can usually apply filters to allow you to search across a specific date range. Think carefully about your search terms, too (for example, historically there might have been multiple ways of spelling a particular name or object). Digital and/or analogue photographs may also accompany a catalogue entry or be found within collections records. It is worth dwelling momentarily on the complexity of museum photographs. Recent fine work has interrogated their 'double collections history': as objects collected in their own right (often within the narrow category of 'art photography') and as infrastructure that is essential for all other kinds of museum work, from documentation and information to interpretation, marketing and design.[44] Awareness of this 'duality' pays dividends. In particular, 'non-collections photographs', to use Elizabeth Edwards' category, have been 'fundamental' to the operation of museums since the nineteenth century and, therefore, 'are key markers of other strands of collections history. They inscribe the way other classes of object are thought about.'[45] With this in mind, museum photographs can help careful researchers to establish museum values in the present and, critically for our purposes, in the past.

Once you have found an object which looks promising for your research purposes in one collection, it is always worth searching across other museum and gallery online databases to find comparable types of object. This can allow you to build up a larger body of material evidence and often make a more convincing argument. The next step, if at all possible, is to arrange to view or handle objects in person. In most institutions, viewing is more likely than actual hands-on inspection. Individual galleries and museums will have their own policies on access, but many will allow you to arrange an appointment (often weeks or months in advance) to view an object in the museum stores, in the presence of an institutional professional, such as archivist, store manager or curator. When contacting the museum or heritage site you will typically need to provide background information as to the nature of your project and your reason for viewing the collections (for example, research for an MA dissertation, or investigation of one's family history, as appropriate). You will also, of course, need to provide the basic information about the object/s you wish to view; the museum/ accession number will be crucial. This is an invaluable opportunity to gain a deeper understanding of the object's making, meanings and wider contexts. We will consider material methodologies in greater detail in Chapter 5.

Material cultures

There are a number of recent research guides on material cultures which offer detailed advice on locating suitable objects, and the application of suitable methodologies:

- Leonie Hannan and Sarah Longair, *History through Material Culture* (Manchester, 2017).
- Anne Gerritsen and Giorgio Riello, *Writing Material Culture History* (London, 2014).
- Karen Harvey (ed.), *History and Material Culture: A Student's Guide to Approaching Alternative Sources*, 2nd edn (London, 2017).

ORAL HISTORY

If you want to undertake your own oral history interviews, then be prepared to invest a significant amount of time and planning in organising, carrying out and transcribing them. The first step is to consult and complete the ethics procedures as required by your institution, as there are strict rules in place to deal with any research that involves living participants. You will be expected to address issues around the collection and storage of data, privacy issues and the practical and safety requirements of yourself and participants when doing the interviews.[46]

Your institutions will probably provide training on oral history interviews, and usually issue a set of protocols for this type of research methodology. The Oral History Society also offers training that addresses the practical, technical and conceptual issues around oral history interviewing, and its website provides a wealth of information for anyone interested in this method of research.

When planning oral history interviews, think carefully about what you would like them to do and what their function will be within the overall research project. One of the key considerations is about recruiting participants, and it is important to think practically about whom you want to interview, how many and where you will conduct the research. Building prior relationships with participants – perhaps via local history societies, social media, broadcast media or relevant heritage organisations – can be crucial in gaining the trust and confidence of potential interviewees. Perhaps one of the surprising issues for historians is the unwillingness or modesty of those whose stories we are interested in, and it is worth factoring in extra time to make links with the communities that you would like to engage with. Also, can you think of ways that the communities or individuals you would like to work with might benefit from your engagement? Considering potential links with and contributions to local history projects or public heritage events is an important way to make sure that your research enhances the world of those who take part in your project.

In advance, prepare the questions you would like to ask your participants, making sure they are open ended and flexible enough to respond to issues or themes that the interviewee raises. Be prepared for interviews to take you in new and interesting directions, while not losing sight of your key research questions. Consider the location of the interview and how this might shape the participant's willingness to speak, particularly regarding sensitive or difficult topics. What technology will you use to record the interviews, and how does the participant feel about your approach? Finally, how does your identity as an interviewer shape or influence what the participant will say, with some eager to please, others shy or defensive, intimidated by talking to an academic researcher? Are there language or cultural barriers that need to be addressed? Undertaking oral history interviews is valuable but very time consuming. It can be challenging to recruit the appropriate (and willing) interviewees, and it is important that researchers are prepared to invest appropriate time and energy into their careful delivery.

With the above in mind, many researchers may find it more practical to make use of the many oral history collections that have already been established, some of which need to be visited in person, while others are available online. Some relevant collections include the following.

- **The British Library** has a vast and important collection. Some interviews are accessible online, while others must be accessed via the library's Reading Room. Collections include oral histories of architecture and landscape design; Sounds, including accents and dialects; Family Life and Work Experience before 1918; and The Millennium Memory Bank. A helpful guide titled 'Finding very particular material in oral history collections: a research toolkit and user journey', is available on the library's website.
- **Local studies collections:** Most local archives have oral history collections that relate specifically to people's experiences in that particular town or city. Many of these collections were created in the 1980s and 1990s and often include interviews with inhabitants who recall the early twentieth century. For example, Tameside Local Studies and Archives includes a taped interview and transcript with an anonymous male interviewee born in Surat, India in 1936, who moved to Manchester in 1972, and discusses the employment challenges he faced; another, with a female interviewee born in 1915, narrates her experiences of family and home life in the Wythenshawe Estate. A comprehensive guide to these kinds of oral histories was collected by the British Library in its 2015 report 'Directory of UK Sound Collections', which can be downloaded from its website.
- **Race, ethnicity and migration:** Oral history has been crucial to the recording and collection of the historical experiences of migrants to Britain; particularly valuable collections include the Roots Family History Project and The Distance We Have Travelled, held by the Ahmed Iqbal Ullah Race Relations Resource Centre in Manchester; the East Midlands Oral History Archive has a collection of British Empire and Commonwealth Related Material; and the Black Cultural Archives in London has a collection of interviews, including with members of the British Black Panther Movement. The Irish in Britain organisation has a collection of forty interviews from its Heritage Lottery-funded project, Irish Voices, which have been made easily accessible on its website; and Birmingham City

Council has also made The Irish Experience oral history project available online.

- **History of everyday life:** As we have already seen, oral histories have been fundamental to retrieving women's experiences and narratives of the past. The British Library's Sisterhood and After online repository contains a range of interviews that may be relevant to urban historians, including regional perspectives and experiences of feminism, and forms of protest and activism. Some funded academic research projects deposit oral history interviews for wider use, such as Housing, Everyday Life and Wellbeing over the long term in Glasgow, 1950–75, which has published extracts of oral history life narrative interviews on the University of Glasgow web pages. The Economic and Social Research Council-funded UK Data Service is also a valuable repository for a range of quantitative and qualitative data collected for use by researchers, including the Coventry and Liverpool Lives Oral History Collection, c. 1945–1970.
- **International collections:** Since so many oral history interviews have become available online, there are new opportunities for historians of the city to take comparative or transnational approaches. This opens up exciting ways to think about urban experience and utilise oral histories in relation to other primary sources.

Open-access oral history collections
A short selection of free, accessible collections of oral histories includes:

- Glucksman Ireland House Oral History Collection in the Archives of Irish America: https://as.nyu.edu/irelandhouse/academic-initiatives/oral-history-of-irish-america-project/oral-history-podcasts.html
- Senator John Heinz History Center Italian American Oral History: www.heinzhistorycenter.org/collections/italian-american-program/oral-history
- The National Archives of Singapore, Oral History Interviews: www.nas.gov.sg/archivesonline/oral_history_interviews/
- University of California Berkeley Library, Oral History Center: www.lib.berkeley.edu/libraries/bancroft-library/oral-history-center/collection-guides
- University of Minnesota Immigration History Research Center, Immigrant Stories: https://immigrantstories.umn.edu/

IN SUMMARY

This chapter has outlined some of the key bodies of primary evidence which might be used for your research project, and has also suggested first steps in locating primary sources. We have seen how many spatial projects will use multiple bodies of evidence. Different sources can enrich your approach to a building, place, concept or theme. In all cases, it is wise to start looking for evidence, archives and repositories early in the research process. It is also best to be broad minded in your search for sources initially; you can focus in on particular bodies of evidence and networks as you become more familiar with the material. You should be open to the new ideas, concepts and connections that will be raised by your interaction with archival and material evidence. Your research project will also be enriched by communication with experts in the field, such as university tutors, librarians, oral historians, archivists and curators. In the next chapter we will extend our discussion of primary evidence by considering different ways of analysing sources.

NOTES

1 For a thought-provoking intervention, see: T. Sasson *et al.*, 'Britain and the world: a new field?', *Journal of British Studies*, 57:4 (2018), 677–708.

2 For a rich discussion of archives, see: M. Ogborn, 'Archive', in J. Agnew and D. N. Livingstone (eds), *The Sage Handbook of Geographical Knowledge* (London: Sage, 2011), pp. 88–98; for accounts of the role of collections and collections management in the development of modern knowledge disciplines, see: S. Alberti, *Nature and Culture: Objects, Disciplines and the Manchester Museum* (Manchester: Manchester University Press, 2009); S. J. Knell, 'Museums, reality and the material world', in Knell (ed.), *Museums in the Material World* (London: Routledge, 2007), pp. 1–28; C. Whitehead, *Museums and the Construction of Disciplines: Art and Archaeology in Nineteenth-Century Britain* (London: Duckworth, 2009).

3 C. R. Lounsbury, 'Architecture and cultural history', in D. Hicks and M. C. Beaudry (eds), *The Oxford Handbook of Material Culture Studies* (Oxford: Oxford University Press, 2010), pp. 484–501 (p. 485).

4   K. Giles, 'Seeing and believing: visuality and space in pre-modern England', *World Archaeology*, 39 (2007) 105–21 (p. 110): 'the idea of the palimpsest, both as a metaphor for the multiple layers of paint, plaster and meaning, which we encounter, and as an analogy for the interpretive process itself'.

5   For a useful introduction to archival practices, see: *Archival Principles and Practices: An Introduction to Archives for Non-Archivists* (London: The National Archives, 2016).

6   K. Grannum and N. Taylor, *Wills and Probate Records: A Guide for Family Historians*, 2nd edn (Kew: The National Archives, 2009), Chapter 6.

7   The National Archives, Kew [hereafter TNA], AT 41/84 [Thamesmead town map, post-enquiry correspondence, 1968].

8   TNA, CO 42/67 (f. 433).

9   See for example: A. Prescott, 'The imaging of historical documents', in M. Greengrass and L. M. Hughes (eds), *The Virtual Representation of the Past* (Aldershot: Ashgate, 2008) pp. 7–22.

10 See, for example: E. Tierney, '"Dirty rotten sheds": exploring the ephemeral city in early modern London', *Eighteenth-Century Studies*, 50:2 (2017), 231–52.

11 The 'making, unmaking and remaking' of Thamesmead is detailed in the following: V. G. Wigfall, *Thamesmead: Back to the Future. A Social History* (London: Greenwich Community College Press, 1997); A. Markowitz, 'The making, unmaking and remaking of Thamesmead. A story of urban decline and renewal in postwar London', *DPU Working Paper No. 193* (London: Bartlett Development Planning Unit, UCL, 2017); P. Ford and K. Baikie, 'Thamesmead: kickstarting the transformation of a stalled New Town', *Geography*, 103 (July 2018), 102–4.

12 London Metropolitan Archive [hereafter LMA], MSS 4462; 4463. See also the excellent 'global-local' analysis of Catherine Impy's scrapbook and visitor book in: C. Bressey, *Empire, Race and the Politics of Anti-Caste* (London: Bloomsbury, 2013), pp. 1–15.

13 See for example recent publications that have emerged from the 'Snapshots of Empire: Governing a Diverse Empire Everywhere and All at Once' project: K. Boehme, A. Lester and P. Mitchell, 'The centre of the muniment': archival order and reverential historiography in the India Office, 1875', *Journal of Historical Geography*, 63 (2019), 12–22; 'Reforming everywhere and all at once: transitioning to free labor across the British empire, 1837–1838', *Comparative Studies in Society and History*, 60:3 (2018), 688–718.

14 TNA, MFQ 1/1379/59 ['Nouveau Plan du Caire dressé par R. Huber Major du génie e.r. ...'].

15   T. C. Whitlock, *Crime, Gender and Consumer Culture in Nineteenth-Century England* (Aldershot: Ashgate, 2005); E. S. Abelson, *When Ladies Go A-Thieving: Middle Class Shoplifters in the Victorian Department Store* (New York: Oxford University Press, 1989).

16   'Woman shoplifter sent to prison', *Manchester Guardian*, 17 March 1925, p. 20.

17   'Women shoplifters fined', *Manchester Guardian*, 3 November 1927, p. 13.

18   C. Wildman, 'An "epidemic of shoplifting"? Working-class women, shop theft and Manchester's new retail culture, 1918–1939', *Social History*, 46:3 (2021), 278–99.

19   E. Moss, *Night Raiders: Burglary and the Making of Modern Urban Life in London, 1860–1968* (Oxford: Oxford University Press, 2019), pp. 110–31.

20   S. Daniels, 'Mapping the metropolis in an age of reform: John Britton's London Topography, 1820–1840', *Journal of Historical Geography*, 56 (2017), 61–82 (p. 63).

21   I. Wray, *Great British Plans: Who Made Them and How They Worked* (London: Routledge, 2015), pp. 64–6; Alan Tate, *Great City Parks*, 2nd edn (London: Routledge, 2015 [2001]), pp. 19–21, 394.

22   House of Common Debates (21 February 1833), vol. 15, cc1049–59; Report from the Select Committee on Public Walks, Session 1833, HC 449.

23   Wray, *Great British Plans*, p. 66; Tate, *Great City Parks*, p. 189.

24   Tate, *Great City Parks*, p. 189; Wray, *Great British Plans*, p. 68.

25   J. L. Crompton, 'The genesis of the proximate principle in the development of urban parks in England', *Annals of Leisure Research*, 9:3–4 (2006), 214–44.

26   Wray, *Great British Plans*, pp. 61–3.

27   D. di Zerega Wall, N. A. Rothschild and C. Copeland, 'Seneca Village and Little Africa: two African American communities in antebellum New York City', *Historical Archaeology*, 42:1 (2008), 97–107 (p. 98).

28   TNA, CRES 2/1736. See also: Tate, *Great City Parks* (2015), 229–31.

29   TNA, WORK 32/65.

30   LMA, MBW/OW/VP/8.

31   Wirral Archives Service, B/821/1.

32   See for example: H. Schoenefeldt, 'The Crystal Palace, environmentally considered', *Arq*, 12:3–4 (2008), 283–94.

33   *Official Catalogue of the Great Exhibition of the Works of Industry of All Nations* (Cambridge: Cambridge University Press, 2011 [1851]), p. 125.

34   For a richly illustrated account of the opening of the London Central Mosque in 1977, see: R. Lewcock, *The Architects' Journal*, 166:32 (1977), 255–69.

35 See for example: F. Scarlett, 'Competition design, unexecuted for London Central Mosque', c.1965, RIBA: AO1/H/1 (1–14).

36 Tate, *Great City Parks*, p. 301.

37 Donald Insall Associates [for Wirral Council, 'Birkenhead Park Conservation Area Appraisal and Management Plan' (Chester: Donald Insall Associates, 2007). Available here: www.wirral.gov.uk/sites/default/files/all/planning%20and%20building/built%20conservation/birkenhead%20park/Birkenhead%20Park%20Appraisal.pdf [accessed 4 June 2021].

38 For further discussion of these matters, see: E. Edwards, *The Camera as Historian: Amateur Photographers and Historical Imagination, 1885–1918* (Durham, NC: Duke University Press, 2012), esp. Chapter 5.

39 San Juan, *Rome: A City out of Print*, pp. 198–204.

40 Ruth Hibbard, 'What in the world is jobbing printing?', *V&A Blog*, https://vam.ac.uk/blog/museum-life/what-in-the-world-is-jobbing-printing [accessed 4 June 2021].

41 Good advice about approaching and exploring private collections can be found in: Hannan and Longair, *History through Material Culture*, pp. 113–14.

42 K. Harvey (ed.), *History and Material Culture: A Student's Guide to Approaching Alternative Sources*, 2nd edn (London: Routledge, 2017), pp. 47–8.

43 S. Jilani, 'How to decolonize a museum', *Times Literary Supplement*, 7 June 2018. See also the podcast series on contemporary approaches to decolonising museums, 'The Wonder House', curated by Dr S. Jansari, https://thewonderhouse.co.uk/ [accessed 24 February 2022].

44 E. Edwards and C. Morton, 'Introduction: between art and information', in Edwards and Morton (eds), *Photographs, Museums, Collections: Between Art and Information* (London: Bloomsbury, 2015), p. 7.

45 E. Edwards, 'Location, location: a polemic on photographs and institutional practices', *Science Museum Group Journal*, 7 (Spring 2017), http://dx.doi.org/10.15180/170709 [accessed 24 February 2022]; Edwards and Morton, 'Between art and information', p. 7.

46 For an informed discussion of these important issues, see 'Is Your Oral History Legal and Ethical?', https://ohs.org.uk/advice/ethical-and-legal/ [accessed 23 September 2020].

RECOMMENDED READING

S. Barson (ed.), *Understanding Architectural Drawings and Historical Visual Sources* (Swindon: Historic England, 2019).

W. C. Booth, G. G. Colomb, and J. M. William, *The Craft of Research*, 2nd edn (Chicago: University of Chicago Press, 2003).

A. Brundage, *Going to the Sources: A Guide to Historical Research and Writing*, 6th edn (Hoboken, NJ: John Wiley & Sons, 2018).

E. Edwards, *Photographs and the Practice of History: A Short Primer* (London: Bloomsbury, 2022).

F. Grant and L. Jordanova (eds), *Writing Visual Histories* (London; New York: Bloomsbury, 2020).

S. Gunn and L. Faire (eds), *Research Methods for History*, 2nd edn (Edinburgh: Edinburgh University Press, 2016).

L. Hannan and S. Longair, *History through Material Culture* (Manchester: Manchester University Press, 2017), Chapter 4.

K. Harvey, *History and Material Culture: A Student's Guide to Approaching Alternative Sources*, 2nd edn (Abingdon: Routledge, 2018).

A. Tovell and J. Knight, 'Directory of UK Sound Collections', 2015, www.bl.uk/projects/uk-sound-directory.

✻ 5 ✻

ANALYSING PRIMARY SOURCES

INTRODUCTION

Having located a suitable body of primary evidence, perhaps sought permission to view these materials and ascertained your key research questions, your next important task is to analyse your sources. This chapter considers different techniques of analysis for your spatial research project. Scrutinising primary sources – which often involves asking pertinent questions of your materials – is central to the professional practice of historians, and yet, from the outside, this process can be rather opaque. As readers we are typically presented with the finished product, such as a published book or journal article. Little explanation is usually given by historians of the significant stage between locating evidence and constructing a persuasive historical argument. So, another way of understanding the purpose of this chapter is to pose the question: how do we do spatial history?

There are some central questions, or routes of investigation, which are key to all forms of primary historical research; these are significant, whether you are interpreting a manuscript, an object or a building.

Key questions to ask of your primary evidence can be summarised as follows:

- date of authorship/production;
- author (who made/produced it);
- language(s) (and transcription or translation);
- reason(s) for its production/purpose;
- where was it produced (and later archived/stored);
- who might have seen/viewed/used it;
- what materials it is made from;
- whether a distinct design can be identified;

- whether this is a very unusual source, or representative of a body of similar evidence;
- whether we can identify changes over time; effects on a material substance (including restoration work).

The approach that we take to get the most out of our primary evidence will also vary somewhat, according to the aims of a particular research project. The methodology, or indeed methodologies, which you adopt in order to scrutinise your primary evidence will of course depend on the types of sources under examination. Analysis of an architectural plan will require a different set of skills from interpreting large amounts of quantitative data (as might be needed for an HGIS project). The approach required to understand the meanings and significances of a material object will differ, in some respects, from the approach taken when analysing manuscript materials, such as inventories. Different methodologies can, however, be applied to the same evidence. In previous chapters we discussed how originality can stem from a new approach applied to a familiar body of sources. An architectural historian, an archaeologist and a cultural historian might all bring distinctive techniques of analysis to bear on a single building, for example. The architectural specialist might identify period-specific design features of the structure; the archaeologist might recognise certain construction techniques and the cultural historian might ascertain particular social and gendered divisions of space within the building, based on interior spatial organisation. Their different approaches to the same evidence are closely linked to their central research questions, priorities and training.

Following on from the structure and approach of the previous chapter, we continue here to examine categories of primary evidence, and ways of analysing them, in turn. We begin with the built environment, and then move on to archival evidence, personal testimony (including oral histories), visual sources and material cultures. This organisation of types of evidence is intended to make the chapter as accessible as possible to readers encountering these approaches for the first time. We are not, however, suggesting that approaches and sources should be treated as discrete entities; far from it. As you read through this chapter you will find that our approach to sources repeatedly encourages you to make interpretative connections between buildings, things, visual evidence and archival materials. Different types of sources enrich contextualised spatial histories; studies might also engage with varied scales of spatial analysis – from a particular building to local, urban and even global networks.

THE BUILT ENVIRONMENT

There are multiple possible methodologies available for interpreting the extant built environment. Archaeologists, architects and architectural historians, philosophers, anthropologists and art historians, among other disciplinary traditions, have developed techniques for interpreting the meanings, contexts and values of buildings. Here we suggest a basic approach to architectural interpretation which does not tally precisely with a particular scholarly discipline, but borrows from different traditions to help you explore, in the words of architect Adam Sharr, 'the close reading of buildings as cultural artefacts'.[1] Above all, if at all possible, you must gain first-hand experience of the built environment, and thus visit the site in person. Other forms of evidence are no real substitute for this experiential understanding: 'No photograph, film or video can reproduce the sense of form, space, light and shade, solidity and weight that is gained from a personal visit. These qualities are lost in photographs, for an external view of a building can rarely indicate how thick the walls are, or give a sense of the space around the building or inside it.'[2]

Whatever approach we take, the interpretation of architectures comes with a particular type of scholarly health warning! This is because buildings are especially complex types of evidence, similar to and yet distinct from other human art forms. As architectural historian William Whyte contends, 'Architecture is instrumental as well as ornamental and symbolic; it serves a function; it is subject to the laws of physics; and it is also an art form.'[3] In other words, while buildings might signify meanings, say through the ornamentation of the exterior walls, or the layout of the structure, people also physically inhabit and experience buildings in a way that is quite unique to this form of primary evidence. This awareness has implications for our methodology. Our interpretive approach must, as far as possible, take into account the different dimensions of architecture, including design, construction, use and contemporary understandings. Where at all possible, we should aim to investigate the intentions of designers, architects, patrons and city planners, but also the multiple users of that space (remembering that, across history, uses, experiences and meanings of built space have been rooted in social, racial, gendered and generational distinctions).

The functional and symbolic intentions of designers and architects do not dictate how a structure is used or understood. This has been the case across human history. In 1570s London, for example, the Royal Exchange was constructed as a magnificent luxury shopping emporium, and as a site for mercantile meetings and transactions. And yet, though it 'was not planned for women's transactions and conversation', women did have a visible presence at the Royal Exchange. Court records reveal that by day women sold 'apples, oranges and other fruit', and female 'prostitutes used the Exchange at night; illegitimate mothers abandoned their newborn babies there'.[4] In a very different era and context, when the twentieth-century Finnish-American architect Eero Saarinen was commissioned to build the Trans World Airlines terminal at New York City's John F. Kennedy International Airport, 'his self-declared aim was to "express the drama and specialness and excitement of travel." Yet his audience soon understood the building in other terms. They compared it to a bird in flight.' As Whyte explains, whereas Saarinen, 'with his modernist aesthetic and belief that architecture could inspire emotion, had hoped to express the drama of flying. His audience, by contrast, using a non-architectural rhetoric, had responded more literally, and seen a bird rather than flight.'[5] Ultimately, we should remember that there is no single 'right' interpretation of a building. Uses and readings are always highly subjective.[6]

Analysing the built environment

Examination of the urban fabric requires you to be highly observant. In your investigations you must play close attention to design, materials and scale. It is imperative also to remain attentive to human inhabitations and interactions.[7] In a classic guide entitled *Looking at Cities* from the mid-1980s, city planner Allan B. Jacobs suggested that observation of the urban environment involved looking for 'clues'. He wrote that: 'clues help the observer understand the nature of the urban environment being examined. They help answer some of the questions about the past, the evolution, and the present state of an urban area.' But what exactly are these pointers? Jacobs suggested that, in order to understand the social, political and economic lives of an urban area (in his case, 1980s San Francisco), we might consider features such as: architectural style, purpose (are we looking at a home, a place of worship or a commercial building), building size (and subdivision), level of maintenance, intensity of land use (the amount of human activity within a given place), artefacts (details on buildings), the 'quality' of design, building materials and workmanship.[8] As historians encountering a particular built space, we might consider the following issues as important clues for understanding its meanings and significances:

- Where is it located in the urban environment (e.g. on the outskirts of a city, on the edge of a marketplace, on a major commercial street)?
- Can you ascertain its function, or functions (e.g. religious worship, commercial activities, social exchange)?
- What can you say about its scale and dimensions? Compared to other built structures in the area, is it especially large or diminutive? Can you estimate its width, or the height of the building (number of storeys)?
- What is the structure made of? Types of materials used for construction (e.g. wood, stone, steel, reinforced concrete) will obviously vary widely, depending on the age and status of the built environment. Remember that different types of materials might be used for different elements of the building: frontages of buildings might have different material properties to structures.
- What are the key external design features? These might include numbers, words, symbols or other visual representations on exterior surfaces (Figure 5.1). Buildings might feature engravings, they might also be ornamented with applied motifs, such as plaster mouldings.
- Does it have a single or multiple entrance and exit points?
- Can you deduce anything about the workmanship?
- Are there obvious marks of use or wear (like stains and scuffmarks)?
- What is the relationship between the particular building under examination and any ancillary or adjoining buildings?

If you are able to gain access to the building, then you will also need to think about the spatial organisation of the structure. Can you determine a basic building layout? Does the structure have few, or multiple rooms? What are the purposes of these different spaces? Do they have the same or different types of decoration and material cultures? Is there a sequential hierarchy of rooms? Is there a single route through the building, or multiple pathways? Are some chambers seemingly more 'public' or 'private'? The questions suggested here are by no means exhaustive. You can adapt the routes of enquiry depending on your particular research questions.

Figure 5.1 Almshouses, dated 1880, Cambridge.

When undertaking this on-site analytical work, it is also important to look for any clues as to multiple periods or phases of building (Figure 5.2). This can be a tricky process at first, but the more you practise this technique of close observation, the better you will become at detecting evidence of change and adaptation over time. Evidence might take the form of differences in material (e.g. sections of a wall made from brick, rather than stone); differences in wall alignment or thickness; variations in structural technique (e.g. changes in brickwork, or timber framing) (Figure 5.3); blocked windows and doors; and, of course, 'stylistic differences in architecture and decoration'. It is also worth paying attention to any evidence of changes in plan design. Clues for such adaptation can take the form of alterations to partition walls, inserted floors and removed staircases (look for scars in the fabric of walls).[9]

It is helpful, when viewing the exterior or interior of a building, to record your thoughts and observations when you are on site. These might take the form of words, sketches or digital photos. You might even record a spoken narrative account as you move through the building

Figure 5.2 Nineteenth-century house, with twenty-first century extension, Cambridge.

(most mobile phones have the appropriate technology for this). First impressions of primary evidence can be important, and once you are further into the research process it is easy to forget these valuable experiential insights. Basic impressionistic drawings are a useful way of recording evidence, and the process of close observation can often draw attention to details of which you were previously unaware. If you are able, it might also be useful to take measurements – for example, of the thickness of the walls, or the dimensions of windows in different parts of the building.

Of course, as historians we are gathering all these clues relating to the built fabric not really because they are ends in themselves, but because they can further illuminate a huge range of social, economic, political and technological ideas, and changes over time. Where a building is located might tell us about land values, or the priorities of urban planners (large industrial buildings tend to be on the outskirts of urban areas – where land is cheaper, and more noxious and noisy activities can be kept apart from trade and governance and salubrious domestic

Figure 5.3 Nineteenth-century house, with twenty-first century extension, Cambridge.

areas). The exterior features of a building can reveal regulatory and environmental details (such as attempts to control the spread of fire), but also notions of status and wealth. The height of a building may indicate the social and political status or pretentions of its owner (think how intimidating it can feel, standing adjacent to a castle or a cathedral – the sheer scale and mass of the building were in part intended to provoke such a reaction), but it can also reveal economic features, and even ideas about faith and spirituality. Modern skyscrapers are immensely tall, some even hundreds of storeys high, in part because land values are so great in metropolitan areas (so it makes sense to build upwards), but also because for many urbanites elevation and city views are associated with social status and financial success (penthouse apartments at the top of modern skyscrapers are among the most expensive and socially exclusive urban dwellings). The scale of a building may also relate to religious ideas and notions of the cosmos. In many religious traditions spaces of worship are relatively tall (traditionally, before the arrival of modern factories and skyscrapers, religious buildings were the tallest structures in an urban environment), with a huge distance between human inhabitants and ceilings – precisely to express a sense of awe-inspiring divinity.

Interior building plans and the spatial organisation of structures can be highly revealing of particular political, social and gender orders. If a whole family, or multiple households, are living in one or two rooms, this tells us something important about their economic status and living conditions. By contrast, a house with multiple rooms of highly specialised functions (with separate spaces to eat, store foodstuffs, cook, sleep, socialise, read, work – and we could of course go on with other specific uses) suggests relative affluence, material comfort and the ability and perhaps desire to maintain some element of privacy. Multiple routes through a building – for example back staircases in addition to a main central staircase, have been developed in many different cultures in order to maintain a physical and social distance between members of a family and their household staff. Of course, our reading of design and spatial organisation must be sensitive to cultural difference and variation. Communal living arrangements, such as student dormitories, may indicate particular political ideals – as in early Soviet Russia.[10] The organisation of the built fabric may reflect and reinforce particular gender ideals. Traditionally, houses in Bahrain and the Persian Gulf were organised around a courtyard, all rooms facing inward except those of the male inhabitants, as it was the men who received guests, and thus had outward-facing windows.[11] We could give innumerable examples relating to the scale, materials and exterior and interior design and furnishings of the urban built environment across space, time and cultures. The overall point here is that buildings reflect particular political, cultural and social circumstances, and they also work to shape and reinforce those circumstances. In our interpretations of the built environment we must pay attention to all the material and spatial clues which point toward these varied contexts.

When studying a specific building, or building type, we should avoid simply analysing the structure(s) in isolation. Rather, in researching and writing meaningful spatial histories it is best to remain mindful of broader urban, environmental and human settings. Methodologically, this means taking into account other primary sources in addition to the extant built fabric. Are there visual depictions (such as paintings, prints or photographs) of the building and its wider urban milieu? Can you find first-hand descriptions of the building and the broader urban environment (for example in diaries, surveys, letters or oral histories)? Can you identify change over time in these textual and visual representations?

Applying theoretical approaches

Once you have contextualised the built environment that you are researching, the next step might be to consider the theoretical and analytical frameworks that will facilitate your deeper assessment of the meaning and significance of the sources you plan to draw on. It can be daunting when you start engaging with theoretical approaches to historical analysis, and embedding cultural frameworks within your research is often challenging. You may find it helpful to look at some of the ways that other historians of the built environment have applied cultural theory to their research. Certainly, there is no shortage of scholarship that has utilised Foucault's work in analysing the relationship between power and the built environment, such as Chris Otter's study of Victorian lighting technologies as a method of controlling and governing urban populations, Ishita Pande's history of childhood, age and citizenship in colonial India, and Frank Mort's re-evaluation of post-war social change through an account of London's spaces of power, sex and culture.[12] These are useful examples that take a specific site – say, London or colonial India – and apply Foucauldian models relating to governmentality, power and knowledge to a specific body of primary evidence, including technologies of light; medical and legal tracts; social surveys; and police records. The theory underpins the authors' analysis, but their assessment of the primary evidence remains central, and they avoid long discussions of the theoretical work itself. You may find this light-touch approach to theory works well. Most historians who take a spatialised approach tend to avoid including long theoretical sections in their research, in favour of subtle but informed references to the most crucial theoretical scholarship.

ARCHIVAL SOURCES

Archives should always be handled with care. In the powerful and influential thesis of archivists Joan M. Schwartz and Terry Cook:

> Through archives, the past is controlled. Certain stories are privileged and others are marginalized. And archivists are an integral part of this story-telling. In the design of record-keeping systems, in the appraisal and selection of a tiny fragment of all possible records to

enter the archive, in approaches to subsequent and ever-changing descriptions and preservation of the archive and its patterns of communication and use, archivists continually reshape, reinterpret, and reinvent the archive.[13]

These processes, steered by archivists, from selecting and classifying to losing or even throwing away, all impact upon the kinds of histories we write and, more importantly, the misconceptions within which we work.

In other words, archives are not neutral repositories of information but are informed by, produce and reproduce power relationships. Theoretical and historical writing, influenced by Foucault's work on the underlying systems that structure Western thought, implicates archives in histories of the state, governance, colonialism and imperialism.[14] In one version of this story, the emergence of 'official' centralised archives across Europe in the late eighteenth century and first half of the nineteenth was entangled with ideas of nation and national patrimony, and the development of the modern state.[15] More recent interventions have complicated the picture, challenging its chronological assumptions, and showing why archives should be treated 'not merely as the object but also the subject of enquiry'.[16] Urban environments are at the heart of these stories. The archives and collections that became increasingly formalised and centralised were inseparable from the business of governance, organisation, surveillance and, in some cases, simply keeping track of activities in cities. Importantly, for our purposes, this worked at different spatial and geographic scales, from activities that took place within a single building, such as the daily routines of a hospital in medieval Bologna, to operations that were urban, regional, national and, indeed, global and transnational in scope. Moreover, many archives relating to specific urban environments are rife with activities that relate to the management of space and place: from the maintenance of social and spatial boundaries by means of curfews and city walls in the medieval and early modern city, to the impact of new transport infrastructure on city limits and urban zoning in the modern city, to attempts to drive growth and prosperity through targeted transformation of the urban built environment in the twentieth-century metropolis.

With these thoughts in mind, you will get more out of your source material if you are aware of the following issues. First, archives are always **selective**: this is relevant to the information captured in the first place – the sorts of lives documented – and also the information kept and, just as importantly, lost or discarded over time. This selectiveness is inscribed in how archival materials, broadly defined, are **ordered** so that information can be retrieved. As discussed in Chapter 4, archives, irrespective of scale or purpose, are intensely spatial. This is evident in the physical organisation of materials in places we call archives, and also in the relational and contextual nature of archival classifications. Some kinds of information are captured and made 'discoverable' (to use the parlance of contemporary digital culture) by means of methods of classification. Card catalogues and, in some cases, additional print and manuscript registers, will be available to help you surface historic systems of ordering and classifying. Most importantly, archival 'infrastructure' will not be immediately apparent to the researcher and, in most cases, will have been revised many times over the years. Take, for example, the shift from handwritten inventories, registries and card catalogues to computer databases and digital metadata. Getting the most out of your archive means having a good grasp of multiple, often overlapping, forms of ordering, classification and organisation that have been used. It also means being mindful that 'different orders may produce different accounts of the past.'[17]

Moreover, archives, archivists and archival practices are shaped by social, professional and technological **conventions and prejudices**. Technologies of reading and writing have had considerable impact on what has been preserved in archives and, in turn, on who has been able to access this. Geographer Miles Ogborn's work on the East India Company in the seventeenth and eighteenth centuries combines the concerns of imperial history, book history and history of science with approaches from STS.[18] Looking at a mixed economy of writing, across manuscript and print, Ogborn 'takes seriously the different forms of writing around the East India Company in order to understand how changing relationships of knowledge and power shaped the encounter between Europe and Asia in the seventeenth and eighteenth centuries'.[19] For our purposes, his study also suggests how to carry out networked contextualisation of materials found in archives and other collecting institutions. Close analysis and comparison of the expectations and use of different kinds of writing results in a rich picture of the social, spatial and material dimensions of manuscript and printed sources, from letters and ledger books to printed travellers' accounts. Focusing on the use, circulation and reception of writing in its many forms brings Britain and the East Indies 'into a single interpretative frame'.[20] Ultimately, this enables 'geographies of knowledge and power that are both firmly located in particular places and stretched half way across the globe'.[21]

Linked, the **privileging of textual records** found in particular kinds of archive can also result in the displacement and devaluing of other kinds of testimony, including oral forms of collective memory and history-making. This prompts questions about whose voices are most prominent in histories of spatial practice and the transformation of the urban built environment. Think back to Thamesmead in South London, briefly touched upon in the previous chapter. The development of London's only 'new town' in the 1960s and 1970s resulted in a variety of archival sources. Much of this material was generated by local, regional and national government. In this instance, recent community-focused work, including oral histories, offers a counterbalance to the 'official' archival voice.[22] As this example suggests, in tandem with the discussion of oral history interviews in Chapter 4 and of counter-archives below, some projects may require you to create or remake an archive, broadly defined, in order to support your work.

Twenty-first-century historians must also deal with issues thrown up by the technological developments that have revolutionised the way many of us work. Since the turn of the century we have seen increasing emphasis on the production of digital and online resources for research, including archival and collections databases, and digitised manuscript and printed texts. While these are extremely useful, historians should also be alert to the challenges they pose. Whenever possible, consulting the online version of something should be followed up by a visit to the archive in person. This will allow you to consult manuscript catalogues, card indexes and registries on site, which may provide clues to additional, as yet undigitised materials that are vital for your project. Seeing your archival materials in the original means that you can also check the accuracy of online transcription. Even more critically, your analysis will benefit from deep engagement with original material evidence. In some cases, digitisation projects – or their recent ancestors, microfilm and microfiche – cut archival evidence down to size, cropping and, in some cases, reorientating it or even scaling it up.[23]

Getting a feel for your evidence is an important part of its contextualisation. You will experience the original evidence at its full size, feel its weight and see how it relates, quite literally, to other documents, in unsorted archive boxes, tied bundles of papers, heavy bound albums, paper folders and, in some cases, as inserts stuck into other things.[24] Moreover, you will have an unrivalled opportunity to build up a picture of the multiple traces left by past users of your archival materials, including the archivists, cataloguers and collection managers charged with its ordering and preservation at various points. Pay attention to how your archive is organised (e.g. in boxes, paper envelopes or bound albums, on card supports, within acid-free tissue paper, tied up with string or fabric tapes ...) for clues about when it was last consulted or rearranged. Look out for the overlay of mark-making – from numbers, letters, even words and sentences in pen and pencil, to stickers and professional hieroglyphs – that might shed light on past modes of arrangement and classification.

With all this in mind, good archival practice should include careful and close **observation** of individual archival 'documents'. This means transcribing materials accurately – work that can be impeded by historical handwritings. For projects focusing on medieval and early modern subject matter, you may need to receive training in palaeography (the study of ancient and historical handwriting) from your university or a local archive or history centre. In addition to noting the content of texts, pay close attention to the material dimensions of the materials you work with. What is the paper like? Does it feel thick and smooth? Does it have a watermark you can follow up in a relevant guide? What colour ink is used? Is all the writing in the same type of handwriting? Or does some of it look older or newer? Is the material typewritten only, or a combination of type and handwriting? Are the papers bound together? Were these materials always bound together, or is this something that was done retrospectively? Are there any ties or strings holding papers together? These observations will enhance your understanding of the purpose of the records. Critical here is the issue of readership: was a 'document' meant to be read by lots of people? Was its readership restricted? Or, even, was it secret? How does this shift your understanding of what you have found out? This work means paying heed to the contexts within which archival materials sit. We might take Ann Laura Stoler's work on colonial archives in nineteenth- and twentieth-century Indonesia as a model, in particular, her idea of 'reading along the grain' to feel the archival 'pulse'.[25] Spend time getting to know the rhythms and routines of the papers you are working with, as well as reading between the lines and against the grain.

Think about where **comparison** with similar or adjacent materials will deepen understanding. As the examples above suggest, no single piece of archival evidence can stand alone. Useful lines of enquiry include: is a document part of a series? Is it related to other orders or pronouncements in the same archive? Was it part of a chain of command? Was it part of a correspondence? Are there details of names and places that you can follow up? Will you need to consult materials in another archival series or collecting institutions to follow the trail? What does a document's relationship to other materials tell you about the record-keeping and administrative routines of, say, trade and commerce, government or the archive? Framing questions like these may result in you working across archives. Refer back to the essay by Goebel we looked at in Chapter 3. In this case, restoring to view the networks of anticolonial activists in interwar Paris was possible only because Goebel worked with archival materials generated by multiple departments of the French state.

Above all, make deft use of **supplementary information**: place processes of archiving and histories of archives within wider institutional, social and cultural contexts. In this part of your work, reflect on how best to use primary and secondary supporting information to make optimum sense of the materials you are working with. The contexts needed will be determined by the subject and primary sources you work with, but from terminology to epistemology, take nothing for granted!

Counter-archives

As we have seen in earlier chapters, historians have turned to new methodologies to address the silences and gaps that we find in archives. One example of a spatial history that powerfully engages with non-archival sources is Anindita Ghosh's analysis of colonial India, which reveals that urban space was an important site of resistance for marginalised groups. Drawing on illustrations, songs, local histories and amateur photographs, Ghosh challenges the idea, put forward by colonialists, that nineteenth-century Calcutta was a problem to be managed, where order was 'threatened by an unruly and disease-ridden Indian section'. She also readdresses contemporary nationalist discourse that suggests that the city 'represented exploitation, corruption, and decadence, while the ancestral rural home was a haven of peace'.[26] Using the example of Kobi songs – originally emerging in harvest festivals in rural Bengal and subsequently appropriated by the prosperous households in Calcutta – which were adapted to depict contemporary urban life and responded to the rapid urban change taking place, Ghosh argues that 'their vigorous presence rendered the streets of Calcutta a contested site for class, caste, community, and gender encounters'.[27] This approach shows how the colonial city could be resisted in spatial terms, particularly through the influence of popular culture that allowed Bengalis to reshape and contribute to urban processes.[28] Likewise, Farina Mir focuses on the Punjabi vernacular language to challenge narratives about the causes of Partition in 1947. She uses the tradition of *quissa* storytelling to foreground depictions of social space that promoted harmony, rather than sectarian divisions.[29] The use of vernacular sources, rather than the perspectives of the colonialists, offers important new insights into identity formation and valuable ways to consider the relationship between popular culture, resilience and resistance within colonial urban space. Such sources also remind us not to be deterred if the topic we are researching has scant records in the archives. Broadening what we think of as historical evidence can lead to more imaginative and path-breaking insights and findings.

To take another example, we can look at the waves of inner-city violence that occurred in areas such as London's Brixton, Manchester's Moss Side and in Liverpool 8, known as Toxteth, in the summer of 1981. Characterised by clashes between police and Black working-class youths, the disturbances emerged due to high youth unemployment and escalating police harassment. In Liverpool in July 1981, a heavy-handed police response to the suspected theft of a motorbike led to weeks of violence and rioting, with over 450 policemen injured, more than 160 buildings damaged, 500 arrests, one death and the first use of tear gas by police in Britain. If we look at the press coverage, we see that youths were blamed for the disturbances, and reportage focused on the damage allegedly caused to the bulldozers, scaffolding and building materials that were attempting to 'regenerate' the area. *The Times* compared the damage as being like 'the Blitz' and described the aftermath: 'smoking ruins … Twisted wrecked lampposts … A pool of dry blood could be seen on the pavements. A mechanical excavator was being dragged away from Jamaica House, a community bank; it had been used to ram the building.'[30] By emphasising the destruction and bloodshed, the press implied that mindless violence had taken place, ignoring the wider problems that had caused the disturbances.

In contrast to this official discourse and cultures of reportage, however, Jacqueline Nassy Brown's ethnographic study of Liverpool used the disturbances as an example of how the local and the global should be conceived of as racial and spatial categories. Rather than relying on official archival resources, Brown spoke to locals who took her through the sites where the disturbances had occurred to reflect on their own perspectives and experiences. Describing an interview with Cecelia who took part in a march in protest at the treatment of Black people in the city following the 1981 disturbances, Brown notes that Cecelia 'relived a moment of unmitigated joy … Cecelia felt elated during those marches for a long time afterward.' Through conversations with Brown, Cecelia drew similarities with the significance of American civil rights movements and:

> wondered aloud whether it must have felt the same for Black Americans in the days of the first marches of the civil rights movement … She thought all things were possible now. Political change for Black people was occurring right there through the actual, physical presence of Black people in all their numbers. White people, Cecelia remembered, were standing on the sidelines confounded by the spectacle – 'at a loss,' in her words. 'Blacks,' she said, 'were taking over the city.'[31]

Here, Brown's attention to Cecelia's recollections facilitates her interpretation of the clashes as an important moment that challenged the established spatial relationships between race and identity, suggesting that the physical attack on Liverpool's streets and buildings paved the way for equality and the breaking down of entrenched xenophobic and racist inequalities in the city. Brown's ethnographic approach and use of alternative sources beyond those found in official or government archives exemplifies the way that different types of evidence can help researchers to achieve new understandings that may reveal reciprocal, fluid and flexible relationships between identity and space that may not be uncovered otherwise. These issues are worth bearing in mind as you begin analysing your sources, particularly if you are interested in retrieving the experiences of those communities who may be underrepresented or silenced within formal archives or dominant cultural sources, such as the press.

Crime records

A subset of archival records, crime records often tell us as much about the spatial environment in which a crime occurred and the social and cultural worlds of offenders and victims as they do about a particular crime that has taken place. Statements by offenders, victims and witnesses can be rich in detail. But, as Natalie Zemon Davis has influentially demonstrated, historians should not read these kinds of sources as 'fact', due to the manipulation of the evidence and narratives presented by those involved in the court system.[32] Let us take the 1931 deposition of a twenty-five-year-old man, on remand for burglary in Manchester. His statement claimed that he had been out of work, and so travelled by bus from Scotland to Manchester. Staying at a hostel, he testified that he had had £4 10s stolen from his coat, leaving him penniless: 'I walked through Piccadilly and I was in such a state of mind through losing my money that I wandered into the outskirts of the city', where he broke into a house and stole some jewellery. He went on to explain that 'I went to Liverpool … to try and sell the jewellery and I was arrested … I was not myself at the time this happened. I was almost frantic with despair.'[33] His statement is of course an attempt to elicit sympathy and to attract lenient treatment from the criminal justice system, but it also tells us about the geographical mobility of offenders moving between Scotland, Manchester and its suburbs and Liverpool within a remarkably narrow window of time, and gives us a rare insight into how young, working-class male criminals moved between spaces.

As a recent edited collection by historians Anne-Marie Kilday and David Nash demonstrates, this type of micro-historical approach to the history of crime can be useful, because it facilitates 'a greater understanding of context with investigative research involving knowledge of a range of attendant social, cultural, political and economic factors' and is 'a particularly good way of capturing such aspects of the everyday history of behaviour that are so frequently hidden from view'.[34] This kind of approach might be especially fruitful for historians of the built environment who are interested in using crime records, because they can provide a range of perspectives and draw our eyes to different parts of towns and cities or distinct ways of utilising space that might otherwise go overlooked. Close attention to changing patterns in the use of microspaces, for instance, can help to draw out the complexities and contradictions in the ways in which space could be utilised by those deemed to be criminals, and the responses of these individuals to changing patterns of surveillance.

PERSONAL TESTIMONY

Personal testimony – including oral histories, letters and memoirs – can be especially valuable in retrieving the experiences of those often marginalised from more official archival sources. Yet they are not unproblematic sources and cannot give us an individual's objective view of the past, nor should we try to aim to achieve this. Rather, what these types of sources give historians is an insight into the ways in which individuals interpreted, recorded and made sense of their experiences and of the world around them. Arguably, this is much more valuable and useful to historians. There is a wealth of scholarship on undertaking and analysing personal testimony, such as that which engages with important concepts such as composure and memory.[35] One of the key questions when analysing oral histories is to think about why, when and how the interviews were undertaken and how this shaped the narrative produced by the subject. Interviewees often want to please the interviewer, and can express concern about their inability to remember an event that took place long ago. But 'accuracy' usually matters less to historians analysing oral histories than an interest in exploring how interviewees construct their own narrative of the past. This might be concerned with what interviewees do not say explicitly but communicate through other cues. Barry Hazley's analysis of interviews with women who migrated from Ireland to Britain in the post-1945 period states that one of his subjects 'hinted at suppressed feelings of loss' in her account of moving to Britain. Hazley argues that 'to the extent Brenda's personal feelings were audible, these emerged indirectly, through sighs and silences as well as depictions of aspects of her external environment that intimated interior feelings of alienation'.[36] This example is an important reminder of the value in listening to recordings of interviews when possible, in order to address how subjects narrate and articulate their story, what is said, or not said, and how it is expressed.

If interviews are unavailable and transcripts are used instead, we can address the descriptions and asides that would usually be included, from the interviewer's responses. For instance, the transcripts of Madeline McKenna's interviews with those who moved to the suburban estates in Liverpool during the 1920s and 1930s reveal how several subjects were offended by some seemingly innocuous questions:

> How old were you Miss B when your parents were allocated this house?
> I'm sorry but I don't really want to answer very personal questions. My age is my own business.
> I'm sorry to offend you ...[37]

It is difficult to know how annoyed Miss B was with the question, without hearing her response in full, but her apparent willingness to continue with the questions suggests that she was probably not too upset. Interestingly, at first her answers were brief, but they got longer as the interview continued, indicating that her initial hostile response may have been an expression of nerves or anxiety. However, she was not the only one of McKenna's interviewees to respond with hostility to that opening question, and this may have reflected a wider defensive attitude towards questions about life on council housing estates. It is worth bearing in mind that the interviews were being undertaken in Liverpool during the 1980s, when the city and the working classes more generally experienced a particularly challenging period under Thatcherism. Many of McKenna's interviewees expressed a keenness to emphasise that the estates had been home to 'a better class of people' in the 1920s and 1930s.[38] A common statement made negative comparisons between the estates in the 1980s and how interviewees had remembered them in the 1930s: 'Well, the Corporation has certainly changed. These houses were well looked after years ago ... The houses are just neglected today, look, a lot are boarded up because they can't be bothered to repair them.'[39] This is a revealing example of how researchers need to engage with the context in which subjects are narrating their experiences. Here, the interviewee used their story to make complaints about what they perceived as the failure of local government at the time when the interview was taking place. It is not difficult to imagine this interviewee looking out of the window and being displeased with what they saw in comparison with the newly built estate they could recall from their childhood. Any analysis of oral histories therefore needs to take into account the context in which a subject is narrating their experience, and the ways in which their present has influenced their reporting of the past.

VISUAL SOURCES

As with oral histories, the 'golden rule' is not to treat visual sources as uncomplicated documentary representations of the past – as what somewhere 'was like'. Instead, as with all other primary evidence, you need to establish purpose, genre 'rules' and expectations. Despite the temptation to engage in a 'deep dive' into the analysis of a single image, part of this work will always involve looking at your visual source in the context of other, related depictions. It is worth keeping in mind that some representations are copies, done after older views, plans or maps. The drawing in Figure 5.4, by Sir John Soane, is after a lost original by

Figure 5.4 Plan and elevation of garden alcove and screen wall at Lansdowne House, Berkeley Square, London, drawn by Sir John Soane, after lost original by Charles-Louis Clérisseau.

the French artist, architect and antiquarian Charles-Louis Clérisseau. It shows the garden alcove concocted by Clérisseau for Shelburne (later Lansdowne) House, a large residence in Berkeley Square, London, designed by Robert Adam. As noted in pen on the drawing, the alcove 'failed'– or collapsed – in about 1776, making this an important piece of evidence that tells us about one of the few projects Clérisseau completed during his two-year stay in England.[40] You will need to take into account the possibility of copying and reproduction when analysing representations of urban environments, especially if you are working with medieval and early modern materials, where there is more chance the 'original' has not survived.

Such examples also make an additional important point. Modes of representation at any given time were informed by available technologies, and by social and cultural conventions and expectations. Thinking specifically about the subject of this book, the production, consumption and use of representations of urban environments were often inextricably tied to other aspects of city life, such as trade and manufacturing. For example, the story of design drawings in Britain is linked to the availability and cost of paper, most notably the availability of mass-produced sheets of paper in different sizes by the nineteenth century.[41] Reflecting more recent innovations, AnnMarie Brennan explores how digital design tools, such as computer numerical control (CNC) fabrication and software, have transformed the appearance of twenty-first-century cities. Initially used in the aeronautical and automobile industries, computer-aided design (CAD) and CNC tools have enabled architects to produce buildings with ever more complex curved surfaces.[42] Here we might think of Frank O. Gehry's Disney Concert Hall in Los Angeles – a project that marked a paradigm shift in the use of digital design methods in the context of architecture.[43] The relationship between technology and representation also reshaped urban subjectivities. One example is Rosa Salzberg's work on the production, sale and consumption of fliers, pamphlets and broadsides in Renaissance Venice. Salzberg deftly combines close object study, drawing on approaches from book history, with deep engagement with the Venetian Archivio di Stato to show how the proliferation of 'cheap' print transformed the city's cultural life.[44] Or we could refer back to Lynda Nead's appraisal of photography in 1890s London, which we considered in Chapter 3, and her argument that increasing access to photographic equipment and technologies fundamentally shifted how urban life was perceived and experienced.

All visual sources come with agendas that, as historians, we need to tease out. It is always worth starting by dwelling on the relationship between the form of your representation and what you can glean of its purpose. Let us use a case study to see this in action – the building of the Crystal Palace in London. This was the temporary building that housed over 100,000 exhibits from across the arts, sciences and industry which were shown at the Great Exhibition in 1851.[45] Despite being the then largest enclosed space on Earth, the cast-iron, laminated-timber and glass structure was erected in London's Hyde Park in less than nine months.[46] Joseph Paxton, whom we met in Chapter 4 in relation to Birkenhead Park, was broadly responsible for its design. His first stab, a quick sketch on blotting paper (Figure 5.5), was, famously, produced on 11 June 1850 during a business meeting of the London

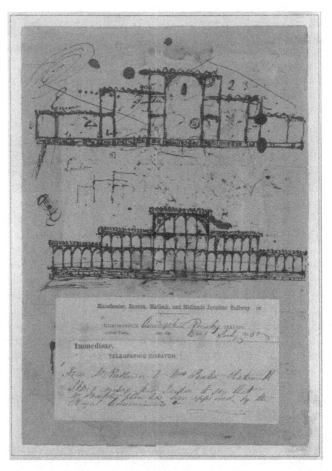

Figure 5.5 Joseph Paxton's initial sketch on blotting paper of the Great Exhibition building, 11 June 1850.

Midland Railway, of which he was a director.[47] Paxton's rough idea was passed to Henry Cole, one of the Great Exhibition's organisers, who agreed that the Royal Commission (the body with oversight of the event) would consider the proposition if he could produce more detailed plans and an estimate of costs.[48] Figure 5.6 shows one of the drawings that Paxton, working with William Barlow, an engineer from London Midlands Railway, managed to make in just over a week.[49] As

Figure 5.6 Joseph Paxton and William Barlow's presentation drawing of the Great Exhibition building shown to the Royal Commission in late June 1850.

you can see, this vision of the Crystal Palace is a much more carefully rendered perspectival view in colour and was intended to show the project in its best light. Even at this point, and with Robert Stephenson, one of the building committee, on board, Paxton's design was not a done deal. Somewhat sneakily, he pushed the issue by having the same view of the building printed in the 6 July 1850 edition of the *Illustrated London News*, where it met with press and popular acclaim.[50] The final image for us to consider is a watercolour by Edmund Walker (Figure 5.7), who specialised in architectural views, and shows the finished building surrounded by visitors on a gloriously sunny day. It belonged to Charles Fox, of the engineering firm Fox & Henderson, who was to build the Crystal Palace. The date of the image's production, 1850, is important: at this point, the site of the Great Exhibition was still under construction, making this, at best, an idealised depiction of a semi-finished building or, indeed, of a project that had barely broken ground.[51]

Figure 5.7 Watercolour by Edmund Walker, painted in 1850, showing the Great Exhibition building in an unrealistic state of completion.

Looking at these drawings, each with a different purpose, emphasises the critical importance of detailed, properly contextualised understanding of visual sources. Although we cannot anticipate precisely the visual sources you will use in your research project, the following broad strands of enquiry may help.

- **Purpose:** What was the visual source used for? Was it part of the design or construction process? If so, where and when? Does it show a completed project or one that was not built? Was it intended to document an existing building or built environment? Why? What were the genre conventions that informed its production? What other things is it similar to or different from? How have these changed over time?
- **Authorship:** Do we know who, individually or collectively, made it? Does it have any handwriting on it, and where? Can you use other sources or expertise to identify the handwriting or date it? Are there indications that more than one person has annotated it? Does it have any other features (choice of paper, use of colour, style of lettering, notation of scales or dimensions) that make it similar to other architectural drawings or visual depictions securely attributed to known people (i.e. architects, architectural offices or studios, draughtsmen and draughtswomen, military engineers)?
- **Materials and production:** What media were used (e.g. ink, chalk, watercolour, CAD software …)? What is its ground or surface made from? Is it vellum (calfskin) or paper? If it is paper, does it have any watermarks that you can identify in relevant secondary literature? How typical (or not) were the choice of materials and/or the

mode(s) of production used? How expensive? In what ways was this mode of production rooted in urban contexts and networks?

- **Comparison and visual contextualisation:** Does your visual source look like anything else? Can this comparison help you to work out its purpose? Was this point of comparison made in the same way as your source, broadly speaking? Or was it created using different formats, conventions, materials and techniques (e.g. your visual source is a manuscript drawing, the point of comparison is an engraving)? Does your source exist in multiple forms? Can you trace how it has circulated across time (chronologically) and place (geographically)?

- **Consumption and ownership:** How many were there? How exact or rough is this calculation? Who had access to this kind of thing? How was it used? How much did it cost? Was it repurposed at any point in its 'life'? How? Do we know who owned it? If so, do we know how these owners used/interacted with it?

- **Spatial presence:** Was this visual source displayed as part of its use? If so, who saw it and where was it kept? Were people required by law or custom to have one on display? If it was not displayed, how and why was it concealed? Was it a prohibited or taboo object? Was it displayed on special occasions (e.g. religious festivals, celebrations)? Did this require particular ritual actions or activities?

Many stages in the development of buildings and built environments were marked by distinctive visual sources, which were often the work of many different hands. A broad array of materials is relevant to this discussion. Due to the breadth of available sources, and the necessity of understanding their distinctive historical and geographical contexts, it is impossible to be comprehensive. For this reason, we will focus on some important strands of visual evidence. We begin by looking at visual representations of urban space, including architectural drawings, before moving on to discuss early modern and modern maps, and then finishing with a brief discussion of images in newspapers.

Visual representations of the urban

Historic England's extremely useful guide *Understanding Architectural Drawings and Historical Visual Sources* draws on the insights of expert contributors to establish the main categories of architectural drawings and other forms of historical visual sources in Britain from the sixteenth century to the present day.[52] Its headings and descriptions are included here to suggest the complexity of the landscape of visual sources – in this instance, the range of distinctive forms of architectural drawing in Britain – and also to signal the importance of getting a grasp on the historical and geographical specificity of forms of representation that are most relevant to your project. It is well worth consulting in conjunction with the discussion in the Historic England guide, which includes illustrations of each of the different categories of drawings and designs referred to here:

- **Sketch:** a basic outline or quickly rendered idea (like, for example, Paxton's initial proposition for the Crystal Palace in Figure 5.5), typically not to scale.
- **Preliminary design:** shows further development of an idea, done to scale. Examples often include multiple scenarios on the same page, allowing clients and patrons choice at this early stage in development.
- **Finished design:** a fully worked out scheme for a building, comprising a plan, elevation and possibly sections, with a scale. These were sent to a masons' workshop to enable the preparation of construction or working drawings, meaning that few survive from the sixteenth or seventeenth centuries, as they were 'either lost or destroyed in the process'.[53]
- **Working drawing:** a rendering that conveyed the information needed in order to construct a building, most notably the different kinds of materials used. As with finished designs, more survive from later periods.
- **Competition drawing:** from the nineteenth century, produced by an architect in response to a national or civic project that was put out to tender, to demonstrate what they and their office could do, in order to secure a contract. Paxton and Barlow's perspective view (see Figure 5.6), shown to the Royal Commission for the Great Exhibition on 22 June 1850, is an example of this kind of drawing.
- **Measured plans, views and surveys of monuments and buildings:** produced by taking measurements of sites as part of antiquarian, archaeological and architectural work.
- **Contract drawing:** first used in late seventeenth century, and proliferating from the nineteenth century with the emergence of building contractors. These were the final design before execution. The presence of the signatures of the contractor, client and architect explain the terminology.

- **Record drawings:** used to mark a finished project or to capture a building's appearance before it was altered or, in some cases, demolished. Typically done by an architect or professional draughtsperson, record drawings were employed as reference material by an office or provided the basis of printed depictions that were shared more widely.
- **Models:** three-dimensional renderings of full buildings or components of projects; in use by the medieval period, but more common from the nineteenth century onwards.

Categorisation of objects will only get us so far. We also need to choose tools for analysis – you may want to look back to Chapter 3, on methodology, to do this. Let us return to the list of different kinds of architectural drawings outlined above. Implicit in their descriptions is the timeline of a building project, from idea, through realisation, to retrospective representation. To make more sense of this list, we could use the concept of 'black-boxing', discussed in Chapter 1, to help think through the practical and conceptual work performed by visual sources during the transformation of urban environments. We might think about how relevant visual materials fulfilled distinctive purposes in the design, realisation and reception of built environments. While some visual materials, such as working drawings produced before construction, show architects, builders and engineers working through the challenges of a particular project, other forms of representation, such as the leaflet in Figure 5.8, combining illustration and graphic design, were part of the repertoire of press, marketing and advertising. This example was intended to entice prospective exhibitors to apply for a snug '6 foot high by 3 foot high' booth at the 1940 World's Fair in New York. There is scope, too, to explore the impact of changing conventions in the production of architectural representations. For example, from the nineteenth century onward, models, along with perspectival drawings and prints, were more widely used to communicate designs to clients and, increasingly in the twentieth century, to local communities.[54]

Visual sources such as the ones we have reviewed in this chapter, were also historically and geographically specific. As historians, we must build up our sensitivity to the contexts that informed the conventions, modes of production and expectations of visual sources. Some of these will be 'false friends', like the scales and numbers found on some architectural drawings, which will, most likely, relate to historical systems

Figure 5.8 Detail from a printed leaflet inviting exhibitors to show their products at the 1940 World's Fair in New York.

of measurement and require conversion into contemporary metrics. In 1660, painters, sculptors and master craftsmen signed a series of *marchés*, or contracts, with Paris's Bureau de la Ville (the city's municipal government) to build the five massive triumphal arches that were the main feature of Louis XIV's entry into the city, a celebration that marked the beginning of his majority, his recent marriage and the end of over two decades of war with Spain.[55] Although these contracts set out in detail the scale, materials and decorative elements, all dimensions were in '*toise*' (or '*thoise*'), with one *toise* being roughly equivalent to six feet. The first challenge for historians working with this material is to convert historical measurements into contemporary ones.[56] The *toise* is just one example of the many kinds of 'highly contextual' weights and measures that existed in the medieval and early modern periods.[57] Just how contextual these were can be illustrated by the 'original' *toise*. It was an actual iron bar affixed to one of the walls of the Grand Châtelet in Paris – a complex that encompassed a courthouse, police headquarters and a prison – presumably because this location invested the *toise* with authority *and* rendered it spatially accessible. The bar can just be glimpsed at letter 'B' in the etching in Figure 5.9, an illustrated plate from an early eighteenth-century book on geometry.

Let us follow French measures into the late eighteenth and nineteenth centuries. The subject provides an excellent demonstration of just how socially and historically constructed even the most seemingly neutral or 'scientific' information is. During the 1790s in France, centralised efforts were made to replace thousands of often highly localised frameworks for envisaging distance, including the *toise*, with a single

Figure 5.9 View of the Châtelet's courtyard, with the *toise* 'bar' fixed to the wall in the right-hand corner.

measure, the metre.[58] This development has been linked to the broader spirit of rationality, universality and quantifying that historians have located in the French Revolution and Enlightenment, forming a 'new language for the material world [that] would create an autonomous and egalitarian citizenry able to calculate its own best interest'.[59] What actually happened was much more complicated and contested, as people across France, including artisans, merchants and consumers, resisted the new system. Scientists, politicians and bureaucrats had not factored in how far economic activity was also social – rooted in tried and tested customary practices that people trusted.[60] In the face of ongoing opposition, the metric system was partially withdrawn by Napoleon in 1812 and replaced by the equally unpopular '*mesures usuelles*' ('ordinary measures'), a sort of 'halfway house' that brought back *ancien régime* units, such as the *toise* (still approximately equivalent to six feet), for everyday calculations.[61]

This case study warns us against heroically teleological accounts of scientific and technological 'progress', especially those which are disencumbered of their social, cultural and political contexts. Elsewhere, scholarly accounts of architectural drawings and visual sources also tend to stress progressive narratives. An example is the shift in practice from pictorial representations to the increasingly standardised use of scaled plans and elevations, as evident in the print depicting a temporary pavilion built for a firework display in eighteenth-century London (Figure 5.10), which were informed by the wider use of surveying tools and knowledge of geometry.[62] While this trajectory explains the development of specialised, often exclusionary, forms of professional knowledge, it is not the full story. Other ways of representing place continued (indeed, continue) to exist, such as the depiction of a building on the lid of a seventeenth-century embroidered box (Figure 5.11); nor were the forms of representation universal within or beyond Western Europe. In this case, choosing to describe an embroidered depiction of a building as 'unsophisticated' or 'vernacular' may have a gendered dimension. This word choice proposes that older forms of pictorial representation, evident in much early modern domestic production, were lacking in comparison with perspectival or measured depictions, produced by means of training and education that was almost exclusively open only to men.[63] This case amply illustrates the battlefield of representation: the extent to which power imbalances are present in how we frame and interrogate different modes within visual culture.

Figure 5.10 Plan and elevation by George Vertue of fireworks in St James's Park, London, to celebrate the Peace of Aix-la-Chapelle, 1749.

Maps and plans

Maps and plans may also tell us more than we at first expect. The study of cartography – the practice of making maps for a host of purposes – has proved an especially fertile area for exploring these concerns.[64] The broad narrative about cartography in early modern Europe proposes a shift from chorographic (i.e. pictorial) to ichnographic (i.e. scaled ground plan) maps, made with surveying equipment, initially a compass and measuring rod, later a theodolite.[65] A classic example is John Roque's twenty-four-sheet map of London, published in 1746, which was the most detailed map of the city in its own time and is still widely used by historians of the eighteenth century. Note, for example, its visibility in the digital humanities tool *Locating London Lives*. In this case, as explained in the project's mapping methodology statement, Roque's map has been manipulated, or 'warped', to fit onto

Figure 5.11 Embroidered cabinet showing scenes from the Story of Esther made by (an) unrecorded maker(s), after 1665.

the first reliable nineteenth-century Ordnance Survey map of London (1869–80).[66]

But interpretation of maps has moved far beyond establishing their precision and accuracy. Geographer and map historian J. B. Harley's influential essay, 'Deconstructing the Map', issued a provocation by looking at cartography through the lens of concepts from late twentieth-century philosophy, most notably the work of Jacques Derrida and Michel Foucault. This was intended to show how far 'maps are a cultural text' and restore to view the politics of maps and map-making.[67] In doing so, Harley argued that what maps looked like was meaningful: from decorative elements, like text, printed portraits and topographical views and cartouches (or elaborate frames) to the 'ethnocentrism' that 'has led historical societies to place their own territories at the centre of their cosmographies or world maps'.[68] Focusing on these issues was a deliberate challenge to the idea that maps are uncomplicated, neutral, 'scientific' representations of place – assumptions 'reinforced in the schoolroom and by popular culture' throughout the nineteenth and twentieth centuries to become part of 'the mind's furniture', in Tim Bryars's evocative phrasing.[69] While frequently cited as a key intervention, Harley's work has also been criticised for its sweeping, cross-geographical and cross-chronological conclusions and use of multiple, often contradictory, theoretical standpoints.[70] Subsequent work by other scholars has showed the importance of combining careful empirical research, including appropriate contextualisation, with the conceptual invigoration provided by tools from other disciplines to reveal the military, commercial, governmental and educational applications of mapping.[71]

Let us look at some examples. William Morgan's 1682 map of London (Figure 5.12) 'was based on the first detailed and truly scientific surveys of the City, Westminster and Southwark'.[72] But it was also a carefully constructed image reflecting a tumultuous moment in London's political history. Its publication came in the months after Charles II, 'emboldened by the promise of lavish French subsidies', had wrested power away from the Whigs, roughly equivalent to a modern political party, who were especially powerful in London.[73] Ultimately, the City of London, seen by the king and his advisors as a hot-bed of radical Whig activity, would forfeit its charter – and independence – on the grounds of sedition in 1683.[74] These circumstances make the map's design, especially the selection of inset images, significant. The spectacle of the deceased cartographer John Ogilby, on bended knee, presenting the subscription book of the survey to Charles II and his consort, Catherine of Braganza, and its carefully chosen landmarks, mostly relating to the Crown and Anglican establishment, 'were a wonderful manifestation of pomp and ultra-royalist sentiments'.[75] In a further spatial twist, a 1682 royal warrant urged representatives of England's political elites, including London's Lord Mayor, Court of Aldermen and livery companies, to display copies of the gargantuan map in their 'public rooms' as a show of loyalty.[76]

A hand-coloured manuscript map of Edo (Tokyo), copied from an early seventeenth-century printed version, provides another useful lesson.[77] It demonstrates the importance of not treating Western modes of representation as standards that were universally and uncritically adopted. In this case, the map's anonymous cartographer made careful use of colour coding, symbols and labels to distinguish between commercial districts, areas reserved for temples and shrines, and residential districts. The latter were further divided into high-status samurai neighbourhoods and those inhabited by so-called commoners. In this instance, mapping conventions reflected the extent to which Japanese

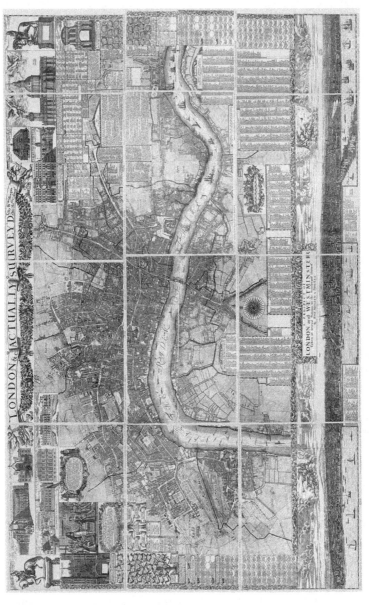

Figure 5.12 William Morgan, 'London &c. Actually Survey'd ...', 1682.

villages, towns and cities were deliberately planned to keep social groups separate. That the segregation was not total is suggested by the small shops located throughout the samurai districts on the map. In another interesting feature, while commoner streets are given names on the map, samurai neighbourhoods are not. Instead, individual parcels of land are labelled with the names of their high-ranking residents.[78]

Mapping has also been identified in scholarship as being fundamental to urban modernity itself. Attempts to modernise and reform the unruly cityscape in the mid-nineteenth century placed cartography at the fore, with Lynda Nead suggesting that maps 'made the modern city legible and comprehensible'. Nead argues that mapping reflected a way to reorder and control the urban fabric as part of a wider attempt to reform the industrial city: 'On the sheets of the map modernity could be absorbed in a single glance; gradient and flow could be plotted and progress could be planned. It was a reassuring sight, in contrast to the incoherent sensory experience of the street.'[79] This reading of maps and mapping helps to approach their evolution as a historically driven process that responded to wider urban development. For instance, the Ordnance Survey of London was introduced in 1851 and emerged from Edwin Chadwick's public health campaigns, reflecting a shift away from previous maps of the city that emphasised decorative or historical features of the city. Nead understands the Ordnance Survey and its focus on order, transparency and accuracy as a wider method of control and a 'determination to build a new social order'.[80] Patrick Joyce goes further, and views mapping as a method of control, particularly by the British state in Ireland, where it mapped fields and parishes for the first time. Joyce argues that this cartographic process ensured that 'what had earlier been relatively unfixed and subject to extra-governmental jurisdiction now became fixed by the state'.[81]

We might think about how Nead and Joyce's approaches offer a useful analytical framework when we look at the example of Charles Booth's cartographic surveys of London in 1889 and 1898–99 (Figure 5.13). Booth led a research team to explore urban life in detail, and colour-coded Ordnance Survey maps of London to present a visual account of poverty in the inner city. We can interrogate Booth's representation of the city and his poverty map of London by reflecting on the processes and aims that created this specific interpretation of urban space. How did Booth and his researchers' status as educated middle class shape their attitudes and readings of 'poor' spaces? To what extent was their view of poverty racialised? How far was this attempt at knowing

Figure 5.13 Sheet 5, East Central District 'Maps Descriptive of London Poverty', 1898–99.

about the poor part of a wider attempt to control them? What was the response of contemporaries to these maps, and how did it alter the way that more affluent urban visitors moved through the city – avoiding or exploring specific areas towards which Booth had drawn attention? This kind of approach can help to conceive of maps and the process of mapping not as a passive depiction of urban space but as an active force in shaping the construction, perception and engagement with the city's urban fabric more directly.

We can also question how the significant number of redevelopment plans produced for Western cities during the first half of the twentieth century can be understood as a method for reconceptualising urban space. The early twentieth century has been heralded as a 'golden age' for planning and civic culture in North America and Europe.[82] These ambitious and comprehensive plans usually encompassed bold and far-reaching redesigns of the city, prolific colourful images, statistical tables and other data, printed in hefty books and accompanied by publicity events and exhibitions. Frank Mort's assessment of the 1943 County of London Plan uses the concept of urban fantasy to think about its impact as an exercise that reimagined the city and allowed both the public and urban planners to invest in a powerful and influential vision of the future of London.[83] For Mort, the impressive plans for London by Patrick Abercrombie and the accompanying film and exhibition allowed the public to engage with and accept the images of a new, revitalised London that aimed to reflect the post-war political consensus – images that in the event were not realised. Similarly, James Greenhalgh has examined the post-war plans for Manchester and Hull, suggesting that they 'represent a time when British cities gazed at the limitless possibilities of the post-war world and imagined a better, healthier, fairer self'.[84] Yet Greenhalgh cautions that we should not oversimplify our reading of these types of sources, or their meaning for the conceptualisation of urban space. He argues that the 'multiple authorship, alongside tensions in the language used within the plans, means that any analysis of the content needs to pay close attention to the way the text interacts with images to gain a better understanding of the intentions behind the documents'.[85] This approach reminds us that these extensive plans and their ephemera need exploration in dialogue with each other and that we can read competing and even contradictory messages in their redesign of the city.

How do these important approaches help us to analyse other plans? Looking at the influential Chicago Plan of 1909 (Figure 5.14) shows

CXXXII. CHICAGO. VIEW, LOOKING WEST, OF THE PROPOSED CIVIC CENTER PLAZA AND BUILDINGS, SHOWING IT AS THE CENTER OF THE SYSTEM OF ARTERIES OF CIRCULATION AND OF THE SURROUNDING COUNTRY.
Painted for the Commercial Club by Jules Guerin.

Figure 5.14 Plate 132 from The Plan of Chicago, 1909: Chicago. View, Looking West, of the Proposed Civic Center Plaza and Buildings, Showing it as the Center of the System of Arteries of Circulation and of the Surrounding Country.

that we can analyse such plans holistically to ask how the images and extensive written explanations accompanying them may have set out a new or distinct conceptualisation of urban space. The extensive images illustrate an emphasis on beautifying and improving the city visually by recommending a significant enhancement of the lake area, rearranging streets and acquiring an outer park area. Yet, an analysis of the detailed explanation shows how the main focus of the plan was the manifestation of clear civic centre, to 'unify Chicagoans by inspiring a civic pride and loyalty in an urban society that provided health, prosperity, and happiness to all those fortunate enough to dwell there'.[86] The work of Daniel Burnham and his peers emerged from the 1900s in response to criticisms that planners had spent far too much time expanding the infrastructure of cities such as Chicago, to the detriment of the quality of urban life.[87] The Chicago Plan therefore prioritised the development of a thriving civic culture and emphasised the importance of developing cities along individual lines in order to engender a strong civic pride, arguing that it 'begets a spirit of loyalty and satisfaction on the part of the citizens'.[88] By focusing on what the plan said, as much as on what it offered visually, we can see that it attempted to shape and define a new urban culture that presented a more inclusive approach to space, complaining that 'the suburb is laid out by the speculative real estate agent who exerts himself to make every dollar invested turn into as many dollars as possible ... In ten years or less the dwellings are dropping to pieces; and the apartment houses, having lost their newness, become rookeries.'[89] Analysing the texts and images together, then, helps us to understand that the motivations behind urban planning might be more overtly political than is perhaps at first assumed, and reflective of specific historical moments that use the urban environment to make wider claims about the role of the local state and its citizens.

Other approaches might explore wider contemporary responses to plans, such as in the press, or their wider influence on other cities and the urban planning movement more generally. Comparative studies, like Tom Hulme's recent study of citizenship and civic education in Chicago and Manchester, are also fruitful and ripe for further development.[90] We might interrogate how such plans conceived of citizenship more specifically, and the implications of this for the relationship between space and identity. For instance, who was excluded and included in Burnham's plan? This is particularly significant in light of Chicago's problems with racism and the poverty experienced by its Black population. Perhaps the most important thing to bear in mind is that just because a plan for urban redesign was not fully realised, this does not mean that it cannot illuminate important historic processes and concepts relating to space, its perceived function and its relationship to those it was being redesigned for. As examples of how and why space was envisioned and imagined, its links to citizenship and ideas about who was included or excluded, unrealised plans provide historians of the built (and unbuilt) environment with rich source material to interrogate the relationship between space and identity.

Newspapers and images

Like plans, it is important to analyse newspapers and images holistically, thinking about their context, production and purpose. While the use

of keyword searches for online newspaper archival databases has revolutionised the way we can use the press for historical research, there
is a risk that we will examine articles in isolation of the wider press culture and reportage. For example, does the manner of representing new
buildings in certain newspapers change over time? One useful tactic
might be to count the number of times a local newspaper reports on
new buildings in a city or complains about a specific urban problem, in
order to chart how important – or 'newsworthy' – it deemed these issues
to be across a defined period of time. We can also address the materiality
of the press by thinking about who read it and the role of the newspaper in cultures of reading. It is also important to situate the newspaper
articles you are interested in within the wider culture of reportage:
where in the newspaper are these events or complaints reported?[91] What
types of news stories do they usually sit next to – world politics, quirky
human interest or specific local news sections? For instance, we might
note that the building of new department stores was considered newsworthy enough and of appropriate significance to warrant appearance
on the front pages of the local press, accompanied by large images and
situated next to world news events in the 1920s and 1930s. How far did
the representation of department stores change across the twentieth
century, and what might this tell us about the relationship between
local commercial culture, civic pride and the press? Reading memoirs
from relevant journalists or, where possible, accessing the archives of
the press, can uncover why the newspaper made important editorial
decisions that shaped its reportage of the urban environment and key
events within it. Can you make links between the editorial team of a
particular newspaper and the investors behind new buildings or certain
businesses? Taking this more comprehensive approach, rather than lim-
iting our assessment to the particular articles that mention the event or
issue we are most interested in, enables us to explore and explain the
wider historical processes and concerns that shaped and produced the
particular aspect of urban space that we are focusing on.

Similarly, when looking at images more directly, we should take a
broad perspective in our analysis. Penny Tinkler's insightful guide to
using photographs in historical research emphasises that we should
evaluate such images by **identifying** further details; **scrutinising** them;
considering their **materiality** as an object; undertaking **contextual**
research; and reflecting on their **meaning**.[92] Tinkler particularly stresses
the importance of contextual research because it illuminates 'the historically and culturally specific practices of making, presenting, circulating,

viewing and using photos in public and domestic contexts' and helps to ensure that the interpretation of the image reflects the historical period in which it was produced.[93] The insightful research by historians of crime such as Alexa Neale and Amy Bell uses crime scene photography to assess how visual clues, particularly those seen as an aberration against domestic space, were framed as evidence of an offence.[94] Bell examines photographs relating to cases of illegal abortion and analyses the images in conjunction with the wider court papers and police records, emphasising the framing of sites of suspected illegal abortions as risky and associated with dirt. Bell argues that 'the furnishings of rooms in crime scene photographs could also be read as depicting an implicit morality. Flats which were dingy, dirty and with visible signs of poverty were construed as backstreet lairs for unsafe abortionists, while signs of prosperity were seen as evidence of the abortionists' ill-gotten gains from exploiting vulnerable and desperate women.'[95] These kinds of approaches produce complex perspectives about space and perceived links with criminality by analysing crime photographs in relation to other historical sources.

A SENSORY APPROACH TO EVIDENCE OF URBAN SPACE AND BUILT ENVIRONMENTS

It can be tempting to presume that spatial histories are primarily concerned with what the built environment looked like and to privilege visual sources, such as the maps, plans and architectural designs that we have just discussed. However, as we saw in Chapter 3, thinking about the senses can be an exciting way to provide new and original insights into the experience of cities in the past. Remember that sight, sounds, smell, touch and even taste would have been historically specific experiences. For example, James Mansell argues that the interwar period was the 'age of noise' in Britain, as the experience of sound was subjected to processes of categorisation and intervention by the state.[96] An urban or spatial history through sound may, as Mansell's, take the approach of examining the ways in which certain sounds were characterised as undesirable and pathologised as harmful, and explore links to wider themes relating to public health or power. Alternatively, we might think about the relationship between musical culture and urban spaces. Scholarship on classical orchestral music and on jazz provides useful examples of how aural culture can help to explore the impact of immigration on urban space and culture, examples being the Manchester Hallé orchestra, a legacy of the city's German diaspora, and the significant role of the Harlem Renaissance in promoting African American arts in the 1920s and 1930s.[97] Listening to historical music (or to music historically) and considering the specific places in which it was performed may provide you with new or interesting ways to think about movement, cultures of listening and the role of sound in shaping, challenging or reproducing the spatial organisation of the built environment.

We can also think more widely about how particular spaces presented distinct sensory experiences that may have been linked to some of the wider thematic issues that we have already addressed, such as spatialised inequalities in class, gender and race. One example is found in the descriptions produced by colonisers, missionaries and philanthropists of the poor in nineteenth-century cities or of indigenous people in colonised spaces that emphasised their perceived physical dirtiness and unpleasant odours of their homes and bodies to convey white, middle-class horror and superiority. Philanthropic approaches to sanitising these bodies – often through the use of unpleasant methods of very hot water or astringent detergents – can be understood as a form of controlling and exerting power over these pathologised groups.[98] Concepts of touch and the emphasis on softness of hands have therefore been interpreted by historians as having racialised and class-based connotations linked to the sexual commodification of particular bodies.[99] Contrastingly, accounts of commercialised and transformed cityscapes have considered scent and smell as a way to understand the implications of the commodification of urban spaces. David Harvey's influential analysis of the 'Haussmannisation' of Paris drew on literature, including works by Gustave Flaubert, to claim that the portrayal of scents reflected wider contemporary ideas that the city had been reduced to a backdrop to human action, writing: 'the city becomes a dead object ... [and] entirely loses its character as a "sentient being" or "body politic"'.[100] These examples have largely used contemporary literary or visual sources to try to retrieve an understanding of how smell and touch reflected wider spatialised practices and power dynamics. If the senses are a new area of historical investigation for you, then reading some of these examples may provide ideas and opportunities for exploring urban space in new ways, or help you to appreciate the sheer range of historical sources you have at your fingertips (or at your nose, mouth or ears).

MATERIAL CULTURES

As with analysis of the urban built fabric, research involving material cultures requires you to be observant, looking carefully for clues relating to materials, designs, functions, users and meanings. It is worth reflecting on our terminology here. Historian Karen Harvey suggests that 'material culture' is an especially apposite term for this source material. She writes that 'unlike "object" or "artefact", "material culture" encapsulates not just the physical aspects of an object, but the myriad and shifting contexts through which it acquires meaning. Material culture is not simply objects that people make, use and throw away; it is an integral part of – and indeed shapes – human experience.'[101] This awareness of our language of description has methodological implications. As historians working with this primary source base, we are interested in investigating both 'material' and 'cultural' dimensions. In other words, our methodology should encompass both close observation of physical features of the thing (such as materials, dimensions, designs) and an attempt to situate it within networks of objects, people and places. Both avenues of enquiry are necessary in order to grasp the full meanings of 'material culture'.

Object viewing

When it comes to material cultures, rather than relying on pre-existing images and catalogue entries, it can be really helpful to view, or even handle, the object directly (in the previous chapter we considered how you might go about setting up an object viewing at a gallery or museum). First-hand observation of a particular artefact can bring to light important features of its making, uses and significances which might be overlooked if you were simply relying on existing object descriptions.

When you visit the storeroom or archive and encounter the object for the first time, bring a pencil and paper, and note down your immediate impressions of the object, as well as any questions which spring to mind. It might help also to take a quick impressionist sketch of the object – this practice can help to focus the mind on particular details. If you are allowed (and always check beforehand), bring a digital camera, or mobile phone, in order to take photographs. These should be for private use (for your own personal research purposes and understanding). If you want to put images online, or include them in a printed publication, you must seek specific permission from the institution. It might be worthwhile to take photos of particular details – such as patterns, signs of use or makers' marks.

The viewing appointment in the store or archive might also be the best opportunity to ask questions of the storeroom manager or curator. These professionals have extensive object and collections-based expertise and are thus best placed to answer your specific object queries. You might, for example, be curious as to how representative or unusual the object is (do they have many more things like it in the store, and, if so, can you view them too)? If the object has signs of use, are these patterns of wear usual, or atypical? Has the object undergone historical or recent conservation work? It is good practice, and entirely appropriate to reference in your dissertation or subsequent published work, any help or particular research steers which you received from museum professionals. It is also considerate to send a copy of your final dissertation or publication (in the first instance in electronic form) to curators or store managers who have provided guidance in the course of your material culture research. Your research and findings might inform future users of the collection.

In their guide on *History through Material Culture* Leonie Hannan and Sarah Longair offer specific advice on the physical examination of things.[102] Here we offer general guidance for close observation. There is no precise checklist of attributes that one has to pay attention to when encountering an object for the first time. The following questions are intended to be helpful pointers, to get the most out of the viewing experience (but this list is certainly not exhaustive, and you may have other object-based queries to consider).

- What materials is the object made from?
- What colours is it?
- What can you say about its construction or making?
- Who made it?
- When was it made?
- What are its distinguishing design features?
- What are its dimensions?
- Does it have any decoration?
- Does it have a particular function(s)?
- Can you discern any signs of use, wear or display?

- Are there any marks of adaptation or repair?
- Is this a highly distinctive object, or representative of a group of things?

Let us take a specific case study in order to make the process of close looking more concrete. Here we consider a drug jar, also known as a pharmacy jar. The object shown in Figure 5.15 comes from the collection of the V&A in London (museum number: 247–1866). A basic object description might run along the following lines:

A white earthenware drug jar covered with a tin glaze and painted in monochrome blue. Crafted by an unknown maker from Marieberg (Sweden), c. 1760–1765. It has several marks or inscriptions. In capital letters the drug name: P:S: STAPH:AGR (likely stands for 'pulvis simplex staphisagriae', simple powder of stavesacre); three crowns; MB in monogram; E.S in blue. The word 'Georgii' is painted on the reverse of the jar. Chipped glaze along base.

Figure 5.15 Swedish tin-glazed earthenware drug jar, c. 1760–65.

Your observations about this particular object, complemented by information gleaned from museum catalogues and specialist literatures (in this case of earthenware jars, and pharmacy jars more specifically), will form the basis of further routes of research enquiry. For this case study, the online museum record usefully informs us that this particular jar was made for the pharmacy of the Serafimer hospital in Stockholm. "Georgii" refers to John Christian Georgii who worked as pharmacist at the hospital from 1753.

Repeated observations

You will likely get only a single opportunity to view (or even handle) an object at very close quarters in museum or gallery stores, if at all. However, if the object is on public display this potentially gives you the opportunity to return to view it – even if behind a protective case – multiple times. But why would a researcher repeatedly return to look at a thing; is a single, thorough observation not enough? Perhaps not. The method of repetition, of repeatedly returning to look at the same object, can be highly beneficial for the student of material culture; it is also an established method extensively used by literary scholars and art historians in their close textual and visual analysis. This is not meant to be a process of simply reaffirming what you thought on the first material encounter. As historians Kate Smith and Leonie Hannan have written, in support of the return and repetition approach, 'By returning, researchers create an opportunity to move in directions that, at first, might not be apparent. At the very least, repetition can enhance critical insight about any assumptions that accompanied a first viewing.'[103] Repeated exposure to a particular object, or 'repeated acts of attention', might be especially beneficial to the historian engaging with material culture.[104] Since historians are typically trained in close textual analysis, and more rarely in the study of material culture, object-based research can feel a quite intimidating process at first. In this respect, regularly repeating the process of close material observation is an essential way of developing your skills in this methodology.

A final thought concerning object viewing within the context of a museum display or gallery: bear in mind that objects are often decontextualised when on display to the public. To return to the eighteenth-century drug jar example: when displayed in a museum of decorative arts (which highlights the most exemplary extant objects), it is very unlikely that this artefact will be surrounded by the types of things that inhabited an eighteenth-century pharmacy or hospital (drugs and medicines, instruments like mortars and pestles, furniture; not to mention medical practitioners and their patients). To build up a sense of the space within which the object operated requires you to undertake further research and contextualisation.

Further contextualisation: building layers of interpretation and meaning

Close (and perhaps repeated) object observation is but one aspect of your material culture analysis. It is essential also to investigate further contexts within which your object was (and is) situated. We should not see close observation and deeper contextualisation as separate processes but, rather, as mutually informing practices. A number of further frameworks for analysis might have been raised by your object examination (such as object design, ornamentation and symbolism, maker's marks and patterns of use). Here we are primarily interested in the spatial dimensions of historical research, and thus we might see this process as a means of locating material cultures within meaningful networks of things, human agents, built and natural environments. These networks might be very local, city-wide, or even on a global scale. This is not a quick task; it is a time-intensive methodology through which you gradually add layers of meaning to your historical analysis.

Let us return to the eighteenth-century earthenware drug jar from Marieberg in Sweden. Our observations and preliminary research have suggested a number of routes of analysis. We might first locate the object within collections of comparable drug jars, both within the V&A and in many other international museum collections besides. Our search of paper and online catalogues shows that there are thousands of extant examples of this type of object. Can we find jars decorated in a similar style? Did these jars contain similar substances? Can we find other examples of specifically named practitioners (who can in turn be located in particular apothecaries' shops, pharmacies or hospitals)? What can we discover about the output of earthenware drug jars from Marieberg more generally? Were they used locally; can we find examples of exported artefacts?

Another related line of enquiry would be to locate the drug jar within the eighteen-century pharmacy or hospital. Can we find any documentary sources (such as a will, inventory or tax document) relating to the pharmacist, John Christian Georgii, mentioned on the jar? Research on early modern apothecaries' shops has shown how 'one of the key devices that apothecaries used to address the problems of medical consumption [for example, the reliability and authenticity of the product] was the material form and arrangement of their shops', including the 'prominent displays of drug jars and collections of exotica'.[105] Are there any documentary or visual sources, such as building plans, for the eighteenth- or nineteenth-century Serafimer hospital in Stockholm (or other urban hospitals) that would enable a comparable exploration of material arrangements of space? What about primary evidence for the organisation of urban space within eighteenth-century Sweden more generally?

An additional research route could involve tracing the spatial networks of the drug originally contained within the pharmacy jar (were these substances local or imported, did they have global trajectories)? The market for drugs was vast in the early modern period and these substances were major, often highly valuable, commodities. Sources such as eighteenth-century herbals and books of recipes – pharmacopoeia – might help to provide context here. These routes of investigation are not exhaustive, but they offer a number of perspectives on starting from the material object and working out, taking in various spatial scales of analysis as you go.

IN SUMMARY

In this chapter we have outlined different approaches to the analysis of varied bodies of primary evidence. These approaches have all been adopted by historians undertaking spatial research. You may engage with one or more of these methodologies in the process of writing up your dissertation. This short account cannot possibly be comprehensive, and there are other routes which we have not discussed here which require highly specific technical training, such as HGIS.[106] Overall, we should be aware that reading about these approaches to primary evidence is just the first step. Practice and experience are essential to all skilled exercises. Historical analysis is a craft; it takes practice and dedication. In the final chapter we turn to the last stage of research – writing up your findings.

NOTES

1 A. Sharr (ed.), *Reading Architecture and Culture: Researching Buildings, Spaces and Documents* (London; New York: Routledge, 2012), p. 2.

2 H. Conway and R. Roenisch, *Understanding Architecture: An Introduction to Architecture and Architectural History*, 2nd edn (London: Routledge, 2005), p. 4.

3 W. Whyte, 'How do buildings mean? Some issues of interpretation in the history of architecture', *History and Theory*, 45:2 (2006), 153–77 (p. 154).

4 Gowing, 'The freedom of the streets', p. 143.

5 Whyte, 'How do buildings mean?', pp. 175–6.

6 Sharr, *Reading Architecture and Culture*, p. 8.

7 *Guide to Recording Historic Buildings* (London: Butterworth Architecture, 1990), p. 43, 'This process has been called "analytical recording" – it involves a close examination of the building, during which the building recorder seeks to disentangle its history using the many strands of evidence and the many analytical techniques available to him.'

8 A. B. Jacobs, *Looking at Cities* (Cambridge, MA; London: Harvard University Press, 1985), Chapter 3.

9 *Guide to Recording Historic Buildings*, pp. 73–5.

10 A. Willimott, *Living the Revolution: Urban Communes and Soviet Socialism, 1917–1932* (Oxford: Oxford University Press, 2017), Chapter 2.

11 Conway and Roenisch, *Understanding Architecture*, p. 61.

12 C. Otter, *The Victorian Eye: A Political History of Light and Vision in Britain, 1800–1910* (London: Chicago University Press, 2008); I. Pande, *Sex, Law, and the Politics of Age: Child Marriage in India, 1891–1937* (Cambridge: Cambridge University Press, 2020); F. Mort, *Capital Affairs: London and the Making of the Permissive Society* (New Haven, CT: Yale University Press, 2010).

13 J. M. Schwartz and T. Cook, 'Archives, records, and power: the making of modern memory', *Archival Science*, 2:1–2 (2002), 1–19 (p. 1). See also: T. Cook and J. M. Schwartz, 'Archives, records, and power: from (postmodern) theory to (archival) practice', *Archival Science*, 2:3–4 (2002), 171–85; J. Schwartz, '"Having new eyes": spaces of archives, landscapes of power', *Archivaria*, 61 (2006), 1–25.

14 See, in particular: M. Foucault, *The Archaeology of Knowledge*, trans. A. M. Sheridan Smith (New York: Pantheon, 1972); idem, *The Order of Things: An Archaeology of the Human Sciences* (London: Routledge, 2002).

15 See, for example: A. Blair and J. Milligan, 'Introduction', in A. Blair and J. Milligan (eds), 'Toward a cultural history of archives', special issue, *Archival Science*, 7:4 (2007).

16 A. Walsham, 'The social history of the archive: record-keeping in early modern Europe', *Past and Present*, Supplement 11 (2016), pp. 9–48 (p. 10). See also: Ogborn, 'Archive', pp. 88–98.

17 Ogborn, 'Archive', p. 89.

18 M. Ogborn, *Indian Ink: Script and Print in the Making of the English East India Company* (Chicago: University of Chicago Press, 2007).

19 *Ibid.*, p. xxii.

20 *Ibid.*

21 *Ibid.*, p. xxiii.

22 See, for example, the following brief issued by the Thamesmead Community Archive seeking to appoint (an) artist(s) to work with residents, past and present, to capture their memories and histories of Thamesmead: 'Thamesmead Community Archive: Artist Engagement Commission', *Thamesmead Now*, 2019, https://thamesmeadnow.org. uk/media/3062/archive-artist-engagment-brief.pdf [accessed 22 June 2021].

23 For a recent invigorating overview of the pitfalls of historical research in the age of digitisation, see: A. McShane, 'Digital broadsides: the upsides and the downsides', *Media History*, 23:2 (2017), 281–302.

24 Two classic ruminations on the material, emotional and sensory dimensions of archival research: A. Farge, *The Allure of the Archives*, trans. T. Scott-Railton (New Haven, CT: Yale University Press, 2013); C. Stedman, *Dust* (Manchester: Manchester University Press, 2001).

25 A. L. Stoler, *Along the Archival Grain: Epistemic Anxieties and Colonial Common Sense* (Princeton, NJ: Princeton University Press, 2010), pp. 1–53.

26 A. Ghosh, *Claiming the City: Protest, Crime, and Scandals in Colonial Calcutta, c. 1860–1920* (Oxford: Oxford University Press, 2016), p. 3.

27 *Ibid.*, p. 123.

28 See also: R. Guha, 'A colonial city and its time(s)', *The Indian Economic & Social History Review*, 45:3 (2008), 329–51; S. Baerjee, *The Parlour and the Streets: Elite and Popular Culture in Nineteenth Century Calcutta* (Chicago: University of Chicago Press, 2019).

29 F. Mir, *The Social Space of Language: Vernacular Culture in British Colonial Punjab* (Berkeley: University of California Press, 2010).

30 'The community', *The Times*, 7 July 1981, p. 5.

31 J. N. Brown, *Dropping Anchor, Setting Sail: Geographies of Race in Black Liverpool* (Princeton, NJ: Princeton University Press, 2005), p. 78.

32 N. Z. Davis, *Fiction in the Archives: Pardon Tales and Their Tellers in Sixteenth-Century France* (Stanford, CA: Stanford University Press, 1987). See also, R. B. Shoemaker, 'The Old Bailey proceedings and the representation

of crime and criminal justice in eighteenth-century London', *Journal of British Studies*, 47:3 (2008), 559–80.

33 Statement 27 October 1931. Manchester Quarter Sessions Depositions, Manchester Central Library: M116/2/5/65.

34 A. Kilday and D. Nash, 'Introduction', in Kilday and Nash (eds), *Law, Crime and Deviance Since 1700* (London: Bloomsbury, 2017), pp. 1–16 (p. 7).

35 G. Dawson, *Soldier Heroes: British Adventure, Empire and the Imagining of Masculinities* (London: Routledge, 1994); P. Summerfield, 'Culture and composure: creating narratives of the gendered self in oral history interviews', *Cultural and Social History*, 1:1 (2004), 65–93.

36 B. Hazley, 'Ambivalent horizons: competing narratives of self in Irish women's memories of pre-marriage years in post-war England', *20th Century British History*, 25:2 (2014), 276–304 (p. 281).

37 McKenna, 'The Development of Suburban Council Housing Estates in Liverpool Between the Wars', Appendix 13, Interview Number 4 (PhD thesis, University of Liverpool, 1986), p. 394.

38 *Ibid.*

39 *Ibid.*, Appendix 13, Interview Number 6, p. 405.

40 P. de la Ruffinière du Prey, *Sir John Soane: Catalogues of Archaeological Drawings in the Victoria and Albert Museum* (London: V&A, 1985), p. 27 [catalogue entry 2].

41 S. Barson (ed.), *Understanding Architectural Drawings and Historical Visual Sources* (Swindon: Historic England, 2019), p. 6.

42 A. Brennan, 'Measure, modulation and metadesign: NC fabrication in industrial design and architecture', *Journal of Design History*, 33:1 (2020), 66–82 (pp. 73–6).

43 *Ibid.*, p. 67.

44 R. Salzberg, *Ephemeral City: Cheap Print and Urban Culture in Renaissance Venice* (Manchester: Manchester University Press, 2015).

45 J. Auerbach, *The Great Exhibition of 1851: A Nation on Display* (New Haven, CT: Yale University Press, 1999), p. 32.

46 *Ibid.*, p. 32; B. Addis, 'The Crystal Palace and its place in structural history', *International Journal of Space Structures*, 21:1 (2006), 3–19 (p. 13).

47 Addis, 'Crystal Palace', p. 4.

48 Auerbach, *Great Exhibition*, p. 48.

49 Addis, 'Crystal Palace', p. 4.

50 Auerbach, *Great Exhibition*, p. 49; Addis, 'Crystal Place', p. 5.

51 J. Bryant (ed.), *Art and Design for All: The Victoria and Albert Museum* (London: V&A Publishing, 2011) pp. 114, 124.

52 Barson, *Understanding Architectural Drawings and Historical Visual Sources*, pp. 4–38.

53 *Ibid.*, p. 4.

54 See, for example, the model made to show the renewal of Thamesmead town centre that we considered in Chapter 5.

55 E. Tierney, 'Contested ideals: designing and making temporary structures for Louis XIV's entrée into Paris in 1660', in J. R. Mulryne, M. Shewring, K. De Jonge and R. M. Morris (eds), *Architectures of Festival in Early Modern Europe: Fashioning and Refashioning Urban and Courtly Space* (London: Routledge, 2018), pp. 139–67.

56 R. E. Zupko, *French Weights and Measures before the Revolution: A Dictionary of Provincial and Local Units* (Bloomington, IN: Indiana University Press, 1978), pp. 175–6.

57 A. Velkar, *Markets and Measurements in Nineteenth-Century Britain* (Cambridge: Cambridge University Press, 2012), p. 29.

58 K. Adler, *The Measure of All Things: The Seven-Year Odyssey and Hidden Error that Transformed the World* (New York: Free Press), p. 89.

59 Velkar, *Markets and Measurements*, p. 54; Adler, *Measure of All Things*, p. 317.

60 Velkar, *Markets and Measurements*, pp. 54–6.

61 Alder, *Measure of All Things*, pp. 315–17.

62 See discussion: A. Gerbino and S. Johnston, *Compass and Rule: Architecture as Mathematical Practice in England, 1500–1750* (New Haven, CT: Yale University Press, 2009), pp. 17–64.

63 The following discussion provides a rich overview of the multiple forms of visual representation with which early modern people made sense of their built world: M. Howard, *The Building of Elizabethan and Jacobean England* (New Haven, CT: Yale University Press, 2007), pp. 165–80.

64 For a good overview of the conventions of British maps and cartography, see: *Understanding Architectural Drawings and Historical Visual Sources*, pp. 39–54; 'Introduction to Maps and Plans', University of Nottingham Manuscripts and Special Collections, University of Nottingham, 2006, https://nottingham.ac.uk/manuscriptsandspecialcollections/researchguidance/mapsandplans/introduction.aspx [accessed September 2021].

65 J. A. Pinto, 'Origins and development of the ichnographic city plan', *Journal of the Society of Architectural Historians*, 35:1 (1976), 35–50; Barson, *Understanding Architectural Drawings and Historical Visual Sources*, pp. 39–54.

66 'Mapping Methodology', *Locating London's Past*, 2011, https://locatinglondon.org/static/MappingMethodology.html [accessed September 2021].

67 J. B. Harley, 'Deconstructing the map', in M. Dodge (ed.), *Classics in Cartography: Reflections on Influential Articles from Cartographica* (London: John Wiley, 2011 [1989]), pp. 273–94 (p. 281).

68 *Ibid.*, p. 279.

69 T. Harper (ed.), *Maps and the 20th Century: Drawing the Line* (London: British Library, 2016), p. 99.

70 See for example a recent special issue that covers in depth the main critiques of 'Deconstructing the map': R. Rose-Redwood (ed.), 'Deconstructing the map: 25 years on', *Cartographica: The International Journal for Geographic Information and Geovisualization*, 50:1 (2015) 1–8.

71 S. Elden, *The Birth of Territory* (Chicago: University of Chicago Press, 2013); M. H. Edney, *Mapping an Empire: The Geographical Construction of British India, 1765–1843* (Chicago: University of Chicago Press, 1998); 'Deconstructing the map: 25 years on', *Cartographica*; T. K. Mondal, 'Mapping India since 1767: transformation from colonial to postcolonial image', *Miscellanea Geographica: Regional Studies on Development*, 23:4 (2019), 210–14.

72 P. Barber and T. Harper, *Magnificent Maps: Power, Propaganda and Art* (London: British Library, 2010), p. 132. See also: R. Hyde, 'London actually survey'd by William Morgan, 1682', in A. Saunders (ed.), *The A to Z of Charles II's London 1682* (London: London Topographical Society), pp. 7–10.

73 P. Barber, 'Maps and politics: London &c. actually survey'd and a large and accurate map of the City of London', in A. Saunders (ed.), *A to Z of Charles II's London* (London: London Topographical Society), p. 2.

74 T. Harris, *Restoration: Charles II and His Kingdoms, 1660–1685* (London: Penguin, 2006), pp. 296–7.

75 Barber and Harper, *Magnificent Maps*, p. 132; Hyde, 'London actually survey'd', pp. 13, 5.

76 Hyde, 'London actually survey'd', pp. 8–9.

77 T. Tetsuo, 'The urban landscape of early Edo in an East Asian context', in K. Wigen, F. Sugimoto and C. Karacas (eds), *Cartographic Japan: A History in Maps* (Chicago: University of Chicago, 2016), pp. 75–80 (pp. 75–6). This map is viewable as part of the online exhibition, 'Edo Tokyo. Digital Museum': www.library.metro.tokyo.lg.jp/portals/0/edo/tokyo_library/english/modal/index.html?d=5389# [accessed 4 June 2021].

78 R. P. Toby, 'Spatial visions of status', in *Cartographic Japan: A History in Maps* (Chicago: University of Chicago, 2016), pp. 78–80.

79 Nead, *Victorian Babylon*, p. 13.

80 *Ibid.*, p. 22.

81 Joyce, *The Rule of Freedom*, p. 45.

82 C. S. Smith, *The Plan of Chicago: Daniel Burnham and the Remaking of the American City* (Chicago: University of Chicago Press, 2006), p. 11; J. W. Reps, *The Making of Urban America: A History of City Planning in the United States* (Princeton, NJ; Oxford: Princeton University Press, 1992), p. 517.

83 F. Mort, 'Fantasies of metropolitan life: planning London in the 1940s', *Journal of British Studies*, 43:1 (2004), 120–51 (p. 124).

84 J. Greenhalgh, *Reconstructing Modernity: Space, Power and Governance in Mid-Twentieth-Century British Cities* (Manchester: Manchester University Press, 2017), p. 29.

85 *Ibid.*, p. 53.

86 Smith, *The Plan of Chicago*, p. 103.

87 *Ibid.*, p. 9.

88 D. H. Burnham, *Plan of Chicago* (Chicago: Chicago Commercial Club, 1909), p. 29.

89 *Ibid.*, p. 33.

90 T. Hulme, *After the Shock City: Urban Culture and the Making of Modern Citizenship* (London: Boydell and Brewer, 2019).

91 For a useful example of this approach, see J. J. Sharpe, 'Reporting crime in the north of England eighteenth-century newspaper: a preliminary investigation', *Crime, Histoire & Sociétés / Crime, History & Societies*, 16:1 (2012), 25–45.

92 P. Tinkler, *Using Photographs in Social and Historical Research* (London: SAGE, 2013), p. 19.

93 *Ibid.*, p. 24.

94 A. H. Bell, 'Abortion crime scene photography in metropolitan London 1950–1968', *Social History of Medicine*, 30:3 (2017), 661–84; A. Neale, *Photographing Crime Scenes in Twentieth-Century London: Microhistories of Domestic Murder* (London: Bloomsbury, 2020).

95 Bell, 'Abortion crime scene photography', p. 675.

96 J. G. Mansell, *The Age of Noise in Britain: Hearing Modernity* (Urbana, Chicago and Springfield: University of Illinois Press, 2017).

97 A. Kidd, *Manchester* (Edinburgh: Edinburgh University Press, 2002), pp. 160–2; T. Gioia, *The History of Jazz* (Oxford: Oxford University Press), pp. 84–118; W. Martin, 'Jazz and the Harlem Renaissance', in R. Farebrother and M. Thaggert (eds), *A History of the Harlem Renaissance* (Cambridge: University of Cambridge Press, 2021), pp. 345–60.

98 E. Moss, C. Wildman, R. I. Lamont and L. Kelly, 'Rethinking child welfare and emigration institutions, 1870–1914', *Cultural & Social History*, 14 (2017), 647–68; L. Murdoch, *Imagined Orphans: Poor Families, Child Welfare, and Contested Citizenship in London* (New Brunswick, NJ:

Rutgers University Press, 2006), pp.33–6; K. van Dijk, 'Soap is the onset of civilization', in K. van Dijk and J. Gelman Taylor, *Cleanliness and Culture: Indonesian Histories* (Leiden: Brill, 2011), pp. 1–40.

99 A. McClintock, *Imperial Leather: Race, Gender and Sexuality in the Colonial Contest* (London: Routledge, 1995) pp. 99–101; Z. Magubane, *Bringing the Empire Home: Race, Class and Gender in Britain and Colonial South Africa* (London: Chicago University Press, 2003).

100 D. Harvey, *Paris, Capital of Modernity* (London: Routledge, 2003), p. 88.

101 Harvey, *History and Material Culture*, pp. 30–1.

102 Hannan and Longair, *History through Material Culture*, pp. 122–5.

103 K. Smith and L. Hannan, 'Return and repetition: methods for material culture studies', *Journal of Interdisciplinary History*, 48:1 (2017), 43–59 (p. 52).

104 *Ibid.*, p. 47.

105 P. Wallis, 'Consumption, retailing, and medicine in early-modern London', *The Economic History Review*, New Series, 61:1 (2008), 26–53 (p. 27).

106 Methods and approaches specific to HGIS (such as turning primary evidence into a GIS database), are discussed in detail in: I. Gregory, D. DeBats and D. Lafreniere (eds), *The Routledge Companion to Spatial History* (London: Taylor and Francis, 2018).

RECOMMENDED READING

S. Barson (ed.), *Understanding Architectural Drawings and Historical Visual Sources* (Swindon: Historic England, 2019).

H. Conway and R. Roenisch, *Understanding Architecture: An Introduction to Architecture and Architectural History*, 2nd edn (London: Routledge, 2005).

E. Edwards, *Photographs and the Practice of History: A Short Primer* (London: Bloomsbury, 2022).

Guide to Recording Historic Buildings (London: Butterworth Architecture, 1990).

A. Higgott and T. Wray (eds), *Camera Constructs: Photography, Architecture and the Modern City* (Aldershot: Ashgate, 2012).

L. Jordanova, *The Look of the Past: Visual and Material Evidence in Historical Practice* (Cambridge: Cambridge University Press, 2012).

M. Ogborn, 'Archive', in J. Agnew and D. N. Livingstone (eds), *The Sage Handbook of Geographical Knowledge* (London: Sage, 2011), pp. 88–98.

A. Sharr (ed.), *Reading Architecture and Culture: Researching Buildings, Spaces and Documents* (London; New York: Routledge, 2012).

P. Tinkler, *Using Photographs in Social and Historical Research* (London: SAGE, 2013).

✤ 6 ✦

WRITING UP FINDINGS

INTRODUCTION

Writing is an essential part of the historian's craft. It is primarily through writing that you communicate your ideas and research findings to a broader audience. For an undergraduate or master's dissertation this audience will likely be your supervisors and examiners; but, as is suggested below, the very best student research might also reach a larger public readership through publication. There are many specific guides on writing styles and techniques, and we will not attempt to reinvent the wheel here. In brief, writing style is highly personal. As a humanities student you will develop your own unique writing habits over the course of your studies, and for most degree programmes the final-year dissertation is the masterpiece of historical writing.

The art of concise and persuasive writing requires practice. Thus, while your lecturers and supervisors (and perhaps study skills tutors) can help you develop your writing skills through feedback on essays and drafts, effective writing techniques come, ultimately, through practice. When you are reading history books and journals, and indeed authors in general whom you admire, pay close attention to the writing techniques they employ. As a general rule of thumb, short sentences are more effective than long, meandering statements. Avoid the temptation to pack multiple arguments, ideas, or historical protagonists into a single sentence (or indeed paragraph). In crafting spatial histories informed by theoretical writings, avoid using terminology which the average undergraduate reader would not understand. If you must use specific theoretical language (for example, philosopher Henri Lefebvre's 'spatial triad', which we have encountered multiple times in this research guide), make sure that you explain your terms thoroughly. A glossary of terms might also be a helpful addition to the work.

You should assume an intelligent readership, but one that might also lack specific knowledge or spatial vocabulary relating to your dissertation theme.

For most historians, research and writing are not really separate processes. It is through writing down our ideas and research findings that arguments are fully formulated and a structure to our work emerges. Initially this writing might be in the form of notes, which will develop into a more coherent body of writing over time. It can be very helpful to keep a separate ideas document from the beginning of the research process, into which you place any productive thoughts – relating to primary sources, secondary reading, useful theorists or dissertation structure – that spring to mind. Not only will this stimulate your creative thinking but it will also ensure that when you begin more advanced writing you will not be facing the rather intimidating blank page. Thus, while you will likely have an intensive period of archival research towards the beginning of your dedicated dissertation time, it is best to start writing as soon as your ideas on the topic begin to formulate. Having a plan in place for your dissertation before you begin writing up in full is really important too. This plan or structure should not be excessively rigid; you should have flexibility to move material around at a later stage. But it is very helpful at least to have a sense of which secondary and primary materials might belong in which sections of your work early on.

Even for experienced professionals, the process of writing almost always takes longer than anticipated. Hence, it is good practice at the beginning of the dissertation period to establish a time frame of work – in other words, to set a date by which you begin writing. You don't want to put yourself under unnecessary pressure by leaving all your writing close to the deadline set by your institution. Even if you have not finished absolutely all your reading around the topic, it is helpful to get words on the page (and you can always improve syntax and add in further references later). You might begin by drafting a secondary literature review on the theme under analysis – as we discuss in more depth below, almost all dissertations include a detailed exploration of relevant historiography. Alternatively, if you are making use of particular case studies (say of material culture or the built environment, or a specific body of visual or archival sources), you might begin the writing process by summarising your findings so far. Some writers find it helpful to use certain targets to stimulate the creative process. For example, you could try writing a set number of words (say 500–700 words each day). Alternatively, you might write for concentrated blocks of time (roughly thirty–forty minutes) without any external distractions. The key to setting targets, though, is to be realistic – you will only feel demoralised if you set an unrealistic word count.

The submitted dissertation will not be your first draft. No historian or author writes a final draft as a first draft. Making multiple edits to your text as it develops is a critical part of the writing process (and this is also why you should leave ample time for writing in your dissertation time frame). While you are obviously the sole author of your dissertation it can be exceptionally helpful to get alternative perspectives on drafts as your writing progresses – your readers might be your university tutors, peers or friends. Of course, you do not have to incorporate all your readers' suggestions.

ORGANISING YOUR MATERIAL

By this point, you will have scoped the secondary literature, framed your research questions, chosen an appropriate methodology and located and analysed your sources. With this time and energy in mind, you owe it to your research to organise your material so that you are presenting your findings clearly and convincingly. Key throughout is remembering your reader, who may not know your subject as well as you do. At each stage, reflect on what is needed to convey what is exciting and original about your work.

The introduction is the first piece of text your reader will encounter and, in many ways, is the most important part of the dissertation. From beginning to end, the introduction does the job of setting out your project and making a case for why it needs to be done. This means showing the existence of the gap in knowledge that you propose to address and, more importantly, demonstrating why this is worth doing. It is not enough to state that something has never been done before. There are plenty of projects that fulfil these criteria but do not deserve your reader's attention (e.g. number of men called Henry born in 1808). Unless you can bring to bear other contexts justifying the urgency of the enquiry – how it adds to knowledge, how it makes us think differently – step away from the project or, less dramatically, reconfigure its presentation! Read the introductions to academic writing, from single-author books (or 'monographs') to journal articles, and you will soon notice the 'genre rules'. Readers, including your supervisors and examiners, will expect to see something that includes:

- **An overview of relevant secondary literature(s) on your topic:** Who and what have you read in doing your research? What are the main debates within published work? What are you convinced by? Where does the published literature fall short? What is the logical gap in knowledge?

You will also need to explain to your reader how you propose to address this gap in the existing literature and why your chosen approach is most appropriate. This part of the discussion will cover:

- **Research questions:** What are the two or three main questions that your project pursues? Are there any sub-questions?
- **Methodology:** What methods and/or theoretical approaches will you use to analyse your primary sources? Why are these most useful for the kind of history that you are doing? Is it your choice of methodology that makes your project original?
- **Primary sources:** What main types of sources does your project interrogate? Where are your sources located? What size of sample do you look at? Are there any potential drawbacks to the sources you have chosen to look at? How do you propose to deal with these? Is it your selection of primary sources that makes your project original?

From here, and again with a view to helping your reader to navigate the discussion that follows, your introduction should finish with a brief outline of your structure. In a long essay, this will include a few sentences on your main headings; in longer pieces of writing, like PhD dissertations or books, you should set out briefly what each of your chapters deals with and how this contributes to the research project as a whole. Irrespective of the type of output, this overview should move beyond being descriptive, to give the reader a clear sense of why this choice of subjects and arrangement of material is best suited to communicating the key point(s) of your argument. Again, it will be helpful to have a look at a few introductions, either in work produced by other students (most universities will keep excellent dissertations on file for you to reference) or in published books and articles. In addition to getting a feel for the 'genre rules', this practice should also develop your sense of how writers use the introduction to draw readers in by means of illustrative case studies and striking opening phrases.

But the introduction alone is not enough to make your argument clear, coherent and transparent. You also need to think carefully about how to **structure** your material. Choosing how to arrange your written work under headings or in the form of chapters can be frustrating and time consuming. But it is also one of the most creative parts of the research process, providing an opportunity to reflect on the storytelling that is integral to writing history. Look at what other students have done, and reread published work that you have previously enjoyed. During your reading, keep these questions in mind:

- What is each chapter about?
- How does the writer divide the broader topic into focused 'chunks'?
- How does each chapter begin and end?
- In what order does the author introduce information? How similar is this to other texts you have read?
- How is chronology used as an organising principle?
- How does the writer build their argument across the written piece as a whole? What are the thematic (or other) links between each chapter?
- What kinds of supporting visual and diagrammatic evidence appear in the text? Where is this situated in relation to discussion?

Much of what we have touched on so far is applicable to many different kinds of history writing. But what matters when writing spatial histories? Most likely, your project will be spatial because it does one of two things. First, it may **intervene in an existing spatial history or history of the built environment** by drawing on less familiar source material and/or a distinctive method/theory. Here, we might think back to the essay about the Red Road housing estate in Glasgow discussed in Chapter 1. This adopts an innovative 'birth and death' structure, informed by the science and technology studies concept of 'black-boxing', in order to rethink the relationship between technological, social and cultural drivers in the development of modern high-rise housing.[1] Thinking beyond the specifics of this theoretical framing, your chapters could be determined by different phases in the design, construction and use of a particular building or built environment, as informed by bigger themes or ideas that your argument engages. Sarah Longair's article looking at the deployment of architectural forms and styles in 'early colonial Zanzibar (1890–1925)' shows how built environments were critical sites of colonial entanglement in British-ruled East Africa.[2] This argument, which turns on the reciprocal interaction between local circumstances (skills, labour, materials, environments), issues of style and imperial networks, is reiterated by Longair's structure. She begins with a broad introduction to architecture as a strategy of colonial government, looking in particular at 'the classical in the Colonial World', before moving on to a series of well-chosen case studies. The latter are rooted in the career of John Sinclair, a colonial officer/amateur architect, and allow the article to compare buildings in different East African cities and, crucially, diverse architectural styles. Longair's structure allows the reader to accrue the broader historiographical and case study-focused knowledge that is needed to substantiate her core propositions: that scholars need to be aware of the multiplicity of colonial architectures that co-existed at any one time and, in turn, to be sensitive to what these can tell us about the specific relationships between local situations and imperial governments.

The second broad approach **focuses on spatial issues and/or the built environment in order to shift thinking in another type of historical debate**. Joy Palacios's article about the burial of actors in seventeenth-century Paris considers the tense relationships between the Church and theatre in early modern France, a subject previously explored through analysis of literary texts.[3] Instead, Palacios focuses on the parish of Saint-Sulpice in Paris, using a spatial and performance-led approach, to reveal how fractious theological debates impacted on lives lived in the early modern city. Beginning with the arresting scene of a famous actress being denied a Christian burial, she introduces relevant ideological and theological concepts, establishes the main players in the Church and theatre in and around Saint-Sulpice and draws attention to her main methodological shift – focused attention to 'the way in which priests and actors used resources like gesture, ritual objects and the city streets to negotiate the theatre's rightful place in public life'.[4] Each section that follows expands on, in turn, the social, spatial and ritual dimensions of the relationships between Church and theatre. Specificity is key: the article is rooted in the spatial proximity of the parish church of Saint-Sulpice and Paris's best-known theatres, including the Comédie-Française.[5] This builds a keen sense throughout of places, populations and spatial practices coming into contact and, on occasion, conflict. Decisions about structure and storytelling not only move theological debates off the page but build towards Palacios's conclusion: that Paris was shaped by multiple, sometimes rival, 'performance regimes', each with its own spatial and spectacular qualities.[6]

Across these projects, a shift in focus or approach provides a route into the bigger questions of history: what we think about historical phenomena (such as change and continuity, cause and consequence, everyday experience, cultural interaction) and/or historical themes (class, race, gender, power ...). Whatever your point of entry or main focus, you will seek to show how attention to **where** allows us to think differently about how and why the past is meaningful. Your structure should help your reader to grasp this originality and significance. But there is no 'right' structure for your spatial history: there will be more than one way in which you can effectively communicate your research. While by no means exhaustive, these prompts could be useful to keep in mind:

- What does the reader need to know in order to fully grasp your argument? What do they need to know from the beginning? What can be held back until later?
- Are you making explicit use of a theoretical framework or methodology from another discipline? If so, you may need to dedicate an early section/chapter to setting up these ideas. Could (one of) its key concept(s) be used to structure your work?
- Is there a key theme at the heart of your project? How do you propose to explain this to your reader so they have enough information about its historical, historiographical and (if relevant) theoretical significance? How might this theme inform your decisions about structure?
- What scale(s) of place, space or built environment does the project deal with? Could these scale(s) help shape your chapter headings?
- Does your project deal with multiple nodes on a network? Where are these? Could you use your structure and headings to establish and explain your interpretative frame of analysis? Can you 'follow' people, (an) object(s) or idea(s) to tease out the character and reciprocal relationships underpinning the network?
- Does your research foreground the spatial practices of a particular individual or group of people? Could you use these to 'tell the story' of your argument?
- Have you uncovered a compelling episode or especially juicy source during your research? Could this be used to start or even structure your written piece?
- How might you use comparison to communicate and structure your argument? Does your project deal with spatial practice in different places? Are you looking at the differences between an urban environment and its representation in texts, visual or material sources?

Are you comparing different kinds of spatial practices? Or the same spatial practices used by different sorts of people?

In addition to a sound introduction and careful structuring, your argument will be reinforced through adept deployment of your supporting evidence. This includes academic referencing, your footnotes or endnotes and bibliography. As the bedrock of scholarly writing, you should leave plenty of time to do this work, which includes reading properly the guidelines provided by your university. Referencing matters, because it ensures that your work is convincingly grounded in evidence and transparent, allowing readers to follow your research trail, should they want to. Turning specifically to histories that concern urban space and built environments, it is likely that you will use visual and material sources, including extant built environments, to make your case. Using maps, plans, drawings, designs and photographs as part of your argument deserves careful thought. Visual evidence, employed as illustrations, should not be an afterthought but a specific and integral part of your argument. How, where and why you deploy this material reflects the seriousness with which you take the full gamut of spatial primary sources in your work. Critical is the selection of appropriate historical materials, trying where possible not to use anachronistic visual materials as illustrations – for example, a twentieth-century design drawing to make a point about medieval building practices – and using apt contextualisation. At this point in your project, it may be useful to look back to the discussions of visual sources and the issues raised by representation in other parts of this book.

For these reasons, it is worth keeping in mind a combination of mutually reinforcing practical and intellectual concerns:

- Make sure that your images, most likely digital files, are **high-enough resolution** to print as clear, sharp illustrations that allow readers to take note of the details that you wish them to pay attention to.
- **Size matters:** There is nothing more frustrating for a reader than poring over a postage-stamp-sized reproduction of a nuanced, well-populated painting or print.
- **Place images carefully** within your discussion. Inset your illustrations in your text, adjacent or near to relevant analysis, or place all your visual materials in a separate section after your text. Irrespective of what you decide to do (or what you are advised to do by university guidelines), adopt a consistent policy that makes your written work as

user friendly as possible. This includes precise use of figure numbers so that it is apparent which items of visual evidence your discussion deals with at any given time.

- Precision and accuracy are key when **captioning** images and compiling lists of illustrations. Most captions will include most of the following information, but do check your university guidelines for confirmation of the expected order:
  - figure number
  - name/title/description of object
  - maker (if known)
  - date of production
  - geographical origin
  - materials
  - techniques
  - dimensions
  - accession number (if from an institution)
  - location and/or credit line for institution and/or photographer.

PUBLICATION

It is through publication – primarily in the form of books, chapters in edited volumes and journal articles – that scholars communicate their arguments and research findings to the wider world. Publishing is an essential element of an academic career, a critical requirement of getting hired as a university lecturer. But, of course, historians seek to publish their work not simply because it is central to their job prospects but more fundamentally because engaging in debate and furthering knowledge are at the core of academic life. For an early-career historian, getting published, seeing your work in print and perhaps having readers directly engage with your research are some of the most exhilarating and rewarding aspects of the often challenging academic career path.

It is not unusual in the UK for the very best MA dissertations, or even exceptional undergraduate research projects, to be published in leading journals. Towards the end of a PhD, doctoral candidates frequently adapt a particular dissertation chapter for publication as a journal article or book chapter (attempting to condense the full research findings of a doctoral thesis into a single article is a less successful strategy). If you receive very positive feedback from your examiners and supervisors on your research project, then publication is a route well worth considering. In their length and relatively focused nature, master's dissertations can be well suited for adaptation into published form.

You might choose to publish your work as a book chapter in an edited volume, or as an article in a specific academic journal. Word counts vary, but published pieces usually range from 7,000 to 10,000 words, inclusive of footnotes (journal articles are usually towards the end of this threshold). Edited collections of essays are typically focused on a particular theme and are often the outcome of a conference or seminar panel. You might be asked directly by the volume's editors to contribute, and the editors will be principally (though not solely) responsible for communicating deadlines and carrying out a review of your work once it is submitted (a process that is referred to as 'peer review').

To get your work published as a journal article, especially if it is a stand-alone piece, will take rather more personal initiative. It is also, arguably, the more prestigious route to pursue. First, you must identify a suitable home for your work. Which journals do you read frequently and admire? What are the mission statements of your preferred journals – and do your research focus and themes fit with this? Do your academic supervisors have any sage advice about where your work might be best placed? Spatially themed or informed historical research might be placed in a history-specific journal, but your proposed article might also be a good fit with a more theoretically minded publication or a journal which is explicitly interdisciplinary in its outlook. Journals require that work is original (in other words, it largely does not appear in any other published form), and it is conventional for work to be submitted to only one journal at a time. The particular process for submission and review will be outlined on the website of an academic journal. But in general terms, once you have submitted a piece to be reviewed on an online portal it will be read by the editor(s) and, if of suitable quality, sent out to review by at least two experts in the field. These reviewers, whose identities remain anonymous to the author, will submit their critical (and, ideally, constructive) comments to the editor, who will decide if the proposed article should be accepted and published, accepted with corrections (meaning that you need to make minor or substantial changes to the text in order for it to be suitable for publication) or rejected.

If you have made use of images and material culture in the course of your research – as we have seen, many spatial histories effectively do so – then you may wish to include these in your published work. Each journal will have policies on the number of images in colour, and black and white, that can be included per article. It will be your responsibility to seek permission to use each image and to pay any related costs. Hannan and Longair's *History through Material Culture* provides very useful advice on seeking institutional permissions for image publication.[7]

PUBLIC ENGAGEMENT

Let us finish by looking briefly at how you might disseminate your research through public-facing outputs. As ever, our focus is on spatial histories, but the issues raised here have wider application to other types of study. Indeed, a major context for this discussion is the increasing emphasis in the UK on academic research demonstrating its value to society and the economy – what is broadly termed 'impact'.[8] Some readers of this book will wish to pursue academic careers. Designing research projects that have impact built in from the beginning and communicating research appropriately for a range of audiences are key skills to develop; it is never too early to learn how to do this effectively. These skills are also vital for those who wish to work beyond academia, especially in public history, cultural and heritage sector roles. Most importantly, this work can be creative and fulfilling. Rather than approaching public engagement, in its many forms, as an opportunity to broadcast your research findings, think about how it can be harnessed to develop your ideas and stretch you outside of disciplinary and professional comfort zones. Most notably, the process is always collaborative, either because the end point is a project created with other people or because your thinking is refined through the questions you are asked by your 'publics' and by the knowledge and experience that they will invariably bring to bear on your work.

Historians at all stages in their careers are choosing to **blog research**, whether through personal or themed blogs or as part of research project pages, such as the V&A's Architectural Models in Context project. Good blog writing relies on the author's ability to distil complex ideas so they are interesting and intelligible to a good general reader. Blogging will push you to reflect on the most important questions and issues raised by your research. You will find yourself wondering how to hook readers from the first sentence, how to communicate clearly and concisely and, above all, how to convey your arguments authoritatively without having the mechanics of scholarly writing at your disposal. Research blogging is not without risks. You do not necessarily want to share all your research gems on a blog without publishing elsewhere first. While transparency and accountability are the core of scholarly best practice, not all historians are as careful as they should be with proper attribution of blog posts. With this in mind, rather than setting out the detail of your evidence, think about how you can use blogging and, in particular, the experience it provides in writing for general readers. For example, you might choose to share the headlines of your research process (archives and collections visited, methodological conundrums), or to highlight where issues raised in your project have contemporary resonances.

The following are examples of websites and blogs focusing on spatial histories and/or histories of urban built environments.

- Stanford Spatial History Project: http://web.stanford.edu/group/spatialhistory/cgi-bin/site/index.php
- Architectural Models in Context: Creativity, Skill and Spectacle: www.vam.ac.uk/blog/projects/architectural-models-network

Other online outputs are even more explicitly collaborative. Throughout this book we have made reference to a wide range of **digital research outputs**, some using GIS, and many of which are open access, that is to say, freely accessible online. These are truly interdisciplinary research outputs, requiring historians to develop new skills in using GIS software and, in some instances, computer coding. More often, historians will work with researchers and technicians with distinctive disciplinary and professional backgrounds, from software development and user testing to front-end design. Many HGIS projects also make use of familiar 'everyday' mapping technologies, including Google Maps and Google Earth.[9] For instance, the project Lynching in America, which brings to light stories of the United States' history of racial injustice, has produced an interactive map of racial terror lynchings carried out between 1877 and 1950. This output is a collaboration between the Equal Justice Initiative (an enterprise which challenges racial inequality and works to end mass incarceration) and Google. This scenario of collaboration and cooperation is the norm for many research outputs beyond the academy, where end points are the result of more than one strand of knowledge and expertise, draw on the efforts of many types of people and demand effective, open-minded communication. Your project may push beyond a tight group of collaborators to embrace a crowd-sourced element that encourages the public to map personal and/or subject-specific histories. One such example is the community-generated project Queering the Map, which captures 'queer moments' in the history of Montreal. In this case, the online project is a response to the disappearance, accelerated by gentrification and rising property prices, of LGBTQ+ spaces tied to 'concrete geographical locations'.[10]

Examples of relevant open-access digital projects:

- Artists in Paris: Mapping the 18th-century Art World: www.artistsinparis.org/about.html
- Layers of London: www.layersoflondon.org/
- Interactive Map of the Gulag: https://gulagmap.ru/
- Lynching in America: https://lynchinginamerica.eji.org/explore

You may even have the opportunity to take your research out into the very places and buildings that inspired it in the form of **a guided walk or tour** for a local or university history group or a relevant specialist society (e.g. groups interested in particular periods of architecture and/or building). Less formally, you might propose a tour linked to your research for a university peer group and tutors. Comparatively light touch from an organisational perspective, reconfiguring your research as a tour of a particular built environment has the potential to be an enormously satisfying experience. You will certainly enhance your presentation skills and boost your confidence by conveying what is urgent and exciting about your research to people who are not necessarily experts in your subject. But remember, tour groups are often self-selecting. Participants will come with a genuine interest in your topic and, more often than not, related knowledge which they will be keen to share. Like other forms of public engagement, this activity requires that you contend with practicalities (e.g. 'How many "stops" should I include?' 'What's my "Plan B" if the weather is terrible?') as much as with issues of content and communication (e.g. 'What are my best "stories"?' 'How can I communicate inclusively?').

Through preparing your tour, you will sharpen your skills as a historian of urban space and the built environment. Preparations will build on repeated visits to your site, informed by close observation and attempts to 'read' what is extant in the built environment, including materials, structural and stylistic features, other buildings/structures in the vicinity, scale and dimensions. In turn, you will draw on your wider contextual knowledge to tease out what is no longer there or to restore to view features (e.g. historic street plans) that were subsumed in later developments. Invariably, your framing will be informed by comparisons – between urban environments and their presentation in visual and textual forms, and between modes of representation. Tours can also animate buildings and built environments by foregrounding issues of historical spatial practices by, for example, focusing on the routes taken by individuals or groups in a particular city and/or for specific purposes, or by attending to what were considered to be shared or restricted places within buildings or wider urban environments. Finally, the practice of walking *between* matters, suggesting how you might inhabit your research: the time taken to move between places or buildings that were somehow linked, the proximities, contingencies and sightlines suggested by buildings, streets, squares, alleyways, hills and inclines, some of which are present in contemporary cities, others that are long gone.[11]

IN SUMMARY

In this chapter we have explored the final part of the research process – writing up – as well as other routes by which you can share your research. This has included discussion of the craft of history writing for academic audiences in the form of the thesis or dissertation, and, where possible, for peer-reviewed publication. We also looked at exciting opportunities for sharing spatial histories more widely by means of digital research outputs, including blogs, and through site-specific talks and tours. Such public-facing activities provide invaluable opportunities to hone the skills in communication and collaboration that are critical for most career paths. Overall, and irrespective of your chosen output, it is worth taking the time to reflect on the narrative and creative strategies that are essential for conveying the originality and urgency at the heart of any research project, as well as the practice and resilience needed to develop as an effective communicator of historical research.

NOTES

1   See discussion above, pp. 36–7.
2   S. Longair, 'Visions of the global: the classical and the eclectic in colonial East African architecture', *Les Cahiers d'Afrique de l'Est*, 51 (2016), 161–78.

3 J. Palacios, 'Actors, Christian burial, and space in early modern Paris', *Past & Present*, 232:1 (2016), 127–63.

4 *Ibid.*, 133.

5 *Ibid.*, 135–8.

6 *Ibid.*, 159.

7 Hannan and Longair, *History through Material Culture*, pp. 144–5, 155–6.

8 For further discussion of impact, including the most up-to-date definitions, refer to the website of UK Research and Innovation (UKRI): 'Excellence with Impact', *UK Research and Innovation*, https://ukri.org/innovation/excellence-with-impact/, [accessed 21 January 2020].

9 I. Gregory, D. DeBats, D. Lafreniere (eds), 'Introduction', in *The Routledge Companion to Spatial History* (London: Routledge, 2018), pp. 1–6 (p. 2).

10 'About', *Queering the Map*, https://queeringthemap.com/ [accessed 21 January 2020].

11 For the joys of what walking can reveal: R. Solnit, *Wanderlust: A History of Walking* (London: Verso, 2002).

RECOMMENDED READING

P. Ashton and H. Kean (eds), *People and Their Pasts: Public History Today* (Basingstoke: Palgrave Macmillan, 2008).

L. J. Hare, J. Wells and B. E. Baker, *Essential Skills for Historians: A Practical Guide to Researching the Past* (London: Bloomsbury, 2019).

E. Hayot, *The Elements of Academic Style: Writing for the Humanities* (Chicago: University of Chicago Press, 2014).

H. Kean and P. Martin (eds), *The Public History Reader* (London: Routledge, 2013).

S. Rabiner and A. Fortunato, *Thinking Like Your Editor: How to Write Great Serious Non-Fiction and Get It Published* (New York: Norton, 2002), Part 2: The Writing Process.

F. Sayer (ed.), *Public History: A Practical Guide*, 2nd edn (London: Bloomsbury, 2019).

SELECT BIBLIOGRAPHY

BOOKS

Agnew, J. and D. N. Livingstone (eds), *The Sage Handbook of Geographical Knowledge* (London: Sage, 2011).

Barker, H., *The Business of Women: Female Enterprise and Urban Development in Northern England 1760–1830* (Oxford: Oxford University Press, 2006).

Barson, S. (ed.), *Understanding Architectural Drawings and Historical Visual Sources* (Swindon: Historic England, 2019).

Bressey, C., *Empire, Race and the Politics of Anti-Caste* (London: Bloomsbury, 2013).

Brown, J. N., *Dropping Anchor, Setting Sail: Geographies of Race in Black Liverpool* (New Jersey: Princeton University Press, 2005).

Carpo, M., *Architecture in the Age of Printing: Orality, Writing, Typography, and Printed Images in the History of Architectural Theory* (Cambridge, MA: MIT Press, 2001).

Castree, N. and D. Gregory (eds), *David Harvey: A Critical Reader* (Oxford: Blackwell Books, 2006).

Conway, H. and R. Roenisch, *Understanding Architecture: An Introduction to Architecture and Architectural History*, 2nd edn (London: Routledge, 2005).

Davidoff, L. and C. Hall, *Family Fortunes: Men and Women of the English Middle Class, 1780–1850* (London: Hutchinson, 1987).

Dennis, R., *Cities in Modernity: Representations and Productions of Metropolitan Space, 1840–1930* (Cambridge: Cambridge University Press, 2008).

Edwards, E., *Photographs and the Practice of History: A Short Primer* (London: Bloomsbury, 2022).

Edwards, E. and C. Morton (eds), *Photographs, Museums, Collections: Between Art and Information* (London: Bloomsbury, 2015).

Elden, S., *The Birth of Territory* (Chicago: University of Chicago Press, 2013).

Ghobrail, J. P. (ed.), *Global History and Microhistory, Past and Present Supplement* 14 (2019).

Ghosh, A., *Claiming the City: Protest, Crime, and Scandals in Colonial Calcutta, c. 1860–1920* (Oxford: Oxford University Press, 2016).

Graham, B. and C. Nash (eds), *Modern Historical Geographies* (London: Longman, 2000).

Greenhalgh, J., *Reconstructing Modernity: Space, Power and Governance in Mid-Twentieth-Century British Cities* (Manchester: Manchester University Press, 2017).

Gregory, I. N. and A. Geddes (eds), *Towards Spatial Humanities: Historical GIS and Spatial History* (Bloomington, IN: Indiana University Press, 2014).

Gregory, I., D. DeBats and D. Lafreniere (eds), *The Routledge Companion to Spatial History* (London: Taylor and Francis, 2018).

Griffiths, P. and M. Jenner (eds), *Londinopolis: Essays in the Cultural and Social History of Early Modern London* (Manchester: Manchester University Press, 2000).

Gunn, S., *The Public Culture of the Victorian Middle Class: Ritual and Authority in the English Industrial City, 1840–1914* (Manchester: Manchester University Press, 2007).

Hamlett, J., *At Home in the Institution: Material Life in Asylums, Lodging Houses and Schools in Victorian and Edwardian England* (London: Palgrave Macmillan, 2015).

Hannan, L. and S. Longair, *History through Material Culture* (Manchester: Manchester University Press, 2017).

Harvey, D., *Paris: Capital of Modernity* (London: Routledge, 2003).

Harvey, K. (ed.), *History and Material Culture: A Student's Guide to Approaching Alternative Sources*, 2nd edn (London: Routledge, 2017).

Hazley, B., *Life History and the Irish Migrant Experience in Post-War England* (Manchester: Manchester University Press, 2020).

Hills, H., *Invisible City: The Architecture of Devotion in Seventeenth-Century Neapolitan Convents* (Oxford: Oxford University Press, 2004).

Jacobs, A. B., *Looking at Cities* (Cambridge, MA; London: Harvard University Press, 1985).

Jerram, L., *Streetlife: The Untold History of Europe's Twentieth Century* (Oxford: Oxford University Press, 2011).

Johnson, M., *English Houses 1300–1800: Vernacular Architecture, Social Life* (Harlow: Longman, 2010).

Joyce, P., *The Rule of Freedom: Liberalism and the City* (London: Verso, 2003).

Kean, H. and P. Martin (eds), *The Public History Reader* (London: Routledge, 2013).

Kilburn-Toppin, J., *Crafting Identities: Artisan Culture in London, c. 1550–1640* (Manchester: Manchester University Press, 2021).

King, A., *Colonial Urban Development* (London: Routledge and Kegan Paul, 1976).

Koven, S., *Slumming: Sexual and Social Politics in Victorian London* (Princeton: Princeton University Press, 2004).

Lefebvre, H., *The Production of Space*, trans. Donald Nicholson-Smith (Oxford: Blackwell, 1991 [1974]).

Lester, A., *Imperial Networks: Creating Identities in Nineteenth-Century South Africa and Britain* (London: Routledge, 2001).

Lichtert, K., J. Dumolyn and M. Martens (eds), *Portraits of the City: Representing Urban Space in Later Medieval and Early Modern Europe* (Turnhout: Brepols, 2014).

Massey, D., *Space, Place and Gender* (Cambridge: Polity, 1994).

Massey, D., *For Space* (London: Sage, 2005).

Mayne, A. and T. Murray (eds), *The Archaeology of Urban Landscapes: Explorations in Slumland* (Cambridge: Cambridge University Press, 2001).

McKellar, E., *The Birth of Modern London: The Development and Design of the City 1660–1720* (Manchester: Manchester University Press, 1999).

Mir, F., *The Social Space of Language: Vernacular Culture in British Colonial Punjab* (Berkley: University of California Press, 2010).

Moss, E., *Night Raiders: Burglary and the Making of Modern Urban Life in London, 1860–1968* (Oxford: Oxford University Press, 2019).

Nead, L., *Victorian Babylon: People, Streets and Images in Nineteenth-Century London* (New Haven: Yale University Press, 2000).

Ogborn, M., *Spaces of Modernity: London's Geographies, 1680–1780* (London: Guilford Press, 1998).

Ogborn, M., *Indian Ink: Script and Print in the Making of the English East India Company* (Chicago: University of Chicago Press, 2007).

Robertson, E., J. D. Seibert, D. C. Fernandez, and M. U. Zender (eds), *Space and Spatial Analysis in Archaeology* (Calgary: University of Calgary Press, 2006).

Romain, G., *Race, Sexuality and Identity in Britain and Jamaica: The Biography of Patrick Nelson, 1916–1963* (London: Bloomsbury, 2017).

Rothman, D. J., *The Discovery of the Asylum: Social Order and Disorder in the New Republic* (Boston, MA: Little Brown, 1971).

Salzberg, R., *Ephemeral City: Cheap Print and Urban Culture in Renaissance Venice* (Manchester: Manchester University Press, 2015).

San Juan, R. M., *Rome: A City Out of Print* (Minneapolis: University of Minnesota Press, 2001).

Sharr, A. (ed.), *Reading Architecture and Culture: Researching Buildings, Spaces and Documents* (London; New York: Routledge, 2012).

Shepard, A. and P. Withington (eds), *Communities in Early Modern England: Networks, Place, Rhetoric* (Manchester: Manchester University Press, 2000).

Sklair, L., *The Icon Project: Architecture, Cities, and Capitalist Globalization* (New York; Oxford University Press, 2017).

Smith, C. S., *The Plan of Chicago: Daniel Burnham and the Remaking of the American City* (Chicago: University of Chicago Press, 2006).

Solnit, R., *Wanderlust: A History of Walking* (London: Verso, 2002).

Thrift, N. and M. Crang (eds), *Thinking Space* (London: Routledge, 2000).

Tilley, C. Y., *A Phenomenology of Landscape: Places, Paths and Monuments* (Oxford: Berg, 1994).

Vanhaelen, A. and J. P. Ward (eds), *Making Space Public in Early Modern Europe: Performance, Geography, Privacy* (London: Routledge, 2013).

Walkowitz, J., *City of Dreadful Delight: Narratives of Sexual Danger in Late-Victorian London* (London: Virago, 1992).

Wildman, C., *Urban Transformation and Modernity in Liverpool and Manchester, 1918–1939* (London: Bloomsbury, 2016).

Wilford, J., *Sacred Subdivisions: The Postsuburban Transformation of American Evangelism* (New York: New York University Press, 2012).

Wilson, E., *The Sphinx in the City: Urban Life, the Control of Disorder and Women* (London: Virago, 1991).

CHAPTERS IN EDITED COLLECTIONS

Harley, J. B., 'Deconstructing the map', in M. Dodge (ed.), *Classics in Cartography: Reflections on Influential Articles from Cartographica* (London: John Wiley, 2011 [1989]), pp. 273–94.

Latour, B., 'The Berlin key or how to do words with things', in P. Graves-Brown (ed.), *Matter, Materiality and Modern Culture* (London: Routledge, 2000), pp. 10–21.

Otter, C., 'Locating matter: the place of materiality in urban history', in T. Bennett and P. Joyce (eds), *Material Powers: Cultural Studies, History and the Material Turn* (London: Routledge, 2010), pp. 38–59.

Tuan, Y.-F., 'Space and place: humanistic perspective', in S. Gale and G. Olsson (eds), *Philosophy in Geography* (London: Reidel, 1979), pp. 387–427.

JOURNAL ARTICLES

Arnade, P., M. Howell and W. Simons, 'Fertile spaces: the productivity of urban space in northern Europe', *The Journal of Interdisciplinary History*, 32:4 (2002), 515–48.

Beebe, K., A. Davis and K. Gleadle, 'Introduction: space, place and gendered identities: feminist history and the spatial turn', *Women's History Review*, 21:4 (2012), 523–32.

Bishir, C. W., 'Urban slavery at work: the Bellamy Mansion Compound, Wilmington, North Carolina', *Buildings & Landscapes: Journal of the Vernacular Architecture Forum*, 17:2 (2010), 13–32.

Brennan, A., 'Measure, modulation and metadesign: NC fabrication in industrial design and architecture', *Journal of Design History*, 33:1 (2020), 66–82.

Bressey, C., 'The city of others: photographs from the City of London Asylum Archive', *Interdisciplinary Studies in the Long Nineteenth Century*, 19:13 (2011), 1–15.

Bruslé, T. and A. Varrel, 'Introduction. Places on the move: South Asian migrations through a spatial lens', *South Asia Multidisciplinary Academic Journal*, 6 (2012), 1–12.

Daniels, S., 'Mapping the metropolis in an age of reform: John Britton's London Topography, 1820–1840', *Journal of Historical Geography*, 56 (2017), 61–82.

DeBats, D. A. and I. N. Gregory, 'Introduction to historical GIS and the study of urban history', *Social Science History*, 35:4 (2011), 455–63.

Escobar, A., 'Culture sits in places: reflections on globalism and subaltern strategies of localization', *Political Geography*, 20:2 (2001), 139–74.

Goebel, M., '"The Capital of the Men without a Country": migrants and anti-colonialism in interwar Paris', *American Historical Review*, 121:5 (2016), 1444–67.

Gieryn, T., 'What buildings do', *Theory and Society*, 31:1 (2002), 35–74.

Giles, K., 'Seeing and believing: visuality and space in pre-modern England', *World Archaeology*, 39 (2007) 105–21.

Hanna, E., 'Photographs and "truth" during the Northern Ireland Troubles, 1969–72', *Journal of British Studies*, 54:2 (2015), 457–80.

Herman, B. L., 'Slave and servant housing in Charleston, 1770–1820', *Historical Archaeology*, 33:3 (1999), 88–101.

Hirsch, S. and D. Swanson, 'Photojournalism and the Moss Side Riots of

1981: narrowly selective transparency', *History Workshop Journal*, 89 (2020), 221–45.

Jackson, P., 'New directions in cultural geography revisited', *Area*, 48:3 (2016), 367–70.

Jacobs, J. M., S. Cairns and I. Strebel, '"A tall storey … but, a fact just the same": the Red Road high-rise as a Black Box', *Urban Studies*, 44:3 (2007), 609–29.

Jerram, L., 'Space: a useless category for historical analysis?', *History and Theory*, 52:3 (2013), 400–19.

Kelly, J., '"To Fan the Ardour of the Layman": *The Architectural Review*, the MARS Group and the cultivation of middle class audiences for modernism in Britain, 1933–1940', *Journal of Design History*, 29:4 (2016), 350–65.

Kingston, R., 'Mind over matter? History and the spatial turn', *Cultural and Social History*, 7:1 (2010), 111–21.

Kümin, B. and C. Usborne, 'At home and in the workplace: a historical introduction to the "spatial turn"', *History and Theory*, 52:3 (2013), 305–18.

Laitinen, R. and T. Cohen, 'Cultural history of early modern streets – an introduction', *Journal of Early Modern History*, 12:3–4 (2008), 195–204.

Latour, B., 'Mixing humans and nonhumans together: the sociology of a door-closer', *Social Problems*, 35:3 (1988), 298–310.

Lester, A., 'Imperial circuits and networks: geographies of the British Empire', *History Compass*, 4:1 (2006), 124–41.

Longair, S., 'Visions of the global: the classical and the eclectic in colonial East African architecture', *Les Cahiers d'Afrique de l'Est*, 51 (2016), 161–78.

Männistö-Funk, T., 'The gender of walking: female pedestrians in street photographs 1890–1989', *Urban History*, 48:2 (2019), 1–21.

McKellar, E., 'Tales of two cities: architecture, print and early guidebooks to Paris and London', *Humanities*, 2:3 (2013), 328–50.

McKenna, M., 'The suburbanization of the working-class population of Liverpool between the wars', *Social History*, 16:2 (1991), 173–89.

McQuire, S., 'Rethinking media events: large screens, public space broadcasting and beyond', *New Media & Society*, 12:4 (2010), 567–82.

Mort, F., 'Fantasies of metropolitan life: planning London in the 1940s', *Journal of British Studies*, 43:1 (2004), 120–51.

Nead, L., 'Animating the everyday: London on camera circa 1900', *Journal of British Studies*, 43:1 (2004), 65–90.

Palacios, J., 'Actors, Christian burial, and space in early modern Paris', *Past & Present*, 232:1 (2016), 127–63.

Sasson, T., J. Vernon, M. Ogborn, P. Satia and C. Hall, 'Britain and the world: a new field?', *Journal of British Studies*, 57:4 (2018), 677–708.

Tierney, E., '"Dirty rotten sheds": exploring the ephemeral city in early modern London', *Eighteenth-Century Studies*, 50:2 (2017), 231–52.

van den Heuvel, D., 'Gender in the streets of the premodern city', *Journal of Urban History*, 45:4 (2019), 693–710.

Vickery, A., 'Golden age to separate spheres? A review of the categories and chronology of English women's history', *The Historical Journal*, 36:2 (1993), 383–414.

Walsham, A., 'The social history of the archive: record-keeping in early modern Europe', *Past and Present*, Supplement 11 (2016), 9–48.

Wetherell, C., 'Historical social network analysis', *International Review of Social History*, 43:S6 (1998), 125–44.

Whyte, W., 'How do buildings mean? Some issues of interpretation in the history of architecture', *History and Theory*, 45:2 (2006), 153–77.

Wright, G., 'Cultural history: Europeans, Americans, and the meaning of space', *Journal of the Society of Architectural Historians*, 64:4 (2005), 436–40.

INDEX

Note: page numbers in italics refer to illustrations